Managing Social Anxiety

A Cognitive-Behavioral Therapy Approach

Client Workbook

Debra A. Hope
Richard G. Heimberg
Harlan R. Juster
Cynthia L. Turk

Contents

Chapter 4: Plotting the Road Map for Our Journey: Gathering Information on the Situations That Are Difficult for You

Chapter 5: Identifying the Thoughts That Cause Anxiety

Comments About the Program

"The authors are in the forefront of research on cognitive-behavior therapy for social phobia, the most carefully documented effective treatment for this disorder, and are excellent clinicians. They bring their extensive knowledge of social phobia and their wealth of experience in treating these clients together in a valuable workbook for people undertaking CBT. Although firmly based on empirical research, this is no stodgy manual. It is written in a lively, accessible form with many vivid examples that will help clients apply the concepts to themselves. It contains useful forms for homework assignments and tests at the end of each chapter to enable clients to assess whether they've understood the material. Not every client takes to bibliotherapy, but for the many who do, this manual will prove a valuable adjunct to therapy."

Dianne L. Chambless, Ph.D.
William Leon Wylie Professor
Co-Director, Anxiety Treatment Center
Department of Psychology
University of North Carolina at Chapel Hill

"This outstanding manual brings the latest research findings on social anxiety (many of these findings originate in the authors of this manual!) directly to the socially anxious person. The authors' depth of experience shines through on every page—they have studied and treated thousands of people with social anxiety, and here they share what they have learned. Written in a warm, supportive style and in clear, straightforward terms, this manual describes a step-by-step program to guide readers through the recovery process. Any person who suffers the pain and isolation of social anxiety should read this book."

Jacqueline B. Persons, Ph.D.
Director, San Francisco Bay Area Center for Cognitive Therapy
Associate Clinical Professor, Department of Psychiatry
University of California, San Francisco
Associate Clinical Professor, Department of Psychology
University of California, Berkeley

About the Authors

DEBRA A. HOPE, PHD, received her doctoral degree in clinical psychology from the State University of New York at Albany in 1990 after completing her doctoral internship at the Medical College of Pennsylvania/Eastern Pennsylvania Psychiatric Institute. She is currently Professor of Psychology at the University of Nebraska–Lincoln and Director of the UNL Anxiety Disorders Clinic in UNL's Psychological Consultation Center. Dr. Hope has published approximately 50 papers on social anxiety, cognitive-behavioral psychotherapy, social skills, and schizophrenia. Her research on the similarities and differences between social anxiety and dysthymia has been supported by a grant from the National Institute of Mental Health. She is co-editor of *Social Phobia: Diagnosis, Assessment, and Treatment* and editor of volume 43 of the Nebraska Symposium on Motivation entitled *Perspectives on Anxiety, Panic and Fear*. Dr. Hope is past president of the Anxiety Disorders Special Interest Group of the Association for Advancement of Behavior Therapy.

RICHARD G. HEIMBERG, PHD, received his degree in clinical psychology in 1977 from Florida State University. After two decades as Professor of Psychology at the State University of New York at Albany, he now holds a similar position at Temple University, where he also directs the Adult Anxiety Clinic. Dr. Heimberg is widely credited with the development of the cognitive-behavioral treatment for social anxiety on which this manual is based, and his treatment development research has been supported by the National Institute of Mental Health since the early 1980s. Dr. Heimberg sits on the Board of Directors of the Association for Advancement of Behavior Therapy and the Scientific Advisory Board of the Anxiety Disorders Association of America. He is co-editor of *Social Phobia: Diagnosis, Assessment, and Treatment* and co-author of *Social Skills Training Treatment for Depression*. In addition, he has published over 160 papers on social anxiety disorder, other anxiety disorders, and depression. Dr. Heimberg currently serves as Associate Editor of the journal *Cognitive Therapy and Research* and sits on the editorial boards of nine other scientific journals.

HARLAN R. JUSTER, PHD, received his degree in counseling psychology from the State University of New York at Albany in 1985 and worked for several years as a psychologist at the Veterans Affairs Medical Center in Albany, NY. He joined Dr. Heimberg's research group as a postdoctoral fellow in 1991 and continued there as Assistant Director of the Social Phobia Program until 1997. Dr. Juster has published approximately 30 papers on social anxiety disorder and related topics, including several literature reviews on treatment outcome. He is currently Director of the Anxiety and Phobic Disorders Center at Pine Bush Mental Health, a private practice clinic in Albany, NY.

CYNTHIA L. TURK, PHD, received her degree in clinical psychology from Oklahoma State University in 1996 after completing her predoctoral internship at the University of Mississippi Medical Center/Jackson Veterans Affairs Medical Center Consortium. She is currently a postdoctoral fellow at the Adult Anxiety Clinic of Temple University and Director of the Generalized Anxiety Disorder Program there. Her research interests include social anxiety, generalized anxiety, and behavioral medicine.

Acknowledgements

Development of this manual would not have been possible without the direct and indirect contributions of many people. We would like to thank Jacqueline Persons, whose work has greatly enriched our sophistication regarding cognitive therapy. Edna Foa and Michael Kozak's outstanding contributions to our understanding of emotional processing and exposure therapy are evident throughout the manual. No book about cognitive therapy would be complete without acknowledging the tremendous influence of Aaron T. Beck's work. We would also like to thank Judith Beck for her willingness to share her work on cognitive therapy techniques. David Barlow's strong support of the dissemination of empirically validated treatments, including this one, initially helped inspire us to launch this project. Leslie Cohn and Peter Norton provided valuable clerical and technical assistance. Our thanks to the many people who read portions of the manuscript and provided feedback, and to our families for their support and patience. Thanks as well to the many graduate students and postdoctoral fellows who have worked with us over the years. They have provided the sparks for many of the ideas that came to fruition here and stimulated our own thinking in immeasurable ways. Most of all we would like to salute the many people who sought help for their social anxiety and were also willing to make a contribution to the greater good through their participation in our research. In a real sense, this manual is their gift to others who seek to overcome social anxiety. Finally, we would like to acknowledge the National Institute of Mental Health for their support of our research on the nature and treatment of social anxiety.

We would also like to express our appreciation for the contributions made by various persons at The Psychological Corporation, especially for the support we have received from Joanne Lenke, PhD, president of The Psychological Corporation, and Aurelio Prifitera, PhD, vice president and director of the Psychological Measurement Group. As project director, Sandra Prince-Embury, PhD, has contributed steady support and invaluable guidance to ensure scientific precision and clinical usability of the Client Workbook. Special thanks are also extended to those individuals whose efforts were crucial in preparing the Client Workbook for publication. Among this group are Jennifer Leigh Brown, research assistant; Kathy Overstreet, senior editor; Judi Lipsett, consulting editor; Marian Zahora, designer; and Javier Flores, designer.

Chapter 1

The Invitation: Are You Ready to Begin the Journey to Overcome Social Anxiety?

Have you ever experienced social anxiety? If you are like most people, you have had many such experiences. Social anxiety is feeling tense, nervous, or frightened in situations that involve other people. To help make this definition more clear, let's take a look at Nicole in a situation that many of us will find familiar. (Note that whenever we describe our clients in this book, their names and some details are changed to protect their privacy.)

Nicole recently has received the good news that she is being promoted to a supervisory position in her job. However, the morning before she starts the new job, she finds herself questioning whether the promotion is what she really wants. As part of her new responsibilities, she has to make presentations on her department's activities at weekly management meetings. While preparing what she will say in her first meeting, Nicole notices that she is nervous about speaking in front of the managers, most of whom she does not know very well. She has a few butterflies in her stomach as she worries about making a good impression. After all, she does not want anyone to think that they made a mistake when they offered her the promotion!

Finally, it is time for the meeting, and Nicole takes her place at the conference table. As she listens to others give their reports, her anxiety increases and her heart beats faster than normal. She tries to relax by telling herself that she is prepared and that no one expects her to be perfect on her first day. When it is Nicole's turn to speak, she feels a little rush of anxiety as she looks out at all of the faces, and she stumbles over the first couple of words. However, as she gets into her report and notices that everyone seems to be listening attentively, the anxiety quickly subsides. Afterwards, Nicole wonders what she was so worried about since her report went fine. She thinks she will like her new job.

The nervousness that Nicole experienced when she had to speak in front of the group is one type of *social anxiety*. Social anxiety in public speaking situations is very common, and most people have some of the symptoms that Nicole had—butterflies in her stomach, increased heart rate, worries about what others will think about her, and a bit of difficulty speaking fluently. Many people have social anxiety the first few times they have to do something such as speaking in front of a group, meeting with a new boss, going to a job interview, going to a new class or job where they do not know anyone, or getting to know someone they might like to date. This commonly experienced social anxiety is unpleasant but not unmanageable, and it goes away fairly quickly. However, as we will see in the following example, some people have a very different experience with social anxiety.

Cory and Jodi have been dating for several months, and this dinner will be the first time he will meet her family. Let's take a look at Cory as he is getting dressed to go to dinner with his girlfriend and her parents. He takes a deep breath to relieve his tension as he thinks to himself that worrying about this dinner has ruined his entire week. Every time he thought about it, he felt sick to his stomach. As the time draws near, he feels even more upset and nauseous. Although Cory is in his thirties, Jodi is his first girlfriend, and they started dating only because she actively pursued him. Cory never thought someone as pretty and fun as Jodi would go out with him! Now he is worried that he will make such a terrible impression on her parents that she will be embarrassed to be with him. On the way to the restaurant, Cory nearly runs off the road because he is so distracted by thoughts of the dinner. All he wants to do is run away, as far and as fast as he can. When Jodi introduces him to her parents, his heart is pounding and his palms are sweaty. He becomes convinced that her father thinks he is a loser because he looks so anxious. Throughout the dinner, Cory has to make an effort to keep track of the conversation because he keeps thinking that everything is going wrong. At the end of the evening, Cory declines Jodi's parents' invitation to stay for coffee and dessert, claiming that he has to be at work early the next morning. The next day, Jodi tells Cory that she felt that the dinner was a big success and her mother thought it was "sweet" that he looked a little nervous.

Unlike Nicole, Cory's experience of social anxiety causes him to feel miserable and truly interferes with his life. Not only was he nervous on the day of the dinner, but he had been anxiously anticipating it all week. The social anxiety interfered with his concentration so that he had difficulty driving safely and making dinner conversation. The comment Jodi's mother made about his nervousness made it clear to Cory that his anxiety was visible to Jodi's parents, and he is worried about what they will think of him.

As we can see, social anxiety is a normal part of life, but it can sometimes have a negative impact on an individual's life. The important question is not whether someone experiences social anxiety or not, but to what degree and how often. Thus, experiencing social anxiety is not like having a broken arm—your arm is either broken or it is not. Rather, social anxiety is on a continuum. To illustrate, let's think about how people with differing levels of social anxiety might react in Nicole's and Cory's situations.

Individuals who experience less social anxiety than Nicole might not be at all nervous about giving a report for the first time and, in fact, might welcome the opportunity to demonstrate their talents in front of the management group. Others might have worried for several days about giving the report, perhaps even having difficulty sleeping the night before. People who experience more social anxiety than Nicole might have continued to be anxious throughout the presentation. They may have performed well despite the anxiety, but it is also possible that they would have had difficulty effectively communicating their main points. A person who experiences very high levels of social anxiety might have turned down the promotion, knowing that giving reports was part of the job and the prospect of doing so was too terrifying to even consider.

Someone who experiences much less social anxiety than Cory might have been a little nervous just before meeting Jodi's parents (most people are nervous meeting prospective in-laws!) but would have quickly become more comfortable as they began to talk together. Someone who experiences more severe social anxiety than Cory might have refused to attend the dinner because he felt panicky just thinking about it, despite knowing that this would make Jodi angry and might even threaten the future of their relationship.

Let's consider one more example that demonstrates just how devastating social anxiety can be. Eric was a 30-year-old man who sought help with his social anxiety after reading a story in the newspaper about our treatment program. It was immediately obvious that Eric was very nervous about talking on the telephone. After a lot of encouragement, he agreed to come in and meet with a member of our staff. At the clinic, we could tell that Eric was having difficulty just sitting in the waiting room because he felt so anxious. As he talked with our staff person, he started to feel a little more comfortable and described how his social anxiety had gradually gotten worse. Eric explained that he had always been shy and nervous around people but had managed to get along in school by reading books rather than talking to others. He went to college primarily because he was too frightened to think about getting a job; college seemed a safer prospect because he knew what to expect in a school environment. Throughout college he worked at part-time jobs on campus that did not require contact with people, such as re-shelving books at the library.

After he graduated, Eric was again confronted with the prospect of finding work. He lived for a couple of years off his savings, some money from his parents, and a few part-time jobs that he usually quit after a few weeks because he could not tolerate the anxiety. He had no friends. He spent some time with a cousin and lived with his parents. Finally, his parents insisted that he get a steady job, so he took a position as a night-shift janitor at the college. Eric was very anxious at first but was soon able to develop a routine that allowed him to work alone most of the night cleaning several floors of a large classroom building. Because Eric was bright, hard-working, and reliable, his supervisor tried several times to promote him to more responsible positions, but Eric always refused. Any change might require that he have more contact with other people, and he did not believe he would ever be able to supervise anyone. When he was not at work, he stayed home. His one pleasure was music trivia, and he constantly read books about popular artists, listened to the radio, and watched the music channels on TV.

Eric explained to our staff member that he felt nervous around almost everyone. If he had to talk with anyone, his heart would pound, and he would feel shaky all over and nauseous. When he went out in public, he felt extremely self-conscious and was convinced that everyone could see that something was wrong with him. Eric came to treatment because he was terrified at the way his life was turning out. He wanted friends and a family someday, but it was clear to him that his life was not heading in that direction. Eric's parents were getting older and he feared he would be living on the street if something happened to them.

Defining Social Anxiety

Mental health professionals have traditionally called severe social anxiety "social phobia." Recently the term "social anxiety disorder" has come into use. We will use social anxiety disorder in this manual with one exception. In Chapter 9, we describe how to overcome specific social fears like worrying that others will see your hand shake while writing a check. Because these fears tend to be very focused, we continue to use "specific social phobias" to describe this aspect of social anxiety disorder.

A definition of social anxiety disorder was provided in 1994 by the American Psychiatric Association in the *Diagnostic and Statistical Manual of Mental Disorders*, fourth edition (DSM–IV). DSM–IV defines social anxiety disorder as "a marked and persistent fear of one or more social or performance situations in which the person is exposed to unfamiliar people or possible scrutiny by others. The person fears that he or she will act in a way (or show anxiety symptoms) that will be humiliating or embarrassing" (p. 416). This means that *the heart of social anxiety disorder is anxiety due to concern about what others might think of you*. The social and performance situations feared by people with social anxiety disorder vary widely, but the most common ones are public speaking, conversations with unfamiliar people, dating, and being assertive. In addition, some individuals with social anxiety disorder are afraid of eating or drinking in front of other people, being the center of attention, talking with supervisors or other authority figures, urinating in a public bathroom (usually only men have this fear), or intimate sexual situations. Regardless of the specific situation, people with social anxiety disorder share a common fear that others will think poorly of them. Sometimes this worry about what others think is related to a fear of displaying a particular anxiety symptom such as blushing or trembling.

The following criteria must be met for an individual to be diagnosed with social anxiety disorder: 1) the person must realize that the fear is excessive and that most people would not be as frightened in a similar situation; 2) the person must avoid the situations that cause anxiety or suffer through them despite great distress; and 3) the social anxiety disorder must interfere with the person's life in important ways (e.g., keep him or her from dating, going to school, doing well at work) or the person must be very upset about having the fears.

Social Anxiety or Social Anxiety Disorder?

Up until now, we have been using the terms social anxiety disorder and social anxiety interchangeably. You might be wondering whether there is a difference between the two. As we just saw, social anxiety disorder is an official label or diagnosis that is based on the specific criteria laid out in DSM–IV. Most mental health professionals recognize that these criteria are fairly arbitrary, but it is helpful to have a standardized definition to assist clinicians and researchers in communicating with each other. Social anxiety is much more loosely defined than social anxiety disorder and simply refers to the distress a person might experience when interacting with or performing in front of other people. As we said earlier, nearly everyone experiences social anxiety sometimes, but it is usually short-lived and does not interfere with the person's life. However, as social anxiety starts to become more severe or is experienced more often and in more situations, then it might be called social anxiety disorder. Because the line between the two is so arbitrary, we will use the terms interchangeably in this book. If you experience social anxiety to the extent that it causes you distress or interferes with things you want to do, then this therapy program is probably for you, regardless of whether you technically meet the criteria for social anxiety disorder.

How Do I Know If This Program Is for Me?

Embarking on any change program requires a commitment of substantial time and energy. Before making that investment, it is important to carefully consider whether you are ready to change and whether a particular program will meet your needs. Assess whether this program is right for you by considering the following questions. These questions present ways in which social anxiety may be negatively affecting your life.

1. Does being nervous or uncomfortable around other people keep you from doing things you want to do?

2. If you are honest with yourself, are you in your present job (or school) because you only have to deal with people you know well? If you are unemployed, have you avoided looking for a job for fear of interacting with others? Have you avoided getting a job or changing jobs because you are anxious about job interviews?

3. Are you not dating because the thought of going out with someone makes you very nervous or because you are afraid of what will happen if you ask someone out?

4. Do you limit how involved you become with people because you are afraid of letting them get to know you? Do you worry that if people really knew you, they wouldn't like you?

5. Do people often comment that you are quiet, unapproachable, or withdrawn in social situations or meetings?

6. Do you find yourself turning down invitations to social events because you know you would feel uncomfortable if you went?

7. If you do make plans to go to a social event or a work activity that involves other people, do you feel relief if it is canceled?

8. Does being the center of attention make you feel very uncomfortable and self-conscious?

9. Do you worry about blushing or looking nervous in front of other people?

10. Are you the sort of person who rarely strikes up casual conversations with store clerks, neighbors, passengers sitting next to you on the bus or plane, classmates, or co-workers from other departments?

11. Do people tell you that you worry too much about what others think of you?

12. Are you uncomfortable eating or drinking with others because you worry about spilling your drink or embarrassing yourself in some other way? Do you worry that you don't have good manners?

13. Do you get so nervous talking to people that your voice sounds odd or quivers or you can't get your breath?

14. Do you like other people and daydream about a better social life but doubt your ability to achieve your dream because you are too shy to really get to know people?

15. Do you have trouble stating your opinion or asking for something you deserve because you worry about what others will think of you?

If you said "yes" to any of these questions and would like to make a change in your life, then this workbook applies to you. Some people will find that almost all of these questions describe them. If that is true for you, then you have discovered that social anxiety is probably limiting. Don't be concerned. Answering yes to lots of the questions just means that you are likely to find this program particularly helpful.

Will This Program Work for Me?

This program is a comprehensive approach to the treatment of social anxiety and social anxiety disorder. This may lead you to ask whether this program is effective and, more important, whether it will be effective for you. Because each person is an individual, with a unique background, personality, and daily living situation, it is impossible to guarantee that this program will help you overcome your social anxiety or social anxiety disorder. That's the bad news. The good news is that there are many reasons to believe that you will see a significant decrease in social anxiety if you follow the procedures carefully. That optimism is based on a large body of scientific research. Let us tell you a bit about that research.

The treatment approach described in this manual was first developed by Dr. Richard Heimberg in the early 1980s, at the time that social anxiety disorder was first officially recognized as a unique type of anxiety problem. In the first carefully controlled scientific study using this treatment, 75% of the participants were rated as having made major improvements in their social anxiety disorder symptoms. The participants reported that they were much less anxious in the situations they had feared prior to treatment. Six months after treatment they came back to the clinic for evaluation and were usually still doing well.

We later contacted as many of the people who had participated in this study as we could locate to see if they continued to do well or if their social anxiety disorder had returned. If the positive effects of treatment "wear off" and a person starts to get anxious again in many social situations, then the treatment has not been long lasting. The results, however, were positive: five years after the treatment, most of the participants we contacted continued to show the benefits of treatment.

Since that first study in the 1980s, there have been at least 10 other scientific studies that have investigated whether the treatment procedures described in this manual (or very similar ones) reduce social anxiety and social anxiety disorder. These studies have included hundreds of participants and have been conducted in the United States, Australia, Great Britain, the Netherlands, and other European countries. Overall, these studies show that most people make significant improvement with the treatment. In the studies we have conducted, about 80% of the participants made substantial progress in treatment.

You might be asking yourself what is "significant improvement" or "substantial progress"? Does that mean the participants overcame all of their social anxiety? Since social anxiety is a normal part of life, it cannot be fully eliminated. However, we use careful scientific criteria to assure that the improvement that people make in treatment is large enough that it leads to important changes in their lives.

When Linda first came to our treatment program, she was 35 years old and working as a clerk in a state office. Linda had graduated from college several years earlier and had taken a number of classes toward a master's degree in social work.

She disliked her current job and was eager to finish her degree so she could pursue her chosen profession. However, Linda was extremely frightened about giving presentations in class and was unable to take any class that required speaking, even informally, in the classroom. She worried that she would stumble over her words, lose her train of thought, and generally appear incompetent and foolish. Linda participated in 12 weeks of the group version of the treatment described in this manual. By the end of therapy, she would get a little nervous at the beginning of a presentation in the group but felt the anxiety was manageable. As treatment ended, she signed up for one of the classes she had been avoiding, and felt fairly confident about being able to complete the required class presentation. Although she thought she might always be a little nervous talking in front of others, Linda felt that she would be able to handle any anxiety that arose. About a year later, she sent her therapists a note reporting that she had finished her social work degree and had found a position she was enjoying.

Jim was a 36-year-old man who had never been married when he sought treatment to help with his anxiety in dating situations. Actually, Jim became anxious almost any time he had to talk with someone, but it was worse with women, and he very much wanted to develop a serious relationship. By the end of three months of treatment, Jim felt much more confident in social situations and had become involved with a singles' outdoor recreational group. He was making an effort to ask women for dates on a regular basis, even if he was only somewhat interested in them. These dates were casual in the sense that Jim did not have to be ready to marry someone to invite that person to a movie. Six months after the end of therapy, Jim reported to his therapist that one of these casual dates had turned into a more serious relationship and they had even begun to discuss marriage.

What Can I Do to Get the Most Out of This Program?

There are no guarantees that the therapy described in this workbook will help you conquer your social anxiety, but scientific research has shown it to be helpful for literally hundreds of people. However, there are some things you can do to help you get as much benefit from a therapy program as possible.

Seriously invest in change. No matter what anyone tells you, making personal changes is hard work! Overcoming social anxiety is no exception. To get as much out of this program as possible, you must invest both your time and your emotional resources. This means setting aside time at least several times a week to work on your social anxiety in addition to participating in a structured therapy session. The work might include doing some of the exercises in this book, talking to someone you wouldn't normally talk with, or practicing the self-help skills you will learn. In fact, the more practice the better, so if you can spend even 20–30 minutes a day, you will see progress.

In addition to investing time, you must invest emotional resources. By this we mean two things. First, some of the exercises in this book will make you uncomfortable or possibly even very anxious. Although it seems a little odd, you must be willing to experience some anxiety in order to overcome it. We have a slogan for this—*Invest Anxiety in a Calmer Future.* This means that you must face your fears in order to overcome them. You do not have to face the worst ones first, but you will have to gradually try some things you have been avoiding. Done systematically, that investment will pay off. Second, you must invest emotionally by being honest with yourself and with your therapist. As you start to analyze some of the thoughts and fears you have about yourself and the world around you, you might find that some of them are embarrassing or seem childish to you. Speak up about them. The thoughts and fears that cause you the most distress are the most important ones to talk about. Not talking about what concerns you makes your therapist's job very difficult.

Do the exercises carefully and practice, practice, practice! All of the exercises in this book have been carefully designed to help you progress through the program step by step. Most exercises build on previous ones, so it is important to do each one carefully. Once you have become an expert at all of the skills, you might find shortcuts that work for you. However, doing the procedures carefully at first will assure that you have all the tools needed to cope with the anxiety you might experience as you try the more advanced procedures. The more you rehearse the exercises, the more quickly the skills you learn will become new habits that replace old, problematic habits. And one of the best things about habits is that they require very little effort.

Persevere. If you are like most people, you have had problems with social anxiety for a long time, maybe even most of your life. If overcoming social anxiety were easy, you would have done it already. That is why it is important to stick with the program even if it does not seem to be working right away. We have included techniques to monitor your progress. Change usually starts slowly, so pay attention to small improvements. Small improvements usually lead to larger ones with time, patience, and practice.

Be kind to yourself. It is easy to focus on what you want to change or things you don't do as well as you would like. It is not always easy to give yourself credit for your efforts. As you work through the program, give yourself a pat on the back as often as possible. Look for things you are making progress on and celebrate them rather than beating yourself up for not yet reaching other goals. Later we will devote a lot of attention to "disqualifying the positive" because individuals with social anxiety are often their own worst critics. Most people find that being critical of themselves doesn't help them change. It just makes them feel miserable!

Be willing to try new ways and give up old ways of dealing with your social anxiety. If you have been using drugs or alcohol to help control your anxiety, discuss that openly and honestly with your therapist. This program is unlikely to work if you rely more on drugs or alcohol than the procedures you will be learning. If you use alcohol or street drugs like marijuana to control your anxiety, be honest with yourself and your therapist about how much you drink or smoke. If you cannot do the exercises without "chemical assistance," then you should seriously consider seeking treatment for the substance abuse problem as well.

If you take prescription medication for anxiety on an "as needed" basis, try not to take it when you are doing the exercises, especially the ones that ask you to try to enter new situations. If you take prescription medication for anxiety on a daily basis, discuss with your therapist or physician whether you should stop or reduce the medication before beginning this program. If you are still experiencing social anxiety despite the medication, you might be able to continue the medication for now as you try this treatment. However, these are complicated decisions that should be made on an individual basis, so it is important to discuss them frankly with your therapist. See Chapter 14 for further discussion about medications in the treatment of social anxiety.

To a great extent, whether this program works for you is under your control. If you are honestly ready to invest the time and energy in change and work carefully through the program, our experience treating hundreds of people suggests that you will be able to overcome your social anxiety. If at this point you (or you and your therapist) agree that this approach would be helpful to you, take a deep breath and we'll start this exciting journey together.

Overview of This Treatment Program

This client workbook describes a step-by-step therapy approach for overcoming social anxiety and social anxiety disorder. It is designed to be used while working with a therapist who has been trained to use cognitive-behavioral treatment for social anxiety. Scientific studies show that therapy that uses this approach is effective. If you are reading this workbook and are not in therapy, you may use it to consider whether or not to seek a therapist at this time.

Chapters 2 and 3 provide background information on social anxiety and social anxiety disorder and on related problems like shyness. These chapters will develop a common language that is used in the rest of the manual and will help you understand that many other people experience the same discomfort that you do around people. Chapter 2 also explains how what you do and what you think work together to keep you from overcoming your fears. Most important, Chapter 3 explains the rationale behind the program—what needs to change in order for you to feel more comfortable in the situations that currently make you nervous.

In Chapter 4, you will learn how to analyze your social fears and understand exactly what it is about different situations that makes you anxious. You will also learn some self-monitoring skills that will help you track your progress through the program. Self-monitoring is particularly important because people with social anxiety often ignore any successes they might have in social situations. It is critically important for you to become aware of the things that go well for you in social and performance situations so that you can learn to give yourself credit for them. Right now you probably have no trouble blaming yourself for the things that do not go so well; self-monitoring will help you develop a more balanced approach to how you reward and punish yourself.

Chapters 5 and 6 will help you gain important self-help skills, known as cognitive restructuring skills, to help you overcome your anxiety. Through careful step-by-step exercises, you will become a sophisticated scientist who seeks out problematic thoughts and subjects them to rigorous tests of logic. That is, *you will learn to treat your thoughts about social situations just as if they were the hypotheses in a scientific experiment.*

The cognitive restructuring skills you learn in Chapters 5 and 6 will help you control your anxiety as you begin to do some of the things that your anxiety has kept you from doing. Chapters 7 and 8 describe a systematic approach to putting yourself in anxiety-provoking situations. By starting with situations that cause you only a little bit of anxiety and gradually working up to more difficult situations, you will soon be able to do some of the things you have been avoiding (or doing only with great anxiety!).

Once you have all of the basic skills in place, Chapters 9 through 11 address some common problematic beliefs and difficult situations that we have seen in our years working with socially anxious individuals. Topics like public speaking, making small talk, and worries about specific symptoms of anxiety such as hand tremors will give you further opportunities to practice the skills learned in earlier chapters while addressing a specific concern related to your own profile of social anxiety. Not all of these chapters may appear relevant to you at first, but as you work through each one, you will likely find some helpful pointers.

You should read Chapters 12 and 13 after you have been using the procedures for several weeks. These chapters describe how to consolidate the gains you have already made and to move on to a more advanced level. Chapter 13 also talks about how to handle the "fallout" that comes with making changes in your life, including the reactions of any friends or family.

Chapters 4 through 13 cover the main part of the treatment that we have developed in our research program over the last 18 years. For most people, these procedures will be all that is needed to overcome their social anxiety. The manual ends with a chapter on medication for social anxiety disorder (Chapter 14). We are fortunate to have Michael Liebowitz, M.D., Director of the Anxiety Disorders

Clinic at New York State Psychiatric Institute and an international expert on medication for social anxiety disorder, prepare this chapter. Dr. Liebowitz describes what types of medication are most likely to be helpful for social anxiety disorder and how to know whether medication might be a good option for you.

Self-Assessment

At the end of each chapter we offer a series of self-assessment questions to help you to determine your understanding of key concepts in the chapter. This will help you decide whether you are ready to move on or need to review the chapter again. For each item, circle either true (**T**) or false (**F**), then check your responses in Appendix A at the end of the manual.

1. Social anxiety can be a problem in situations like public speaking, eating or drinking in public, or using a public bathroom.   **T F**

2. Few people experience social anxiety during their lifetime.   **T F**

3. The central theme of social anxiety is fear that others may evaluate you negatively.   **T F**

4. It is important that, throughout this treatment, you recognize the things you do well and the progress that you are making.   **T F**

5. For this treatment program to be effective, it is important to be invested in change and practice the exercises.   **T F**

Chapter 2

Starting Our Journey Together From the Same Place: Understanding Social Anxiety

In the first chapter, we talked about how social anxiety is a normal part of life, but that sometimes it becomes a problem. We asked you to think about a series of questions to help you figure out if social anxiety is a problem in your life. We explained that social anxiety disorder is the official name for more severe kinds of social anxiety that keep a person from doing the things he or she wants to do. In this chapter, we are going to tell you a lot more about social anxiety, including some ideas about what might cause it and how it comes to interfere in people's lives. This will give us a common language and understanding as we begin the journey toward overcoming social anxiety together. But first, let's consider exactly what we mean by the word "anxiety."

Imagine this scene. . .

> Bill is sitting in a meeting and someone hands him a note. The note states that Dennis, who was supposed to give the financial report, has had to leave abruptly for a family emergency. Dennis will not be able to give the financial report and wants Bill to stand in for him. The report is attached to the note. Bill has never seen it before, and he will have no time to study it because it is next on the agenda. As he sits there staring at the report, Bill realizes that it will be impossible to figure it out before he has to stand up and speak in front of the whole group. Bill would be nervous standing up in front of everyone even if he were prepared, but this is much worse. He immediately feels himself becoming very anxious.

What do you think it means that Bill is "anxious"? In this case, Bill feels his heart pounding, and he is getting very warm. He worries that he will look stupid as he tries to present the report, particularly if his voice shakes and his mind goes blank. He considers sneaking out and not giving the report at all. After all, if he is really nervous, he is sure that he will just look down at the report and mumble so no one will be able to hear him anyway.

As we can see in this example, being "anxious" is not just one thing. Anxiety includes what you feel in your body (e.g., the pounding of your heart), what you think (e.g., "I'll look stupid"), and what you do (e.g., sneak out). Psychologists talk about the three components, or parts, of anxiety. These are the *physiological* component, the *cognitive* component, and the *behavioral* component. We'll talk about each of these in detail.

The Three Components of Anxiety

The Physiological Component

This aspect of anxiety describes the feelings you get in your body when you are anxious. This is a very important part of anxiety and often the first that people think about. In the situation described above, we see that Bill had three main physical symptoms—palpitations (the pounding of his heart), flushing (getting "warm"), and shaky hands. Figure 2.1 presents a list of the physical symptoms that people sometimes experience when they are anxious. Obviously, you can experience these symptoms for other reasons—a person can be nauseous because of anxiety or because of the spicy burrito at lunch! On rare occasions, these symptoms may suggest a medical problem as well. For example, chest pain can indicate some sort of heart problem and nausea could be related to an ulcer. However, if you notice that you get these symptoms only when you are worried or frightened about something, then the symptoms are most likely part of your anxiety experience.

Palpitations (heart pounding)	Muscle aches
Tachycardia (heart racing)	Tightness in the chest
Dizziness	Pain in the chest
Nausea	Ringing in the ears
Smothering sensations	Shortness of breath
Lump in the throat	Diarrhea
Shakiness (hands, head, knees)	Flushing
Blurred vision	Blushing
Headaches	Chills
Depersonalization (feeling as if you or your surroundings are not the way they should be)	Parathesias (tingling in the fingers, toes, face)

Figure 2.1. **Common Physical Symptoms of Anxiety**

About one-third of the general population and one of two people with social anxiety disorder have had a very particular combination of physical symptoms called a "panic attack." A panic attack is a quick rush of anxiety that includes at least four of the symptoms listed in Figure 2.2. People sometimes say that a panic attack feels like a sudden rush of adrenaline. The anxiety usually stays at the highest peak for only a few minutes (10–15 minutes at the most) and then starts to subside.

---

1. palpitations (heart pounding) or tachycardia (heart racing)

2. dizziness, unsteady feelings or faintness

3. nausea, abdominal distress

4. shortness of breath or smothering sensations

5. trembling or shaking

6. sweating

7. choking

8. numbness or tingling sensations

9. hot flushes or chills

10. depersonalization or derealization

11. chest pain or discomfort

12. fear of dying

13. fear of going crazy or doing something uncontrolled

Having 4 of these 13 symptoms all together in a rush of anxiety that peaks quickly then starts to subside is considered a "panic attack."

Figure 2.2.   Symptoms of a Panic Attack

Note. Reprinted with permission from the *Diagnostic and Statistical Manual of Mental Disorders,* Fourth Edition (DSM–IV). Copyright 1994 by the American Psychiatric Association.

You may have noticed that the last two symptoms on the list in Figure 2.2—fears of dying or going crazy/doing something uncontrolled—are not physical symptoms. When people experience a panic attack, especially for the first time, they often believe they are having a heart attack or losing their mind. This is because the symptoms can be very intense and frightening, especially if they seem to come from out of the blue. This brings us to an important distinction. If you experience panic attacks but they occur only when you encounter a social or performance situation that frightens you, then the treatment described in this manual is probably appropriate for you. However, if your panic attacks seem to occur spontaneously, or at times you would not expect them to, then you may have a related but different problem called "panic disorder." Individuals with panic disorder are most worried about the physical symptoms they are experiencing (e.g., pounding heart or shortness of breath) and what those symptoms mean for their physical or mental health or mortality (e.g., that they are dying or going crazy). On the other hand, a person with social anxiety disorder who experiences panic attacks is usually much more concerned about other people seeing their anxiety than about the physical symptoms themselves.

If you think you might have panic disorder, discuss it with your therapist. It is also possible to have both social anxiety disorder and panic disorder at the same time. Although some of the treatment techniques used in this manual are similar to those used for panic disorder, there are some special techniques for panic that are highly effective. These techniques are described in another manual in this series: *Mastery of Your Anxiety and Panic–Third Edition* (MAP 3) by David H. Barlow and Michelle G. Craske.

Let's take a minute to think about the physical symptoms you experience when you become anxious in a social or performance situation. Figure 2.3 is a form entitled "Physical Symptoms of Social Anxiety That I Experience." (A sample form filled out for Bill appears in Figure 2.4.) Think about a recent situation in which you became anxious. Describe it briefly in the space provided and check off all of the symptoms on the form that you remember having in that situation in the column labeled "Most Recent." Note any symptoms that are not on the list under "Other." Now look over the symptoms you checked and circle the one or two that are the most severe (or that concern you the most). Then think about the time that your social anxiety was the worst you ever experienced. This may have been recently or a long time ago. Although it will probably make you a little uncomfortable to think about it, try to remember exactly how you felt, where you were, what was happening, and so forth. After you have a strong memory of your worst experience with social anxiety, describe it briefly in the space provided, then check off any of the symptoms you experienced in the column labeled "Worst." People generally have a few more physiological symptoms when they are most anxious but there are usually some symptoms that they "typically" get.

As you can see on Bill's form, he listed the experience with the financial report as the recent situation in which he felt anxious. He checked three physical symptoms for that experience—palpitations, shakiness, and flushing/blushing. For the worst experience with social anxiety he could remember, he wrote about a speech he had to give in his 11th grade English class. This is a very painful memory for Bill because he remembers being extremely anxious. He had been dreading giving the 5-minute speech for weeks but could not figure any way to get out of it. On the day of the speech he felt a little better and thought he might get through it. Then, as he started talking, he felt a huge rush of anxiety. His chest tightened up and he felt like he could not breathe, his heart started pounding, and his voice sounded so funny that a couple of students snickered in the back of the room. He skipped class the rest of the week because he was so embarrassed about what had happened.

The Cognitive Component

As we have seen, Bill was very aware of the physiological component of his anxiety. However, he was probably less tuned into the other components of the experience. Let's look at the cognitive component. "Cognitive" is the word psychologists use for thoughts and thought processes. Bill is thinking, "I'll look stupid," and is concerned that his mind will go blank. Anxious thoughts often involve a prediction that something bad will happen, as was the case for Bill.

Physical Symptoms of Social Anxiety That I Experience

1. Briefly describe the most recent situation in which you felt anxious.

2. Briefly describe the time you experienced the worst social anxiety.

	Most Recent	Worst
Palpitations (heart pounding)	☐	☐
Tachycardia (heart racing)	☐	☐
Dizziness	☐	☐
Nausea	☐	☐
Smothering sensations	☐	☐
Lump in the throat	☐	☐
Shakiness (hands, head, knees)	☐	☐
Blurred vision	☐	☐
Headache	☐	☐
Chills	☐	☐
Tightness in the chest	☐	☐
Pain in the chest	☐	☐
Ringing in the ears	☐	☐
Shortness of breath	☐	☐
Diarrhea	☐	☐
Flushing/blushing	☐	☐
Parathesias (tingling in the fingers, toes, face)	☐	☐
Depersonalization/derealization (feeling as if you or your surroundings are not the way they should be)	☐	☐
Other:	☐	☐

Figure 2.3.

Physical Symptoms of Social Anxiety That I Experience

1. Briefly describe the most recent situation in which you felt anxious.

When Dennis left me to give the financial report without a chance to prepare.

2. Briefly describe the time you experienced the worst social anxiety.

Speech in 11th grade English class.

	Most Recent	Worst
Palpitations (heart pounding)	☑	☑
Tachycardia (heart racing)	☐	☐
Dizziness	☐	☑
Nausea	☐	☐
Smothering sensations	☐	☐
Lump in the throat	☐	☐
Shakiness (hands, head, knees)	☑	☑
Blurred vision	☐	☐
Headache	☐	☐
Chills	☐	☐
Tightness in the chest	☐	☑
Pain in the chest	☐	☐
Ringing in the ears	☐	☐
Shortness of breath	☐	☐
Diarrhea	☐	☐
Flushing/blushing	☑	☐
Parathesias (tingling in the fingers, toes, face)	☐	☐
Depersonalization/derealization (feeling as if you or your surroundings are not the way they should be)	☐	☐
Other: *shaky voice*	☐	☑

Figure 2.4. **Physical Symptoms of Social Anxiety That Bill Experiences**

Individuals with social anxiety often have thoughts about their own performance ("I won't know what to say to her," "I'll stumble over my words and look dumb") or what someone else might think about them ("He'll think I'm weird," "They'll think I'm boring," "She thinks I'm incompetent"). Do these thoughts sound familiar? Let's take a look at some of the thoughts you have when you are anxious.

Go back to the recent anxiety experience you listed when you described your physical symptoms of anxiety and record the same situation on Figure 2.5, "Thoughts Related to an Anxiety-Provoking Situation." A sample form for Bill appears in Figure 2.6. Write down as many thoughts as you can remember having. Put one thought on each line. Consider thoughts you might have had in anticipation of the event and after the event, as well as during it. Sometimes it is the anticipation of something that makes us most anxious.

Now go back and look at the thoughts you listed. Did you ever question these thoughts or ask yourself if they were realistic? Sometimes the thoughts are true but more often they represent our worst fears, rather than what actually happens. Our anxieties often prevent us from looking at a situation objectively. In later chapters we will look carefully at the thoughts you are having and probably uncover some that you may not be aware of at this point. Learning to think differently in situations that make you anxious is an important step toward overcoming your social anxiety.

The Behavioral Component

We have discussed two of the three components of anxiety (physiological and cognitive), and now we turn to the third—the behavioral component. When psychologists talk about "behavior," they usually mean anything that you can observe another person doing. Walking, smiling, sneezing, and juggling are all "behaviors" because you can look at someone and see whether they are doing one of these or not. You do not have to ask them. (Although some psychologists consider thinking an "internal behavior," for our purposes we will consider thinking as separate from observable behavior.)

It is often helpful to think about the behavioral component of anxiety as having two parts of its own. The first is *what you do in an anxiety-provoking situation*. Think of the anxious young man who looks down at his shuffling feet as he attempts to talk with an attractive young woman. Shuffling feet and reduced eye contact are behaviors often associated with anxiety. Let's go back to Bill, whose friend Dennis left him to give the financial report, and see what anxious behaviors he was concerned about displaying. Bill thought that he would look only at the report, not the audience, and that he would mumble. These are behaviors you would be able to observe if you were in the room when Bill gave the report.

The second part of the behavioral component of anxiety is *avoidance*. Avoidance involves either not doing something that frightens you or doing it in a way that you stay away from the most frightening aspects of the anxiety-provoking

Thoughts Related to an Anxiety-Provoking Situation

Briefly describe a recent social or performance situation in which you were anxious:

List as many thoughts as you can remember about that situation. Include thoughts you had in anticipation of the event, during the event, and after the event. List one thought per line.

1. _____

2. _____

3. _____

4. _____

5. _____

6. _____

7. _____

8. _____

9. _____

10. _____

Figure 2.5.

Thoughts Related to an Anxiety-Provoking Situation

Briefly describe a recent social or performance situation in which you were anxious:

Last week Dennis left the financial report for me to give without giving me a chance to prepare.

List as many thoughts as you can remember about that situation. Include thoughts you had in anticipation of the event, during the event, and after the event. List one thought per line.

1. *I'll look stupid.*

2. *My mind will go blank.*

3. *Everyone thinks there's something wrong with me because I'm so nervous.*

4. *I can't believe Dennis did this to me.*

5.

6.

7.

8.

9.

10.

Figure 2.6.   **Sample Form for Bill**

situation. For example, if you experience social anxiety when talking with unfamiliar people, you might turn down an invitation to attend a party where you won't know many people. This would be avoiding the party altogether and is a behavioral sign of anxiety. On the other hand, you might go to the party, even though you are anxious, and spend the entire evening in the kitchen talking with the few people you already know and with whom you feel comfortable. Although you did not avoid the party entirely, you avoided the part that makes you the most anxious, namely talking with strangers. Going back to Bill for a moment, we can see that he considered sneaking out to avoid giving the report.

Avoidance behavior is a particularly interesting aspect of anxiety because it is an effective short-term solution to reducing you anxiety! Let's assume that Bill decided to sneak out of the meeting so he would not have to give the financial report. Imagine Bill getting up and walking out the door. How do you think Bill feels as soon as the door closes behind him? He probably feels an immediate decrease in his anxiety as he realizes he will not have to do something that frightens him. Thus, avoidance is an effective way to reduce anxiety in the short run. However, what happens if we follow Bill for a little longer in our imagination? As time goes by, how might he feel about having avoided giving the report? Again, if he is like most people, he will start to feel badly about himself. He might tell himself that he is weak or incompetent and he might feel depressed. He might be angry with himself for not being able to give the report and angry with Dennis for putting him in the situation in the first place. In fact, Bill might now be in an awkward situation because he has to face Dennis and tell him he did not give the report. It might be difficult for Bill to go back to the next meeting of this group because he may wonder what people were thinking about his leaving so suddenly. So, as we can see, avoidance may decrease anxiety initially but it usually creates other bad feelings and problems as well.

Avoidance is often a big problem for people with social anxiety because avoiding a few situations that make you anxious can quickly snowball into a general pattern of avoiding lots of situations. Trying to stop avoiding anxiety-provoking situations is difficult because of the immediate relief from anxiety that avoidance provides. This sense of relief "rewards" you for avoiding. Anything a person does that gets rewarded is more likely to be done again in the future. If you do something (like leave a situation that makes you nervous) and something good happens (like a decrease in your anxiety), then you will probably do it again. It matters less that avoidance might make you feel bad later. What does matter is that the immediate decrease in anxiety is a very powerful pay-off.

Let's take a moment to examine how often you avoid situations that make you anxious. Think about the last week or two. Was there anything that you should have done or would like to have done but did not do *because of anxiety*? Did you eat by yourself or join your co-workers for lunch? Did you take the opportunity to chat with the attractive single man or woman who started a conversation with you? Did you raise your hand to volunteer when they were looking for help with the new project at work/school/church/community organization? Sometimes avoidance can be very subtle, and most people who have trouble with social anxiety are avoiding more than they think they are. Avoiding means missing out on opportunities to make friends, meet prospective spouses, gain new opportunities at work or school, and make contributions to your family or community. *Avoidance has as much to do with those things you never start as with those you stop.*

Interaction of the Physiological, Cognitive, and Behavioral Components

When a person becomes anxious, he or she rarely experiences just one of the components of anxiety. In fact, the cognitive, physiological, and behavioral components of anxiety interact with each other, and an increase or decrease in one may cause increases or decreases in the other two. Let's look at an example of how this might work.

Cathy started her job as a clerical worker in a large company about a year ago. She had understood that after she had been there a year, she would get a raise in pay if her performance evaluations were good. Her last evaluation was excellent, but nothing has been said about a raise, and her co-workers say that this is unusual. In fact, Cathy took on extra responsibilities after a part-time person quit a few months ago. Cathy has been wanting to speak with her supervisor about a raise but the thought of doing so makes her very anxious. She has a meeting with her supervisor this morning about a project she has been working on and she plans to bring up her salary at the end of the meeting. When Cathy woke up this morning, her first thought was about the meeting: "Something must be wrong with my work, or they would have given me a raise." Since this is a thought related to her anxiety, we have placed it first in Figure 2.7 and labeled it "Cognition."

Let's follow along with Cathy and see how the three components of anxiety interact with each other. As Cathy starts her day, she notices that she has a tight feeling in her stomach, and the muscles in her shoulders and back are tense. She also notices that she is distracted and accidentally knocks an entire stack of files off her desk. As she picks the files off the floor, she thinks, "I'm so incompetent! No wonder they won't give me a raise." Just then she notices that her heart is starting to beat faster and the back of her neck has begun to ache from the tense muscles. Cathy tries to keep working but cannot sit still. Every few minutes she finds herself jumping out of her seat to do some unnecessary task. She thinks to herself that if her supervisor had thought she deserved a raise, she would have already been given one. Asking for a raise is probably too "pushy." Cathy is still worried about being too pushy as she goes into the meeting with her supervisor. By then she is feeling a little short of breath and her hands are shaking as she knocks on the office door. During the meeting Cathy keeps having images of her boss laughing aloud as she thinks, "She'll laugh when I ask for a raise because I'm so nervous that I'll look ridiculous." Throughout the meeting, Cathy's foot taps on the floor and, as the meeting draws to a close, her heart starts pounding. By then she is feeling extremely anxious and thinks, "I'm too nervous to talk with her. I won't do it right and I'll get fired." She leaves the meeting without asking about the raise. She immediately starts to feel calmer as her heart slows down and her muscles begin to relax. However, a little while later she feels sad and says to herself, "I'm such a loser! I don't deserve a raise anyway."

As you can see in Figure 2.7, the physiological, behavioral, and cognitive components of Cathy's anxiety built on each other. As she had an anxious thought, her heart started pounding and her muscles tensed up. Then when she noticed her physical and behavioral symptoms, she had more anxious thoughts until she spiraled down to the point that she was unable to ask for the raise. As described above, when she first avoided asking for the raise, she felt better. Later, however, she was upset about having avoided facing her supervisor, and she still did not have the raise she deserved!

As you can see, the cognitive, behavioral, and physiological components of anxiety work together and can create a downward spiral that leads to missed opportunities and bad feelings. Most people we have worked with say that this situation sounds all too familiar. As you might guess, the solution involves interrupting the process before it gets out of control. Where did things start to go wrong for Cathy? The downward spiral started with a thought: "Something must be wrong with my work or they would have given me a raise." One can well imagine that Cathy's experience would have turned out differently if she had started with a different thought, such as "I deserve to know why they have not given me the raise that was promised." If you can learn to recognize the signs that the anxiety spiral is starting *and* you have the tools to change what is happening, then you can begin to overcome the anxiety and take charge of your life. In the rest of this manual, you will learn more about yourself and about the tools you need to do just that.

Summary

The purpose of this chapter was to develop a common language and understanding about social anxiety. As you have seen, the word "anxiety" does not mean just one thing. Anxiety has three parts and each may be experienced differently by different people. By now you and your therapist should have a general idea of how the physiological, behavioral, and cognitive components of anxiety play out for you. Understanding your anxiety reaction and learning to monitor the symptoms is an important first step in overcoming social anxiety.

1. Cognition
"Something must be wrong with my work or they would have given me a raise."

2. Physiology
Tightness in stomach, tense muscles in shoulder and back

3. Behavior
So distracted that she knocks a stack of files off her desk

4. Cognition
"I'm so incompetent! No wonder they won't give me a raise."

9. Cognition
"She'll laugh when I ask for a raise because I'm so nervous that I'll look ridiculous."

10. Behavior
Foot tapping on floor throughout meeting

8. Physiology
Feeling short of breath and hands are shaking as she goes to the meeting with her supervisor

5. Physiology
Heart beating faster, back of neck starts to ache

7. Cognition
"If my supervisor thought I deserved a raise I would have gotten one. It is too pushy to ask for one."

6. Behavior
Cannot sit still, jumping out of seat every few minutes

11. Physiology
Heart pounding as meeting draws to an end

12. Cognition
"I'm too nervous to talk with her. I won't do it right and I'll get fired."

13. Behavior
Leave the meeting without speaking up about a raise

14. Physiology
Physical symptoms subside almost immediately

15. Cognition
"I'm such a loser! I don't deserve a raise anyway."

Figure 2.7. **The Downward Spiral of Anxiety**

Homework

During the upcoming week, we would like you to monitor all three components of anxiety in one or two situations in which you get anxious. This will give you practice in paying attention to what anxiety feels like for you. You probably already know that anxiety feels uncomfortable and may make you want to leave the situation. Now you can break down that reaction and begin to identify the details (physical symptoms, behaviors, specific thoughts) of your experience. Figure 2.8, entitled "Monitoring the Three Components of Social Anxiety," is to be used with this assignment.

Any situation that comes up during your week will work for this assignment as long as you experience some social anxiety. It does not have to be a particularly difficult situation, but the anxiety should be high enough that it makes you uncomfortable. If you do not encounter an anxiety-provoking situation this week, then sit down and imagine one that you had recently. Try to recreate the situation in your mind, then fill out the form. We have included a completed form in Figure 2.9 for Cathy, the person we just described who wanted to ask for a raise.

Self-Assessment

1. Anxiety includes four components: behavioral, physical, cognitive, and avoidance.   **T F**

2. The physical symptoms of anxiety can include tachycardia (rapid heartbeat), blurred vision, fever, and shortness of breath.   **T F**

3. If you asked three people if they've ever had a panic attack, probably at least one would say yes.   **T F**

4. Anxious thoughts, which occur with social anxiety, are usually predictions that something bad is going to happen.   **T F**

5. Avoidance of scary situations makes you feel better immediately and is also an effective long-term strategy to reduce your social anxiety.   **T F**

Answers to Self-Assessment questions may be found in Appendix A.

Monitoring the Three Components of Social Anxiety

Date _____

Briefly describe the situation in which you experienced social anxiety:

Physiological Component	Behavioral Component	Cognitive Component
The physical symptoms I experienced were …	*The way I acted or things I did that were observable to others were …* *(Also indicate whether you escaped from the situation or avoided it)*	*The thoughts I had were…*

Figure 2.8.

Monitoring the Three Components of Social Anxiety

Date _____ 2/3 _____

Briefly describe the situation in which you experienced social anxiety:

I was planning to ask my boss for a raise after the meeting on our project.

Physiological Component	Behavioral Component	Cognitive Component
The physical symptoms I experienced were ... tight stomach tense muscles shaking hands heart pounding	The way I acted or things I did that were observable to others were ... (Also indicate whether you escaped from the situation or avoided it) knocked files off my desk could not sit still foot tapping Avoided asking for a raise	The thoughts I had were... Something must be wrong with my work or they would give me a raise. I'm so incompetent. If my supervisor thought I deserved a raise I would have had one. It's too pushy to ask for a raise. She'll laugh when I ask for a raise because I'm so nervous that I will look ridiculous. I'm too nervous to talk with her. I'll get fired. I'm such a loser! I don't deserve a raise anyway.

Figure 2.9.   Sample Form for Cathy

Chapter 3

More About Social Anxiety and This Treatment Program

In the first part of this chapter we will examine the possible causes of social anxiety disorder. As you will see, there are no definite answers about the causes of this disorder, but there is good scientific research about what factors may contribute to it. The good news is that we do not have to understand what caused your social anxiety in order to treat it. However, understanding more about how social anxiety makes life difficult will help explain the rationale for this treatment program. The second part of this chapter will describe the rationale for the treatment program underlying this workbook.

Possible Causes of Social Anxiety

Most psychologists agree that social anxiety disorder, like most other psychological disorders, is not caused by just one thing, but results from a combination of factors including genetics, experiences in your family, and other experiences you have had. We will talk about each of these in turn.

Genetics: Is Social Anxiety in Your Genes?

No one has found the gene that "causes" social anxiety disorder, and it is unlikely that one exists. However, scientific research over the last 20 years indicates that social anxiety probably has a genetic component, at least for some people. Two lines of evidence support this belief. First, psychologists have looked at social anxiety disorder in twins and found that if one twin is socially anxious, the other is also likely to be socially anxious. This likelihood increases if the twins are identical twins (come from one egg and have identical genes) than if they are fraternal twins.

The second line of evidence that social anxiety disorder has a genetic component comes from work by Jerome Kagan and his colleagues at Harvard University. Dr. Kagan has described what he calls "behavioral inhibition to the unfamiliar" in some infants who are only a few months old. Dr. Kagan has followed some of these infants to the age of 7 and found that three-fourths of the infants who were uncomfortable with the unfamiliar continued to be shy and three-fourths of the infants who were not uncomfortable were not shy at age 7. Because this discomfort or shyness can be identified so early in life and seems to last as the child develops, it seems likely that it is genetically transmitted.

If you are like most people with social anxiety, you are not surprised that genetics probably contributes to the development of this problem. There are probably other members of your family who are socially anxious or at least a little bit shy. In fact, someone with social anxiety disorder is about three times as likely to have a close family member with the same disorder as someone who does not have any problems with anxiety. It appears that social anxiety disorder "runs in families." If the disorder is caused by bad (or at least unfortunate) genes, then you are probably stuck with it, right? Wrong. If you look back at the twin research described above, you will see that not everybody with an identical twin who had social anxiety disorder was socially anxious themselves. Similarly, about a quarter of Kagan's shy and uncomfortable infants were not shy a few years later. This is because the genetic contribution to social anxiety disorder, as for other psychological problems, is a *predisposition*, not a *blueprint*. A genetic predisposition means that, all things being equal, if you have inherited certain genes related to shyness, there is an increased likelihood that you will be shy. However, regardless of a genetic predisposition, the life experiences you have strongly influence whether or not you will be socially anxious and how severe that social anxiety will be. Families provide most of our experiences in early life so we will look next at how families might contribute to the development of social anxiety.

Family Environment

Much of what we know about ourselves, other people, and how the world operates we learned from our family while we were growing up. Although it is unlikely that our personality is set in stone by age 5 as psychologists once believed, certainly our fundamental beliefs about life start to form in early childhood. These beliefs include whether or not you can trust other people, whether events happen to us in a predictable or unpredictable fashion, whether life is under our control or whether we are mostly vulnerable to the whims of fate and powerful other people. We also start to learn whether we are valuable and worthwhile individuals. We learn all of these basic principles by watching and listening to those around us.

If one or both parents have social anxiety, then their child might learn to be socially anxious by watching how the parents handle social situations. For example, if the parents tend not to socialize with other people, then the child probably will not socialize a lot and will not value social activity as an important part of life. In fact, several studies have found that the families of people with social anxiety disorder tend not to socialize with other families, even compared to people who have problems with other types of anxiety such as agoraphobia. Similarly, a parent who looks nervous around other people and seems worried about what others think communicates to the child that social interactions are not safe and that one must always be on guard. Parents can also teach children to avoid feared social situations by refusing invitations themselves or suggesting avoidance as a coping strategy when the child is anxious. For example, if 7-year-old Andrea is scared about going to her friend's birthday party, a socially anxious parent might be sympathetic and encourage her to stay home, telephoning the friend to say that she is ill. Certainly we are not suggesting that parents should force children to do everything that scares them, but by consistently offering avoidance as an option, parents can teach their child it is better to avoid than to try to push ahead and overcome the fear.

Important Experiences

Sometimes people we have treated for social anxiety disorder say that there were particular experiences that made them socially anxious. A child or adolescent who is "different" in some way from his or her peers may start to develop social anxiety. One person told us that he became nervous around others when he was teased for stuttering. Although the stuttering had mostly disappeared through speech therapy, as an adult he was still uncomfortable talking with people he did not know well. Another man who came from a loving but very poor family said that his social anxiety started during his wedding to a college classmate who came from a wealthy family. He was so afraid that he would do something socially inappropriate during the wedding that he began to sweat profusely. People commented on his nervousness and perspiration, and from that point on, he was nervous around people he perceived as higher in social status than his own family. Although he had achieved significant financial and social success, most of his co-workers and acquaintances caused him serious anxiety as he worried that they would discover that he "didn't belong."

For some individuals, the beginning of their problems with social anxiety is having a panic attack in a social situation. For example, people with very severe public speaking anxiety sometimes remember a particular incident in which they had a huge rush of anxiety symptoms (panic attack) while giving a speech. Some individuals were able to finish their speeches, but others had to stop. Since these experiences often happen in school, people may remember being teased or laughed at by their classmates and feeling humiliated. The memory of this situation often haunts them whenever they need to speak in front of a group, so they are likely to avoid doing so. Avoidance prevents the opportunity to have a more successful experience, and the bad experience continues to control them.

Pulling It All Together: The Interaction of Genetics, Family Environment, and Important Life Experiences

We have seen that there are three primary causes of social anxiety disorder: a genetic predisposition to be anxious and withdrawn, learning experiences within one's family, and other unique or traumatic experiences. These are represented in Figure 3.1 as slices of a pie. Not all of these factors are equally important for everyone with social anxiety disorder. However, we believe that most individuals who seek treatment are probably born with a tendency to be shy and to withdraw from new situations. If this tendency combines with particular experiences as one grows up, then the person may develop dysfunctional ways of thinking about the world and about what happens to them. We will briefly examine some of these dysfunctional thinking patterns.

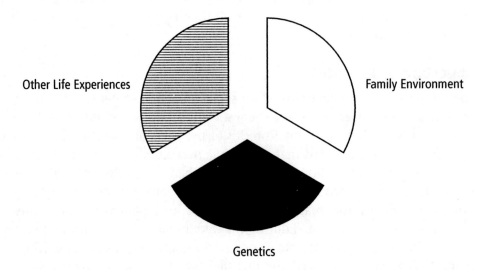

Other Life Experiences

Family Environment

Genetics

The size or importance of each "slice" varies from person to person.

Figure 3.1.   **Contributions to the Development of Social Anxiety**

Dysfunctional Thinking Patterns

1. **External Locus of Control.** There is a great deal of research showing that people who are anxious or depressed have an "external locus of control." That is, the person believes that something outside of him- or herself determines what will happen. Persons with social anxiety disorder believe that other, more capable and competent people control what will happen. Take the example of a man asking a woman to accompany him to a movie. If this man is socially anxious, then he believes it is totally up to her to say yes or no. He probably expects her to say no. However, if the man is not socially anxious, he probably believes he has some influence over her response. He may believe that he can talk her into going, that he will be able to flirt with her so that she will want to go, or that she will be flattered by his interest. This is known as an "internal locus of control" because the person believes that something inside of himself or herself influences what will happen. In most instances, people with social anxiety disorder underestimate the control or influence they may have on other people's positive reactions to them.

2. **Perfectionistic Standards.** Some socially anxious people set very high standards for their behavior in social situations. They also believe that other people's standards for them are unrealistically high. Along with these expectations is the belief that it is not acceptable for them to ever look or feel nervous in social situations. Other standards may emphasize never offending another person, always observing perfect manners, always being dressed just right for every occasion, or always being witty and charming. All of these expectations are perfectly admirable goals but unrealistic to expect of oneself on a regular basis. If achievement of perfection is your goal, you will frequently experience failure and feel badly about yourself.

3. **Low Self-Efficacy.** Self-efficacy is the term psychologists use for self-confidence in how effective one expects to be. One type of self-efficacy refers to the belief that you can do something successfully. Socially anxious people often have low self-efficacy, meaning that they doubt their ability to do the right thing (or to do it well) in a social interaction. They may doubt that they have adequate social skills or the ability to make small talk. Sometimes individuals with social anxiety disorder also experience a second kind of low self-efficacy known as "low outcome expectancies." This refers to the belief that even if you can perform adequately (such as being assertive and asking someone to change his or her behavior), you will still not get what you want (i.e., the other person will not comply). Socially anxious individuals often expect that a situation will go poorly or that they will be rejected by the other person.

As with the other dysfunctional thinking patterns, low self-efficacy beliefs such as these can become self-fulfilling. If you do not believe you can accomplish what you want, then it makes little sense to try. However, not trying to make a new friend, give a speech, or tell someone how you feel means that you never really find out what would have happened if you had reached out or spoken up. Thus you never have an opportunity to disconfirm your dysfunctional belief or discover that you are more skilled and more effective than you previously believed.

How Dysfunctional Thinking Patterns Play Out in an Actual Situation

We have probably all heard the expression "seeing the world through rose-colored glasses." This expression describes the tendency to see people and circumstances in a positive light, even more positively than the situation warrants. People have characteristic ways of viewing the world that act like a filter. Some things get through the filter, and the person thinks about them and acts on them. Other things are blocked out. In the case of rose-colored glasses, positive aspects of people and circumstances make it through the filter. Negative information gets screened out and the person seems to ignore it. Neutral information becomes tinged with pink and is viewed positively.

Following this metaphor, we might say that people who experience severe social anxiety (and probably other forms of anxiety as well) see the world through amber-colored glasses. Like the amber of a traffic light, these glasses warn that danger could be nearby, so watch out and be prepared. Things may be fine now, but they could change at any minute. These amber glasses help the person to pay extra attention to signals that the interaction may not be going well or that the other person is forming a negative impression. In our research we have found that the filtering system is very specific. Socially anxious people pay a lot of attention to information related to social threat but pay no more attention than a nonanxious person to information about other kinds of threat. The amber glasses also filter out information that indicates non-threat, that the situation is safe, proceeding well, or that the other person is forming a favorable impression. If you ask a socially anxious person how they are performing in a conversation, for example, they almost always underestimate how well they are doing. This is because the amber glasses represent a biased view that focuses on their mistakes or imperfections ("I stumbled over my words"). This perspective also leads the person to ignore or disqualify anything that goes well ("I haven't made a total fool of myself because he is very easy to talk to"). It is important to realize that these beliefs—or amber-colored filter—are dysfunctional because they provide a biased view of the situation. This serves to maintain the dysfunctional beliefs, increases the physical symptoms of anxiety, and leads to real or imagined poor performance.

Dysfunctional Beliefs and Increased Physiological Arousal

When we are in danger, our bodies have a built-in mechanism to help us handle that danger. When the caveman or cavewoman walked outside the cave and came face to face with a saber-toothed tiger, the ones with an internal alarm system were more likely to survive. This alarm system, called the fight-or-flight response, means that when our brains identify that shape as a dangerous tiger, our bodies gear up (muscles tense, heart rate and blood pressure increase, adrenaline is released into the bloodstream) to either fight the tiger or run away quickly (flight). Although there are some situations today in which the fight-or-flight system helps us respond to danger, social situations are not among them. Social situations are not dangerous, at least not in the same way that a saber-toothed tiger was dangerous. A pounding heart is useful when facing a tiger, but not when trying to start a conversation with a stranger.

Excessive physiological arousal, such as a pounding heart, can interfere in two ways. First, social interactions require complicated behavior. One has to pay attention to what the other person is doing and saying, figure out what it means, make the appropriate response, and then evaluate how the other person reacts. All of the extra energy from the fight-or-flight response interferes with these behaviors because a conversation does not require the same level of energy as running or fighting. Instead, conversations require calmness and concentration. Actors and athletes often report that they perform best when they feel "pumped up" for a performance, meaning that they are experiencing a little bit of arousal that makes them feel focused and alert rather than lethargic. Too much anxiety, however, keeps actors from remembering their lines or athletes from sinking the game-winning free throw.

How does physiological arousal relate to dysfunctional beliefs? If you have a biased view of a situation, then you might perceive it as more dangerous or challenging than it really is. This would lead to increased arousal that may then interfere with performing well, thus incorrectly confirming the belief that the situation was too difficult for you to handle, and the expected social failure becomes a reality. However, experiencing the arousal itself can also serve to strengthen the dysfunctional beliefs. If your heart is pounding and your muscles have tensed up, then it is easy to think that the situation "must" be dangerous. While the inherited tendency to experience arousal in unfamiliar situations contributes to the development of dysfunctional beliefs about their dangerousness, misinterpreting a situation as threatening can lead to arousal which then serves to confirm that the situation is dangerous after all! This circular reasoning is an easy trap to fall into and can lead to more and more anxiety.

Dysfunctional Beliefs and Behavior

As we just saw, dysfunctional thinking can both result from and lead to physiological arousal. Perceiving social situations through the amber glasses of dysfunctional thinking patterns can also interfere with a person's performance. At every moment we are bombarded by all sorts of sensory information. You see the black words on the white page, feel the pressure of the chair against your back, hear the sound of your own breathing, and so forth. Our attention system can only absorb so much information at one time, so we block out most and only concentrate on what is most relevant at a given moment. Having a conversation with someone or giving a speech requires a lot of attention. However, as you will remember from above, socially anxious people use up part of their attentional capacity by watching for signs of social threat. That means there is less capacity left to listen to what the other person is saying and to notice small nuances or gestures. We have probably all had the experience of not listening to someone because we were thinking of what to say next. It is very difficult to listen and plan to talk at the same time! To some extent the individual with social anxiety does this all of the time. It is hard to fully participate in a conversation when you are thinking about what to say next, whether the other people like you, whether their voice tone means they are angry, never knowing what to say, and hoping the conversation will be over soon because your heart is starting to pound and they might notice your blushing.

Summary of the Development of Social Anxiety and Dysfunctional Beliefs

Let's take a moment to summarize the causes of social anxiety disorder. Social anxiety disorder seems to result from an inherited tendency to be anxious and withdrawn in new situations that then interacts with certain types of experiences in life. Whether the genetic predisposition, early experiences, or traumatic experiences are more important varies from person to person. The combination of these factors leads the person to develop certain patterns of dysfunctional thinking about whether he or she has control over the outcome of social situations and whether that outcome is likely to be positive or negative. These beliefs then serve to color how future social interactions are interpreted in a way that tends to confirm the dysfunctional beliefs. The beliefs may interfere with performance or lead the person to avoid the situation, thus preventing opportunities to overcome the anxiety and check out whether the beliefs are true.

Frequently Asked Questions

When we share this explanation for social anxiety disorder with people, there are some questions that frequently come up as people try to apply it to their own situation. We would like to address some of the most common of these questions now.

1. **Isn't my social anxiety caused by a chemical imbalance in my brain?** Very often people with social anxiety disorder have read or been told that the disorder is caused by a "chemical imbalance" in their brain or nervous system. Usually people take this to mean that being socially anxious is like having an underactive thyroid gland. The body simply is not producing the right chemicals in the right amount and the solution is to change which chemicals are produced by taking medication. This view is only partially correct, however. Research on the brain processes of people with social anxiety disorder has not consistently found differences between individuals with and without the disorder. Yet our thoughts and emotions start in our brain, so there must be biochemical processes underlying social anxiety. The chemical imbalance theory is too simplistic because it ignores the fact that our experiences in the world greatly affect the complex chemical systems and neural pathways in the brain. Recent research with brain imaging demonstrates that the brains of individuals change following successful treatment for emotional disorders, whether the person was treated with medication or with psychological treatments such as the one described in this manual.

   We recognize the significance of biological processes in fully understanding social anxiety disorder. In fact, many people take medication for the disorder and experience substantial benefit. That is why we have included a chapter on medication in this manual. However, scientific research suggests that biological explanations for social anxiety disorder and treatment with medication are not the whole story for most people.

2. **I'm just an introvert or shy. Isn't that OK?** Of course it is OK to be an introvert or shy if it is OK with you. Lots of people prefer a more solitary life and lead rich, fulfilling lives that emphasize pursuits they do on their own. Many are creative, talented people who choose their friends carefully.

However, you are the best judge of whether or not you are happy being an introvert. If being shy keeps you from doing what you want to do, if you are lonely because you lack close friendships, if you want to be with people but it makes you too nervous and uncomfortable, then being an introvert is not OK for you. The treatment discussed in this workbook can help you change. It is unlikely that you will suddenly become an extrovert who is the life of every party, but there is probably a middle ground where you can be quite comfortable.

3. **This explanation doesn't fit me. No one else in my family has social anxiety and I was fine until I got divorced/experienced a traumatic event/had children/etc.** Our explanation of social anxiety disorder assumes that experiences early in life are important in the development of the disorder for two reasons. First, research suggests that individuals with social anxiety disorder say their parents treated them in particular ways that seem to be related to the development of the problem. Second, most people report that they noticed they were socially anxious their whole life or that it started by the time they were in high school. It is relatively uncommon for social anxiety disorder to start when someone is in their 20s or older. When the disorder seems to start after a significant event in adulthood such as a divorce or relocation, we have often found that there were hints of the problem before but that the person had developed a way to manage it. For example, it is not unusual to see someone seeking treatment for social anxiety after being widowed or divorced. They discover that they had relied on their spouse in social situations and now lack the confidence to enter social situations on their own, let alone re-enter the dating scene. If you are one of the few people who developed social anxiety later in life, this workbook may still be useful to you. It may be important to examine what was going on in your life when the social anxiety developed to see how it changed your beliefs about yourself and the world around you.

Cognitive-Behavioral Therapy as Treatment for Social Anxiety

What Is Involved in Cognitive-Behavioral Therapy

We have discussed the three components of social anxiety: cognitive, physiological, and behavioral. Each of these will need to be addressed in treatment. Cognitive changes will involve changing dysfunctional beliefs and expectations to a more functional view of yourself, other people, and the world. Excessive physiological arousal in feared situations will need to be reduced substantially. Behavioral changes need to include both improving performance in social situations (if poor performance is a problem) and eliminating avoidance of feared situations and people. The treatment itself has three components which address each of these aspects of social anxiety. The three components of treatment are *systematic graduated exposure, cognitive restructuring,* and *homework assignments.* Each of these will be discussed in turn.

Systematic Graduated Exposure

Folk wisdom tells us that if you want to overcome the fear of something, you must ultimately face it head on. The same is true for overcoming social anxiety. However, as you well know, this is easier said than done. Psychologists use the word "exposure" to refer to facing one's fears in a therapeutic fashion—in other words, doing the things that make you anxious. Your ultimate goal is to feel more comfortable in the situations that now cause fear. Eventually you will have to enter those situations, some of which you may have avoided for a long time. There are lots of ways to face your fears. We like to use the analogy of learning to swim. You can probably learn to swim by jumping repeatedly into the deep end of the pool and struggling to the side. After repeatedly being very scared and swallowing a lot of water, you would eventually learn how to float and then paddle and kick to move through the water. However, it would not be much fun. On the other hand, you can learn to swim by starting gradually, in the shallow end of the pool. First, you just get your feet wet and get used to being in the water. Then you learn to put your face in the water, and later how to float. Over time you develop sufficient skills to be able to jump into the deep end. You will probably still be anxious when jumping off the diving board for the first time, but you have built up your confidence over repeated practices in easier situations. We believe in doing exposure the same way. If someone is anxious about talking with a co-worker of the opposite sex, we believe that it makes sense to work up to it with a series of conversations with people who evoke less anxiety.

One of the unique aspects of this treatment program is that you start exposure within the treatment session. If you are not currently in therapy, note that one of the advantages of a structured therapy situation is to provide a safe environment within which to confront difficulties that you have been struggling with alone. By first role playing (acting out) interactions in a therapy session, you have an opportunity to try new things in a controlled environment. You can get feedback on how well you are doing, and the situations can be easier because they can be predictable. For example, if you are anxious about being assertive, you can first practice in the therapy session in which you and your therapist can control how the other person will respond. Another advantage of in-session exposures is that you can practice coping with something that you are worried about but is unlikely or unpredictable in real life. For example, we once worked with someone who always worried that his note cards would blow away during a speech. He feared that he would be embarrassed as he tried to gather them up and then would be unable to continue, as his notes would be out of order. Through careful placement of a fan in the therapy room, we were able to create this fairly unusual situation. Once he had lived through the situation once, he realized that he would just need to take a few minutes to re-order his notes, make a humorous comment about what had happened, and then go on.

Why is exposure helpful in overcoming social anxiety? It works in at least three ways. First, as you stay in the situation, your physical symptoms will habituate. Although it may seem like your shaking knees and pounding heart will never stop, this is not the case. *Habituation* is a normal bodily process in which physiological arousal levels off and then decreases over time. Habituation also occurs with repeated practice in a situation so that over time you become less anxious and the anxiety goes away faster. In real life, people often feel so anxious that they do not stay in a situation long enough to find out that their heart will stop pounding and the nausea will go away. Once you have experienced habituation a few times, you can learn to trust that it will happen, which helps you feel more relaxed before you even enter the feared situation.

Second, exposure works because you are practicing exactly what you need to do. Often people have avoided the things they fear for so long that they have had little practice in what to say or do. Exposure allows you to practice the behavioral skills that are involved in asking for a date, making a speech, being assertive, or making conversation in a safe environment.

Third, exposure works because it gives you an opportunity to test the reality basis of your dysfunctional beliefs. If you have a perfectionist belief that you must not look at all anxious, then exposure will help you determine how anxious you actually look by giving you feedback from others. Exposure will help you see how others respond if your anxiety does show a little (or a lot!).

Cognitive Restructuring

Cognitive restructuring is a set of procedures that allow you to directly attack your dysfunctional thinking by systematically analyzing the things you are saying to yourself when anxious. Cognitive restructuring does not mean that you take out the bad thoughts and replace them with good thoughts. It is not just blindly thinking positive thoughts, either. Cognitive restructuring techniques teach you to question your beliefs, assumptions, and expectations to see if they really make sense or are helpful.

Obviously cognitive restructuring targets the cognitive component of social anxiety, but you might be surprised to learn that it helps with the physiological and behavioral components as well. Remember that physiological arousal is a normal response to a dangerous situation. Through cognitive restructuring you can learn to make a more realistic assessment of the danger in a situation and, consequently, you should have fewer physical symptoms. Cognitive restructuring helps the behavioral component of social anxiety in two ways. First, as your thinking becomes less dysfunctional, you will have more mental capacity to focus on the situation, rather than focusing so much on your anxious reaction to it. Second, changing your dysfunctional beliefs helps decrease your avoidance which, in turn, gives you an opportunity to have more positive experiences. As you evaluate your experiences more realistically, you will eventually change the dysfunctional beliefs for good. Exercises described in this workbook are designed to help you with cognitive restructuring. If you are currently in therapy with a person trained in this approach, your therapist will help you with this process.

Homework Assignments

The third component of treatment is homework. It would be fine if you went through treatment practicing the exposures in session, learning the cognitive restructuring skills, and feeling more and more confident in the role plays. However, it is essential that you make changes in your real life outside of therapy as well. Homework is designed to make that happen. Over the course of treatment, your therapist will ask you to do certain things during the week. At first, the homework assignments will involve thinking about something or keeping track of how you are thinking or feeling. Later, after you have completed some of your in-session exposures, you will start to try some exposures on your own in real situations. Again, these are graduated so that you start with easier situations and work up to harder ones. Thus, homework is the bridge between therapy sessions and the changes you want to make in your life.

There are three important things you should know about homework. First, it is negotiated with your therapist. It is your therapist's job to encourage you to try new things, but it is your job to be honest about what you can and will do for homework. Once you agree to something, you need to follow through, so be sure to let your therapist know how you are feeling about a particular homework assignment. Remember that by expressing your discomfort assertively to your therapist, you are helping yourself overcome your fears of assertiveness or talking with authority figures. Second, you do not have to do the homework perfectly to be successful, you just need to make a good effort. If your homework is to start three conversations during the week, then you just need to start the conversation with someone and exchange a few words. You do not need to have a heart-to-heart discussion or start a lifelong friendship! Third, homework assignments for exposure will include cognitive restructuring exercises as well. It is *essential* that you complete this part of the assignment to get the full benefit of the experience. This way any anxiety you feel during the exposure will truly be "invested in a calmer future," just as our slogan says.

Summary of the Rationale for Treatment

As you can see, this is a fully integrated treatment program in which you systematically begin to face your fears, using cognitive restructuring techniques to help control your social anxiety and change the dysfunctional beliefs that underlie it. By working gradually through the program, you can build success upon success as you tackle more and more difficult situations. At each step you are transferring your progress to the real world through homework and identifying and addressing the dysfunctional beliefs that keep you anxious.

Homework

This is the end of the introductory educational material. The next chapter introduces the first steps of the treatment program. This is a good time to stop and think about how you feel about starting this program. After all, making major changes in your life can be both exciting and frightening. It is likely that you have been struggling with social anxiety for many years. If so, it may be hard to be confident that you can become more comfortable making speeches, having conversations, dating, or being in other situations you fear. On the other hand, you may be excited that you finally understand what has been going on and you are optimistic about change. Sometimes finding out that someone else has had similar problems can be a huge relief. In the last three chapters we have shared what the scientific literature and our combined years of experience have taught us about social anxiety. During the week, we would like you to review this material and think about whether it makes sense to you. Use the worksheet in Figure 3.2 entitled "Worksheet for Reactions to Starting This Treatment Program" to help you think through your reactions. Make a rating on the 1-10 scale for each question, then jot down a few notes to explain your ratings. You should bring your worksheet in to the next session in order to discuss your reactions with your therapist.

Self-Assessment

1. Scientists have isolated the specific gene that causes social anxiety.　　　T　F

2. Behaving in an anxious manner (e.g., refusing social invitations, expressing worry about what others think) in social situations can be learned from your family.　　　T　F

3. Individuals who struggle with severe social anxiety often expect others to decline their invitations or react negatively when social efforts are made.　　　T　F

4. Doing exposure helps you get used to the physical sensations, practice behavioral skills, and test your beliefs.　　　T　F

5. Cognitive restructuring is the process of replacing all your negative thoughts with positive ones.　　　T　F

Answers to Self-Assessment questions can be found in Appendix A.

Worksheet for Reactions to Starting This Treatment Program

Instructions: Circle a number that describes how you feel about each item, then indicate why you made that particular rating.

1. How logical does this treatment seem to you?

   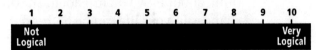

   Explanation for Your Rating:

2. How confident are you that this treatment will be successful in eliminating your fear?

   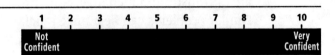

   Explanation for Your Rating:

3. How confident would you be in recommending this treatment to a friend who had social anxiety disorder?

   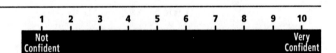

   Explanation for Your Rating:

Use the following scale for questions 4 a, b, and c.

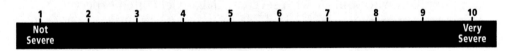

4. a) Currently, how severe is your social anxiety? _____

   b) How severe do you expect your social anxiety to be immediately following completion of this treatment program? _____

   c) How severe do you expect your social anxiety to be one year after completing this treatment program? _____

Explanation for Your Ratings:

Adapted with permission from "Credibility of Analogue Therapy Rationales" by T.D. Borkovec and S.D. Nau, 1972, *Journal of Behavior Therapy and Experimental Psychiatry*, 3, 258. Copyright 1972 by Pergamon Press.

Figure 3.2.

Plotting the Road Map for Our Journey: Gathering Information on the Situations That Are Difficult for You

In the previous chapters, you learned about the cognitive, behavioral, and physiological symptoms that you experience in situations that cause you anxiety. We talked about the factors that contribute to social anxiety disorder, including heredity, things you learn growing up, and experiences you might have in life. We also talked about dysfunctional thinking patterns that can develop as a person grows up and how those patterns can interfere with being comfortable and competent in social situations. The previous chapter ended with a preview of the three components of treatment: graduated exposure to feared situations, cognitive restructuring, and homework assignments. For homework, you were asked to think about how confident you feel about this treatment program. If your ratings indicate that you are fairly confident, that is terrific. You are ready to move on to the next step. A few doubts are normal, but if you are having significant doubts, then you should discuss these with your therapist before moving on to the next step in the program. You might find it helpful to go back and re-read the sections in Chapters 1 to 3 that address the topics about which you have doubts.

Chapter 2 focused on the *symptoms* you may feel when you are socially anxious. In this chapter we are going to start to discuss the *situations* that make you anxious. Although everyone who experiences social anxiety fears being viewed negatively by others or performing poorly in social situations, the situations that evoke those fears vary considerably from one person to the next. Some people become anxious in only a few situations, but others become anxious almost every time they might have to talk with another person. Before you and your therapist can figure out which situations to tackle first, it is important to understand what makes a situation easier or harder for you. Is it easier or harder if you know the person with whom you will have a conversation? Are groups of people easier or harder than one-on-one situations? To answer these questions, you will be constructing a *Fear and Avoidance Hierarchy*. This is a rank-ordered list of situations in which you experience anxiety.

Building a Fear and Avoidance Hierarchy

There are four steps in constructing a Fear and Avoidance Hierarchy: (1) brainstorming; (2) rank ordering the situations; (3) discovering what makes a situation easier or harder; and (4) making ratings of the situations. You will work through each of these steps with your therapist. We have included an example so you can see how the whole process works before you tackle it for yourself.

Step 1: Brainstorming

The first step in constructing a Fear and Avoidance Hierarchy is to make a list of situations that you might want to include. The best way to do this is to "brainstorm" by listing as many situations that make you anxious as you can. Figure 4.1 presents a sample hierarchy brainstorming that Marlene completed. Marlene is an elementary school teacher in her mid-40s. You can see on her list that there are many situations at work that make her anxious but there are also some in her personal life that cause her difficulty. Because she is married, dating is not an issue, but she still gets anxious meeting new people, such as her husband's co-workers. You can see that Marlene listed both general categories such as "talking with students' parents" and very specific situations such as "meeting her husband's ex-girlfriend at the high school reunion." It is OK to have a mixture like this.

As you and your therapist brainstorm together using the form in Figure 4.2, "Brainstorming for Your Fear and Avoidance Hierarchy," be sure to include a wide range of situations. Not all of them will make it onto the final hierarchy, but brainstorming helps assure that you do not miss any important situations. You will want to list at least eight to 10 situations. Do not worry about putting the list in any order at this point. Be sure to include some that you find very difficult as well as others that cause only moderate anxiety and mild anxiety.

If you are having difficulty thinking of enough situations, then consider some situations that people with social anxiety commonly say cause them anxiety. Perhaps some of these apply to you:

- speaking in front of a group
    - large vs. small group
    - familiar vs. unfamiliar people
- being the center of attention
- casual conversations
    - friend vs. acquaintance vs. stranger
- meeting someone new
    - man vs. woman
- eating or drinking in front of others

Brainstorming for Your Fear and Avoidance Hierarchy

Rank	Situation
	Talking with students' parents
	Meeting husband's ex-girlfriend at high school reunion
	Making small talk with husband's co-workers
	Making small talk with husband's boss
	Walking into a meeting late when everyone is already seated
	Returning something to a store
	Having to tell parents their child is failing
	Eating dinner at someone's house that I do not know well
	Speaking in front of a group of adults (kids are OK)

Figure 4.1.   **Sample Form for Marlene**

Brainstorming for Your Fear and Avoidance Hierarchy

Rank	Situation

Figure 4.2.

- writing or typing while being observed

- being assertive

- answering the telephone

- talking with an authority figure

- talking with a very attractive person

- job interviews

- taking communion at church

- unexpectedly seeing an acquaintance

- giving or receiving a compliment

- saying "no" to someone

- attending meetings

  - for work

  - with teachers

  - for a community organization

You can see that there are variations on some situations, such as different types of conversations, that might cause you more or less anxiety. For example, Marlene finds talking with students' parents fairly difficult but she becomes much more anxious if she has to tell the parent that his or her child is failing in school. Maybe you are not very anxious having a casual conversation with someone you know fairly well, but if you have to talk with someone new, then you become much more nervous. By looking over the list of situations provided and considering variations on some of the situations you initially list, you can probably include eight to 10 situations on your worksheet. If you have a lot more, that is fine. Your therapist will help make sure that you have an appropriate range of situations to work on.

Step 2: Rank Ordering the Situations

After you and your therapist have finalized your brainstorming list, it will be time to rank order the situations with 1 being the most difficult, the situation that causes you the most anxiety and that you would most like to avoid. You will count down so that the highest number is assigned to the situation that causes you the least anxiety on the list. You can see the rank ordering that Marlene did in Figure 4.3. "Having to tell parents their child is failing" was the most difficult situation, and "making small talk with husband's co-workers" was the least difficult situation.

Brainstorming for Your Fear and Avoidance Hierarchy

Rank	Situation
7	Talking with students' parents
2	Meeting husband's ex-girlfriend at high school reunion
10	Making small talk with husband's co-workers
4	Making small talk with husband's boss
5	Walking into a meeting late when everyone is already seated
8	Returning something to a store
1	Having to tell parents their child is failing
9	Eating dinner at someone's house that I do not know well
	~~Speaking in front of a group of adults (kids are OK)~~
3	Speaking in front of the congregation at church
6	Speaking in front of the Parent Teacher Association

Figure 4.3. Sample Form for Marlene

As she did her rank ordering, Marlene had trouble ranking "speaking in front of a group of adults" because different variations of that situation caused her different amounts of distress. By dividing the situation into two separate entries on her hierarchy—"Speaking in front of the congregation at church" and "Speaking in front of the Parent Teacher Association meeting" —Marlene was able to complete the ranking.

Step 3: Discovering the Dimensions That Make a Situation Easier or Harder for You

Next Marlene will look over her Fear and Avoidance Hierarchy to see if she can notice any patterns in what makes a situation more or less anxiety-provoking for her. As we look at Marlene's list, we can see that *who* she is making small talk with makes a difference. She is much more comfortable with her husband's co-workers than she is with his boss. As Marlene thinks about it, she realizes that if the other person is an authority figure, it makes the situation more difficult for her. Similarly, she is fairly comfortable speaking in front of a group about work-related topics or as part of her job. She has no anxiety when she is in front of the classroom; that situation does not even appear on her hierarchy. Parent-Teacher Association meetings make her somewhat nervous but everything is related to work so she is confident she knows what she is talking about. However, if she is asked to make an announcement in church or to do some of the readings, she becomes quite anxious. Finally, Marlene finds telling people something they do not want to hear—for example that their child is failing in school—makes her more anxious than just talking about neutral topics. Thus, we can see that Marlene has three *dimensions* that make a situation easier or harder for her: status of the person (her husband's boss is an authority figure), whether the situation is work-related, and the nature of the topic (sharing bad news is harder).

You and your therapist will go over your list and define the dimensions that are important for you. Your therapist will ask if there are patterns in what makes a situation easier or harder. Here are some questions that might help you find the dimensions that are relevant for you. Does it make any difference if . . .

- the person is a man or a woman?

- the person is married or single?

- the person is higher or lower status than you?

- the person is younger or older?

- the person is someone you will or will not see again?

- the person is or is not very attractive?

- the person has or does not have a lot more education than you?

- the situation is one-on-one or involves more than one person?

- the people are friends, acquaintances, or strangers?

- the situation is structured (organized around an activity) or unstructured?

- the situation is formal (like a wedding reception) or casual (like a weekend barbecue)?

- you will be standing or sitting?

- the event will last for a short or long time?

- the event is spontaneous or you have a chance to prepare?

The dimensions that are important for you may be quite different from Marlene's. In fact, what makes a situation difficult for one person may make it easy for another or it may be totally unimportant to them.

Why is it important to identify these dimensions? Because by understanding them, both you and your therapist will be better able to predict how much anxiety you will experience in a new situation that is not on your hierarchy. Later, when you work together to design exposures, it is helpful to be able to make these predictions about situations. Remember the analogy that graduated exposure is like learning to swim by starting out in the shallow end of the pool and working up to the deep end? In a sense, these dimensions define what parts of the "pool" are more shallow or deep for you.

Step 4: Rating Each Situation for Fear It Evokes and the Likelihood You Will Avoid It

The final step in constructing your hierarchy will be to make some ratings about each situation. You will be making two ratings: how anxious the situation makes you (Fear Rating) and how likely you are to avoid it (Avoidance Rating). We will discuss each in detail.

SUDS: Subjective Units of Discomfort Scale

The scale we will be using to make fear ratings is called the Subjective Units of Discomfort Scale or SUDS for short. The SUDS was developed by two of the founding fathers of behavior therapy—Joseph Wolpe and Arnold Lazarus—over 30 years ago. It has stood the test of time because it is simple and easy to use. The SUDS is a 0- to 100-point scale with higher numbers indicating more anxiety/greater discomfort. Here's what the scale looks like:

| 0 | 5 | 10 | 15 | 20 | 25 | 30 | 35 | 40 | 45 | 50 | 55 | 60 | 65 | 70 | 75 | 80 | 85 | 90 | 95 | 100 |

| no anxiety, calm, relaxed | mild anxiety, alert, able to cope | moderate anxiety, some trouble concentrating | severe anxiety, thoughts of leaving | very severe anxiety, worst ever experienced |

We have put descriptive labels at 0, 25, 50, 75, and 100. As you can see, the scale measures "subjective" anxiety just as the name suggests, meaning that it is a measure of how you are feeling. How anxious you feel may or may not match how anxious you look to other people or whether or not you are able to cope with the anxiety and remain in the situation. The SUDS rating is just about feelings. Let's take a moment to talk about various points on the SUDS.

SUDS = 0. A zero SUDS rating means zero discomfort. You may or may not be happy or excited but if you are not feeling at all anxious, then your SUDS rating is 0. Can you think of a recent situation in which your SUDS rating was 0, a time when you felt calm and relaxed? Maybe you felt excited, but not anxious. Record that situation in the box.

Situation When My SUDS Rating Was 0

SUDS = 25. A SUDS rating of 25 indicates that you are feeling mild anxiety with which you can easily cope. In fact, it might mean that you are simply very alert with a little "edge" of nervousness. Performers and athletes often report this type of feeling just before going on stage or onto the playing field. It is more "hyped up" than anyone probably wants to feel all the time, but a little anxiety can help a person focus on the need to perform. Nevertheless, in casual social situations, it is probably a little more anxiety than most people who do not have problems with social anxiety are likely to experience. Think of a recent social or performance situation when your SUDS rating would have been 25.

Situation When My SUDS Rating Was 25

SUDS = 50. By the time a person feels a SUDS rating of 50, the anxiety is definitely bothersome and uncomfortable. There is some difficulty concentrating on what is going on around you, and the feelings of anxiety are distracting. However, at 50 you still feel that you can probably cope and are not yet thinking about leaving or running out of the room. Think of a recent time when your SUDS rating would have been 50 in a social situation.

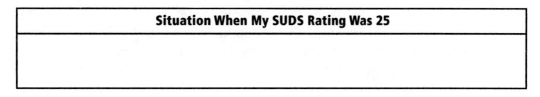

Situation When My SUDS Rating Was 50

SUDS = 75. At a SUDS rating of 75, the person is feeling extremely uncomfortable and is having difficulty coping with the anxious feelings. It is very hard to concentrate and all you can think about is how bad the anxiety feels. If you are having thoughts of running away, then your rating has probably reached 75. Can you think of a situation that you were in recently that fits this description?

Situation When My SUDS Rating Was 75

SUDS = 100. Simply defined, a SUDS rating of 100 is the worst anxiety you have ever experienced or can imagine experiencing. Because the scale is subjective, the feelings that are given a rating of 100 vary from person to person. Some people feel very panicky or have a sense that something terrible is going to happen. Think about the worst anxiety you have ever experienced in a situation related to social anxiety. Now, can you imagine anything worse? Whatever you are imagining is your personal definition of a SUDS rating of 100. Be sure to think about a social or performance situation because the SUDS ratings will be used to track your social anxiety. You may have experienced a traumatic or stressful situation in which you were more frightened but that does not tell us much about your social anxiety.

Situation When My SUDS Rating Was 100

Think about what your SUDS rating is right now. It is OK to use any number between 0 and 100 (e.g., 23, 57, 92), including 0 and 100. Some people just use the "tens" (10, 20, 30, etc.), but you should use the scale however it works best for you. The most important thing is that you communicate to yourself and to your therapist how much anxiety you are feeling so you can track your anxiety as it goes up and down across time.

My SUDS Rating Right Now: _____

Avoidance Ratings

Remember that the list of situations you developed is called a Fear and Avoidance Hierarchy? The second rating for each situation, therefore, will be a rating of avoidance. As we discussed above, avoidance is part of the behavioral component of social anxiety disorder and refers to whether or not you refrain from doing the things that make you anxious. We usually think of avoidance as all or nothing (either you attend a party or not) and that is mostly what we will be considering here. However, you might engage in more subtle avoidance by attending the party but talking only with people you already know and with whom you feel fairly comfortable. You do not initiate conversation with anyone who makes you feel challenged or uncomfortable. We will talk about how to rate that type of avoidance.

As with SUDS, we will rate avoidance on a 0 to 100 scale with a higher number indicating greater avoidance. Here is the Avoidance Scale:

0	5	10	15	20	25	30	35	40	45	50	55	60	65	70	75	80	85	90	95	100
never avoid				avoid once in awhile						avoid sometimes					usually avoid					always avoid

As with the SUDS ratings, you can use any number between and including 0 and 100. If you virtually never enter a situation because of your anxiety, then the avoidance rating would be 100. If you usually enter the situation then your rating for that situation would be low—about 10–20. However, it is possible to engage in more subtle avoidance even if you usually try to enter the situation. Let's go back to the example of attending a party. You may attend the party but only talk with the one person you know. You might actively avoid having to talk with anyone else, even if someone tries to engage you in conversation. In that case, you could honestly say that you do not avoid parties because you do go to them. Your avoidance rating for "attending parties" would be low, maybe even 0. However, the avoidance rating for "talking with strangers at parties" would be high, in this case maybe 95. This rating would not be quite 100 because you at least put yourself in a position where strangers might talk with you rather than avoiding the opportunity altogether.

Sometimes people say that they do not avoid a situation because they do not have the freedom to do so, especially regarding situations related to work or something essential to daily living such as grocery shopping. We have found, however, that it is almost always true that the person could avoid the situation, although the consequences might be extreme. For example, a manager who is anxious about giving a report at a managerial meeting may feel that he cannot avoid the situation because he will lose his job. That may be true, but many people quit jobs (or never even apply in the first place) because they are anxious about giving such reports, even if there are significant financial consequences. Thus, the manager's avoidance rating for giving the report would be low, despite very high anxiety.

Now that you have a good understanding of the Fear and Avoidance Ratings, refer to the Fear and Avoidance Hierarchy form in Figure 4.4. Fill in the situations you rank ordered with the most difficult on top, then make a photocopy of the form. Then fill in the SUDS and Avoidance Rating for each situation on one of the forms, saving the second form without any ratings for evaluating your progress in Chapter 13. Let's look at Marlene's hierarchy and her ratings in Figure 4.5. As we do, we can learn quite a bit about her social anxiety. Both of the top two situations

Fear and Avoidance Hierarchy

Subjective Units of Discomfort Scale (SUDS)

0	5	10	15	20	25	30	35	40	45	50	55	60	65	70	75	80	85	90	95	100

no anxiety, calm, relaxed	mild anxiety, alert, able to cope	moderate anxiety, some trouble concentrating	severe anxiety, thoughts of leaving	very severe anxiety, worst ever experienced

Avoidance Rating

0	5	10	15	20	25	30	35	40	45	50	55	60	65	70	75	80	85	90	95	100

never avoid	avoid once in awhile	avoid sometimes	usually avoid	always avoid

Situation	SUDS	Avoidance
#1 most difficult situation is		
#2 most difficult situation is		
#3 most difficult situation is		
#4 most difficult situation is		
#5 most difficult situation is		
#6 most difficult situation is		
#7 most difficult situation is		
#8 most difficult situation is		
#9 most difficult situation is		
#10 most difficult situation is		

Figure 4.4.

Fear and Avoidance Hierarchy

Subjective Units of Discomfort Scale (SUDS)

0	5	10	15	20	25	30	35	40	45	50	55	60	65	70	75	80	85	90	95	100

no anxiety, calm, relaxed	mild anxiety, alert, able to cope	moderate anxiety, some trouble concentrating	severe anxiety, thoughts of leaving	very severe anxiety, worst ever experienced

Avoidance Rating

0	5	10	15	20	25	30	35	40	45	50	55	60	65	70	75	80	85	90	95	100

never avoid	avoid once in awhile	avoid sometimes	usually avoid	always avoid

Situation	SUDS	Avoidance
#1 most difficult situation is *telling parents their child is failing*	100	25
#2 most difficult situation is *meeting husband's ex-girlfriend at high school reunion*	100	100
#3 most difficult situation is *speaking in front of the congregation at church*	90	90
#4 most difficult situation is *making small talk with husband's boss*	80	40
#5 most difficult situation is *walking into a meeting late where everyone is already seated*	75	90
#6 most difficult situation is *speaking in front of the Parent-Teacher Association*	75	50
#7 most difficult situation is *talking with students' parents*	40	5
#8 most difficult situation is *returning something to a store*	40	100
#9 most difficult situation is *eating dinner at someone's house that I do not know well*	35	50
#10 most difficult situation is *making small talk with husband's co-workers*	25	15

Figure 4.5.   **Sample Form for Marlene**

make her extremely anxious (SUDS = 100). But note that she is much more likely to avoid going to the high school reunion than telling parents their child is failing her class. Because speaking with parents is an important part of her job and she feels it is harmful to the child if she puts off telling parents the bad news too long, Marlene usually does speak with the parents. She gave herself an avoidance rating of 25 because she feels that she occasionally puts off scheduling the meeting for a few days. On the other hand, she finds it easier to avoid meeting her husband's ex-girlfriend at the high school reunion. In fact, her husband is quite angry about her refusal to attend the reunion next month, but so far she does not plan to go.

Looking further down Marlene's hierarchy we can see that she has a fairly low avoidance rating for another situation that provokes quite a lot of anxiety, "making small talk with husband's boss." In that situation, she is more worried about making a bad impression if she seems to avoid the boss than about anything she might say or do during the conversation. On the other hand, two situations that evoke less anxiety are almost always avoided. Situation #5, "walking into a meeting late where everyone is already seated," she avoids by being extremely careful to be on time. Situation #8 is easy to avoid because she either gets her husband to make the return or just keeps the item even though she is dissatisfied.

Final Words on Your Fear and Avoidance Hierarchy

If you are currently in therapy, your therapist will spend quite a bit of time working out the details of your Fear and Avoidance Hierarchy with you. Whether or not you are in therapy it is helpful to become familiar with the material in this chapter and to start thinking about the situations you will want to include on your hierarchy. The Fear and Avoidance Hierarchy serves two important roles in a cognitive-behavioral treatment program. First, as noted above, developing the hierarchy helps you and your therapist understand which dimensions make a situation easier or harder for you. This information can help your therapist develop exposures in the session and for homework that are challenging but not overwhelming. Second, in a few weeks we will ask you to look at your hierarchy again and make new Fear and Avoidance Ratings. This is a good way to track your progress so that you and your therapist can gauge how well the program is working for you.

Homework

Learning to Monitor Your Anxiety

One of the first steps in gaining control of social anxiety is to understand more precisely when and where you get anxious in your daily life. If you go to see a therapist each week, you can (and probably will) describe some of the times you became anxious since your last session. However, there has been a great deal of scientific research suggesting that what clients report to their therapists is not very accurate. People's memories tend to be related to their current mood. If you are having a bad day when you come to see your therapist, you are more likely to remember all of the anxiety you had during the week. Similarly, if you are feeling more relaxed and confident when you see your therapist, you will probably remember the week as more calm, without as many anxiety episodes. In order to overcome the effects of current mood on memory, we will be asking you to make some ratings of your anxiety each day. Then when you meet with your therapist, you can review the ratings and be confident that they are accurate.

Figure 4.6 provides a form to be used to monitor your anxiety during the week, called "Self-Monitoring Form." Make several copies of this form for use in the coming weeks. As you can see in the completed example (Figure 4.7), you will be making three types of ratings. The first is a rating of your average anxiety for the day using the SUDS scale. It should reflect your general sense of how calm/relaxed or anxious/uptight you typically felt during that day and should not focus only on social anxiety. The second rating is an average daily rating of depression. This rating should reflect the extent to which you generally felt down, blue, sad, or depressed throughout the day. Although it may seem odd to be keeping track of your depression during a treatment program for social anxiety, many people with social anxiety also experience difficulties with depression. We have found that most people feel less depressed as they start to make progress toward overcoming their social anxiety. However, if you get too depressed, your therapist may want to talk with you about separate treatment for your depression.

The last rating involves keeping track of your SUDS in one or two situations from your Fear and Avoidance Hierarchy. After completing your hierarchy, you and your therapist should select one or two situations that you would like to monitor. It is best to pick situations that occur fairly often and cause quite a bit of anxiety. You will be monitoring these situations throughout treatment, so avoid picking something that will only occur once or twice.

You should complete the self-monitoring form at the end of the day, perhaps after dinner or at bedtime. It is easier to get in the habit if you make the ratings at about the same time each day. Leave the form in a place where you are likely to see it, maybe taped to your bathroom mirror or on your bedside table. Bring the completed form to session each week to review with your therapist. We have two charts (Figure 4.8 and Figure 4.9) for you to track your progress from week to week. Compute the average for each column on the self-monitoring form and mark the average on the charts. Examples of completed charts appear in Figures 4.10 and 4.11.

Why Do the Self-Monitoring?

Doing self-monitoring every day like this is a bit of a hassle. However, it is also a very important part of the treatment program. As you and your therapist review the self-monitoring each week, you will learn more about the situations that cause

Self-Monitoring Form

Instructions: At the end of each day, record the average anxiety and average depression you experienced throughout the day and your peak anxiety in each of the situations you are monitoring. Use the 0–100 scale. If a situation did not occur that day, indicate N/A for not applicable.

| 0 | 5 | 10 | 15 | 20 | 25 | 30 | 35 | 40 | 45 | 50 | 55 | 60 | 65 | 70 | 75 | 80 | 85 | 90 | 95 | 100 |

| no anxiety/
depression | mild anxiety/
depression | moderate anxiety/
depression | severe anxiety/
depression | very severe anxiety/
depression |

Date	Average Anxiety Today	Average Depression Today	Peak Anxiety in Situation #1	Peak Anxiety in Situation #2

Figure 4.6.

Self-Monitoring Form

Instructions: At the end of each day, record the average anxiety and average depression you experienced throughout the day and your peak anxiety in each of the situations you are monitoring. Use the 0–100 scale. If a situation did not occur that day, indicate N/A for not applicable.

0	5	10	15	20	25	30	35	40	45	50	55	60	65	70	75	80	85	90	95	100
no anxiety/ depression				mild anxiety/ depression					moderate anxiety/ depression					severe anxiety/ depression				very severe anxiety/ depression		

Date	Average Anxiety Today	Average Depression Today	Peak Anxiety in Situation #1 *Conversations with Strangers*	Peak Anxiety in Situation #2 *Speaking up in a group*
5/6	45	20	60	85
5/7	50	20	60	70
5/8	25	0	40	N/A
5/9	25	0	45	60
5/10	60	50	65	70
5/11	50	50	55	N/A
5/12	45	30	50	N/A
5/13	55	30	60	80

Figure 4.7. **Sample Self-Monitoring Form**

Weekly Summary of Self-Monitoring of Average Daily Anxiety and Depression

For each week, plot the number of your average daily anxiety and depression level for that week.

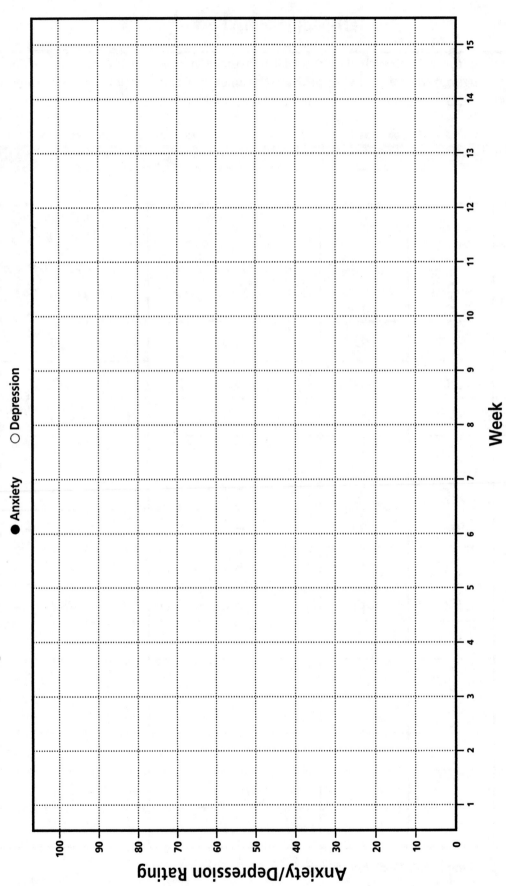

● Anxiety   ○ Depression

Anxiety/Depression Rating

Week

Figure 4.8.

Weekly Summary of Self-Monitoring of Average Peak Anxiety for Two Situations

For each week, plot the number of your average peak anxiety for two situations for that week.

● **Situation 1:** _____   ○ **Situation 2:** _____

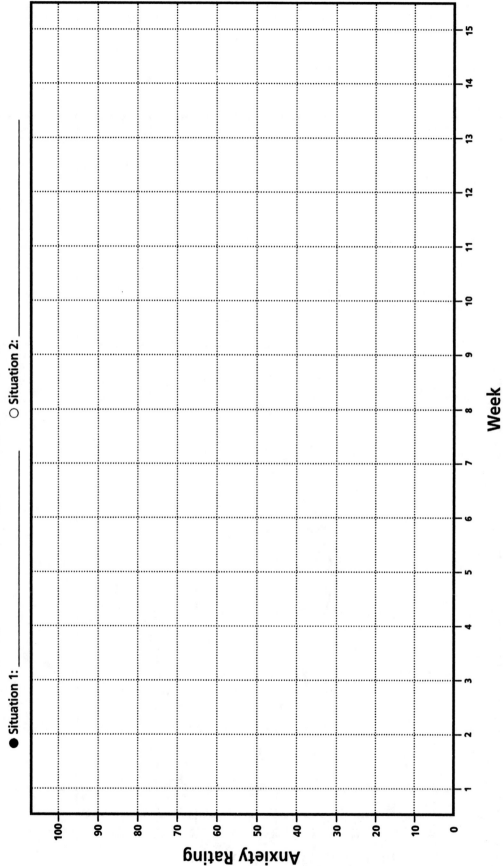

Week

Figure 4.9.

61 ■

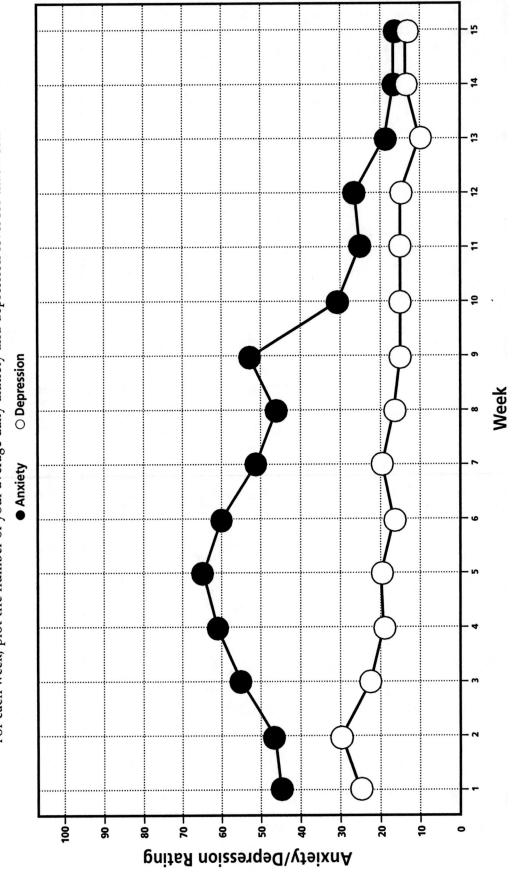

Weekly Summary of Self-Monitoring of Average Daily Anxiety and Depression

For each week, plot the number of your average daily anxiety and depression level for that week.

● Anxiety   ○ Depression

Anxiety/Depression Rating

Week

Figure 4.10.   Sample Completed Weekly Summary of Average Daily Anxiety and Depression

Weekly Summary of Self-Monitoring of Average Peak Anxiety for Two Situations

For each week, plot the number of your average peak anxiety for two situations for that week.

● Situation 1: _Conversations_   ○ Situation 2: _Speaking in a Group_

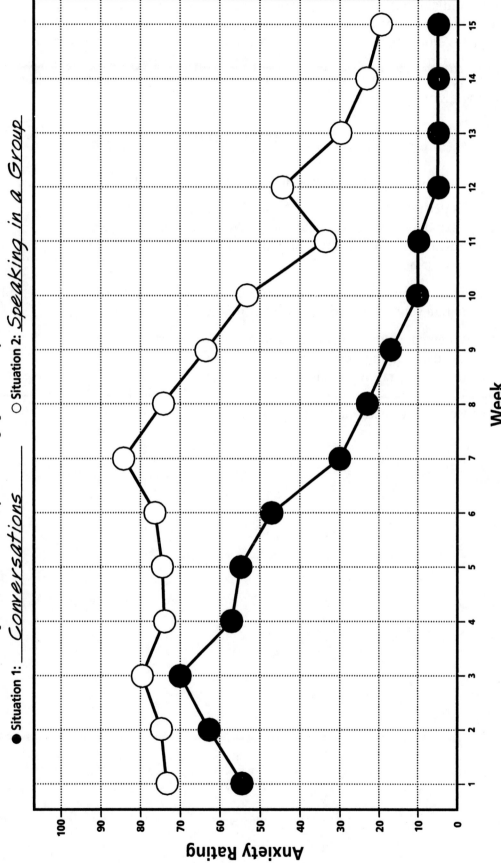

Figure 4.11.   **Sample Completed Weekly Summary of Self-Monitoring of Average Peak Anxiety for Two Situations**

63 ■

you difficulties. This will help your therapist tailor the treatment to fit your particular circumstances. Reviewing the self-monitoring each week also keeps track of your progress through the program. You might notice that your anxiety goes up initially as you stop avoiding situations. It is normal and expected that facing your fears will cause anxiety at first. However, over time you should see progress on the charts.

Self-Assessment

1. The situations that evoke social anxiety are the same for everyone.   **T   F**

2. Understanding the dimensions of situations that you find anxiety-provoking will help you predict how much anxiety you might experience in a new situation that you did not include in your hierarchy.   **T   F**

3. You can use avoidance ratings on the Fear and Avoidance Hierarchy to rate your subjective distress in a situation.   **T   F**

4. When constructing your Fear and Avoidance Hierarchy, if an avoidance rating for an anxiety-provoking situation is low, then the anxiety rating will always be low.   **T   F**

Answers to Self-Assessment questions can be found in Appendix A.

Chapter 5

Identifying the Thoughts That Cause Anxiety

Reviewing Your Self-Monitoring Homework

By the time you start this chapter, you should have been completing the self-monitoring form for a week. As you review the completed form and plot your average ratings for the first week on the graphs, think about what you have learned about your anxiety. What was going on the days that it was the highest and the lowest? Did the two situations you picked to monitor occur during the week? If not, consider whether you are avoiding those situations. In the coming weeks, you will start to reduce that avoidance, so your anxiety may increase for awhile. Later it should decrease as you gain confidence facing your fears.

If you had trouble completing the self-monitoring for this week and you are in therapy, discuss the difficulties with your therapist. If you are not in therapy you may consider consulting a therapist at this time. Perhaps you can pick a better time or place to complete the form. Self-monitoring is extremely important. If you continue to have problems getting it done, then we recommend you stop moving forward in the treatment program and work only on the monitoring for awhile. If you really cannot remember or find time for the monitoring, then maybe this is not the right time to start the treatment program. This program takes a lot of energy and work outside of the session. Be sure you can make the commitment of time and energy before proceeding.

The first four chapters laid the basic groundwork for the treatment program that starts in this chapter. In this chapter and the next, you will learn about how what you think influences how anxious you feel and how to change what you are thinking so you can feel less anxious.

The Importance of Thoughts

Consider two unmarried men, Jerry and Rich, who both moved to town recently for a new job. Neither of them knows anyone and both want to develop friendships and possibly meet a woman to date. As Jerry arrives home from work one evening, he sees an attractive woman about his age getting her mail, apparently arriving home herself. Jerry has seen this woman around and believes that she lives next door to him. He has never spoken with her but would like to get acquainted, so he goes over to her and introduces himself, adding that he has just moved in. She looks up from her mail briefly and says hello. As she continues to sort through her mail, he thinks the following thoughts:

She doesn't want to talk with me.

I'm bothering her.

She thinks I'm weird or something.

I'm so inept that I made a bad first impression just saying hello.

Suddenly feeling anxious and uncomfortable, Jerry then says, "See you around," and picks up his own mail. He walks into his apartment feeling a little angry ("She wouldn't even talk to me") and depressed ("I'll never meet anyone").

Now let's look at Rich's experience in the same situation. Just like Jerry, Rich arrives home from work and sees an attractive woman about his age getting her mail. Rich has also seen this woman around and believes that she lives next door to him. He goes over to her and introduces himself, telling her that he just moved in. She, too, looks up from her mail briefly and says hello. As she continues to sort through her mail, he thinks the following thoughts:

She must be expecting something important in the mail.

Maybe she is tired from work. I'll have to try a little harder.

She is pretty dressed up. I'll have to ask her about where she works.

She might be a little hesitant to talk with a man she does not know.

Rich then makes a comment about the weather and asks if it is typical for this time of year. The woman answers and then asks where he moved from. After talking more about what they each do for work, Rich invites her out for coffee.

Although Jerry and Rich started out in identical situations, the outcomes were very different. Why? Because the thoughts they had about the woman's initial lack of friendliness differed dramatically. In other words, how they *interpreted* her behavior influenced their subsequent actions and, ultimately, whether they had further conversation. It is not events themselves, but our interpretation of events, that causes anxiety.

The Relationship Between Events, Thoughts, and Feelings

Albert Ellis, the world-renowned psychotherapist and creator of Rational Emotive Behavior Therapy (REBT), talks about the relationship between events, thoughts, and feelings in terms of the ABC's.

- A = Activating Event (what happened—the circumstances)
- B = Belief (what a person thinks about the activating event)
- C = Consequences (feelings and behavior)

In this case, the activating event was the woman's lack of response to Jerry's or Rich's introduction. Jerry's belief was that she did not want to continue the conversation. Rich's belief was that she probably would want to continue the conversation but was temporarily distracted or tired. These differing beliefs led to very different consequences. Jerry continued to be alone and felt angry and depressed while Rich was excited about the beginning of a possible friendship. Again, *it is not the events themselves that make a person anxious but how one interprets them.*

Imagine that a stranger is pointing a gun at you. If you are like most people, you will feel frightened because you believe you could get hurt. However, assume that you know the gun is a water pistol. How would you feel now when the stranger points it at you? Probably not very frightened, because you have no reason to believe you are in danger. Again, it is not the gun that frightens us, but our beliefs about the harm the gun could cause.

The same is true of social anxiety. People with social anxiety become anxious not because of the situation itself, but because of what they believe about the situation, the other person, or themselves. Let's look at another example to see how this might work.

Jose is a 38-year-old man who works in a manufacturing firm, and he is attending a party for a newly hired group of managers at the firm. One of the new managers is standing at the refreshment table. He has not met her yet but has heard that she is making a lot of positive changes. He has been thinking that he might try to get a transfer to be in her department. As Jose starts to walk over and speak with the manager, he has the following thoughts:

I'm getting nervous just thinking about going to talk to her.

She'll think I'm too aggressive if I talk to her about the changes she has been making.

She'll think there's something wrong with me if she sees how nervous I am.

I'm going to make a fool of myself.

I must make a good first impression or I will never get the job I want.

These thoughts lead to the following physical symptoms:

- heart beating faster

- breathing faster—feels like he can't get his breath

- butterflies in his stomach

- muscles tensing up

As Jose gets closer to talking with the manager, he notices his mind is going blank and he does not know what to say. He considers detouring to the other end of the table, as if he were only going to refill his glass, but decides to at least say hello and introduce himself. He stumbles over his words as he says his name and has to repeat it for her. After sharing a few words about the party and the food, he excuses himself and slips away. If someone had been watching him, they would have observed the following:

- walking up to her

- stumbling over his words

- blushing

- cutting the conversation short

Before and during the conversation, Jose felt quite anxious. However, as he walked away from the woman, he experienced a number of other feelings as well, and became very upset with himself. Some of the feelings he noticed were:

- guilt and shame over not being able to handle a simple conversation

- sadness and anger that he missed an opportunity to get to know the person better

- foolishness and stupidity at being so incompetent

Not surprisingly, Jose perceived this situation as a failure and felt very poorly about himself. His self-esteem went even lower than usual.

Exploring Your Thoughts

Now imagine yourself at this party and follow through the same analysis that Jose completed. If you do not get anxious at parties, imagine it to be another gathering such as a meeting or reception. You look across the room and see someone you would like to meet standing near the refreshment table. It could be someone that you are interested in dating, someone you admire professionally who could advance your career, or someone famous like a politician, author, or athlete. Pick someone who would cause you at least a little social anxiety if you were to talk with him or her. Imagine that the person is standing alone, eating some of the snacks. Now imagine that you have decided to take this opportunity to go over and talk with the person. As you imagine this, what are you thinking? Write your thoughts in the first section of the form entitled "Learning About Your Reactions" (Figure 5.1). There are a couple of phrases to help get you started.

As you consider the thoughts you recorded above, what physiological symptoms of anxiety might you experience? List these physical symptoms in Section 2 of the form.

As you get closer to the person, with these thoughts running through your head and the physical symptoms running through your body, what would you do? This is the behavioral component of social anxiety. In other words, if someone were observing you, what would they see happening? Record your behaviors in Section 3 of the Learning About Your Reactions form.

Now let's consider how the thoughts you listed above would make you feel. Assume that you either had some difficulty in the conversation or you avoided talking with the person altogether. What emotions might you be feeling? Record them in Section 4 of the form. There are a few examples to get you started.

As you can see from this exercise, the thoughts that you had as you imagined walking over to the person influenced almost every aspect of the way the situation turned out, including:

- whether you experienced certain physiological symptoms

- whether you talked with the person or not

- if you did talk with him or her, how well you did

- what emotions you felt and how you felt about yourself

How Other People Might React To Our Thoughts

Looking back at the thoughts Jose had before approaching the new manager, we can see that he was thinking about how anxious he felt, he anticipated the conversation would turn out poorly, he assumed she would prefer not to talk with him or would think poorly of him, and he placed tremendous importance on making a good first impression.

If Jose's thoughts could magically appear in balloons over his head as if he were a cartoon character, what do you think the manager would say if she could read them? Do you agree with Jose that she would be difficult to talk to or uninterested in what he has to say? Or do you think she would be sympathetic? Do you think she would feel bad that she was making him so nervous? Maybe she would like to talk about the changes she has been making because she has put a lot of effort into

Learning About Your Reactions

1. As I walked over to talk to this person I would think . . .
   "He'll/She'll think . . ." *"I'm going to . . ."*

2. As I consider talking with this person, I would feel the following physical symptoms . . .

3. If someone were observing me they would see . . .

4. If I were thinking these thoughts and acting this way, I would feel . . .
   (Guilty, ashamed, embarrassed, angry, frustrated . . .)

Figure 5.1.

them and likes to hear what people think. Do you think she might say that talking with the bigwigs might be good for her career but that she is always on the lookout for good employees as well?

Now go back and look at the thoughts you wrote down and consider what the person you wanted to talk with would say about your thoughts. Do you think the person would be sympathetic? Do you think he or she would try to make you feel more comfortable? Might he or she tell you not to worry so much?

Most people with social anxiety we have worked with say that they would probably be supportive if they knew that the other person was anxious. Usually people say they would try to make the person feel more at ease. Occasionally we have had clients say that the other person would think they were odd or mentally ill for having such crazy thoughts. Although it is possible that some people would react negatively, it has been our experience that most people try to be supportive and encouraging if they know how nervous a person is. That is probably because social anxiety is a part of everyone's life. Everyone can remember feeling nervous at some time, so it is easier to be empathic than if the feelings of social anxiety were totally foreign to them.

When Jose worried that the manager would think he was too aggressive or that he would make a fool of himself, he did not question those thoughts. Like most people with social anxiety, he accepted his thoughts *as if they were already established facts*. Since he had never met her, what reason did he have to believe that she would think he was too aggressive? Is it not just as likely that she would be impressed by his knowledge of what she had done and be excited about talking with someone about how the changes were working out? Look back over the thoughts you wrote down. Did you question them or did you just assume that they were true? We will return to the notion of questioning your thoughts a little later.

Automatic Thoughts

Aaron T. Beck, the founder of Cognitive Therapy, was one of the first to write extensively about how negative thoughts can make us feel bad. His first work was with people who were suffering from severe depression. Dr. Beck noticed that depressed patients seemed to have a lot of negative, hopeless thoughts such as, "I'm a failure," "I'm never going to get better," and "Nothing ever goes right for me." In fact, the patients regularly shared these thoughts with him. They seemed to come into their minds spontaneously, and the more they thought like this, the worse they felt. In his landmark book entitled *Cognitive Therapy for Depression*, published in 1979 with his colleagues Drs. John Rush, Brian Shaw, and Gary Emery, Dr. Beck called these negative thoughts *automatic thoughts* or ATs for short. He defined automatic thoughts as negative or irrational thoughts about oneself, the world, and the future. Since then, Dr. Beck and many other therapists and researchers have confirmed that people with anxiety also have an abundance of ATs. The good news is that as people learn to change their ATs, they feel less anxious and depressed.

Learning to change the ATs that make you feel anxious is not simply a matter of taking out the bad thoughts and replacing them with good ones. ATs are very persistent and just trying not to have them will not make them go away. Trying to suppress negative thoughts in order to think positively may actually make the ATs worse! Daniel Wegner, a social psychologist, did an experiment in which he asked people to try not to think about a white bear. No one had been thinking about a white bear to begin with, but after they were instructed to not think about it, something surprising happened. All they could think about were white bears! Many experiments since then have concluded that trying not to think about something has just the opposite effect. So what you will be learning in this program is a series of strategies to attack your ATs directly rather than attempting to suppress them and think positively. The first step is learning to identify your ATs.

Identifying ATs and the Emotions They Cause

Let's look at an example of the ATs that one of our clients reported having in a situation that made her quite anxious.

Susan was trying to finish her degree and had enrolled in an evening class in public speaking. It was nearly the last class she needed to finish her program but she had registered and withdrawn three times. Susan was terrified of giving the five required speeches in front of the class. However, this semester she was determined to finish the class. The first assignment was a 3-minute speech about a person you admire. About a week before she was scheduled to speak, Susan started to get nervous. Susan knew that if she was feeling anxious, she must be having some ATs. Let's look at what she discovered she was thinking.

> I don't know who to talk about.
>
> I'm getting too nervous.
>
> I'll look like a complete idiot.
>
> I'll get up there and not be able to say anything.

Looking at these thoughts, is it any wonder that Susan was feeling anxious and worried? Here is what she imagined would happen: The day of the speech would come and she would still not have picked a topic. She would go up to the front of the class without being prepared. She would stand there for the required 3 minutes mostly in silence, feeling very anxious and uncomfortable, and everyone in the audience would conclude that she had very little intelligence. If that is really what was going to happen, then it makes sense that she felt anxious. Anyone would dread having such an unpleasant experience! But how likely is it that her speech would turn out the way she feared? Let's go back and look at some of the questions Susan asked herself about her ATs.

I don't know who to talk about.

Do I have any ideas about who I could talk about?

Does it really matter who I choose?

I'm getting too nervous.

How nervous is too nervous? What does that mean?

Is it any surprise that I am nervous about this speech?

Will anyone else be nervous?

I'll look like a complete idiot.

What do I mean by "complete idiot"?

How much do I think the anxiety will show to others?

I'll get up there and not be able to say anything.

How likely is it that I will not say anything for 3 minutes?

What will happen if I can't fill the whole 3 minutes?

As you can see, Susan is asking herself questions that may help her get a different perspective on some of the thoughts. Try to think of other questions she could ask herself about these thoughts. Do not worry about answering the questions at this point.

To give you some idea about how the cognitive restructuring component of treatment will work, let's assume that Susan is a few sessions ahead of this point in the treatment program and has already learned how to challenge her ATs. After she has identified her ATs, Susan will try to question and challenge them. We will call this a conversation between "Anxious Susan" and "Coping Susan." Here is what she might say to herself:

Anxious Susan: I don't know who to talk about.

Coping Susan: Is it really true that I have no ideas about who I could discuss? I really admire my sister. She was so brave when she had breast cancer. I could talk about that. Or, I could talk about someone famous, maybe a president or an actor. It probably does not matter who I talk about anyway because we are not graded on our choice.

Anxious Susan: I'm getting too nervous.

Coping Susan: I have been avoiding this class for a long time, so shouldn't I expect to be nervous? Anyway, what does *too nervous* mean? I just have to try to prepare my speech, work on my ATs, and get through it. It will probably be easier once I have done it the first time. If it is really horrible, I can always withdraw and try again later.

Anxious Susan: I'll get up there and not be able to say anything.

Coping Susan: Do I really believe that I won't be able to say *anything* for the whole three minutes? Certainly, I'll be able to say something. I can plan ahead and write out what I want to say. Even though we are not supposed to read the speech, I can take notes up there to look at in case my mind goes blank. Maybe I'll take a glass of water as well so that I can take a sip if I get stuck and need to fill some time. The most important thing is just to get through it since I've been avoiding it so long.

How do you think Susan would feel after having a "rational talk" with herself? Usually taking a moment to step back from the ATs, question them, and look at the thoughts more rationally can help reduce anxiety. This is the purpose of the cognitive restructuring portion of the treatment. Cognitive restructuring is not a magic cure for anxiety. It rarely eliminates all anxious feelings. However, it can help you reduce anxiety enough that you are able to cope and get through the difficult situation. These two components of treatment—repeated challenging of ATs *combined with* repeated exposure to the feared situation—work together to reduce anxiety over time.

Identifying Your Own ATs and the Emotions They Cause

Now it is time for you to practice identifying your own automatic thoughts and the emotions they cause. Anyone who decides to make changes in his or her life, such as starting a program to overcome social anxiety, probably has some thoughts about making those changes. Although many of the thoughts may be positive and optimistic, there are likely to be doubts as well. After all, if change were easy, you would have done it already! Let's take a look at some ATs you might have about starting this treatment program.

Take a moment to think about what we have covered up to now. Think about what you have learned about social anxiety disorder and what you have learned about yourself from doing the exercises. Think about the three components of treatment—therapeutic exposure, cognitive restructuring, and homework. Do you have any doubts or fears about anything you have read? Do you have any doubts about whether the treatment will work for you? About whether you will be able to make the changes you want to make? Write down any thoughts you are having on the form in Figure 5.2 entitled "Automatic Thoughts About Starting Treatment for Social Anxiety." Do not worry about grammar or spelling. Do not edit them or try to make them sound better. Just be honest. Try to identify at least three or four thoughts.

Earlier we defined ATs as "negative or irrational thoughts about oneself, the world, and the future." How many of the thoughts you wrote down meet this definition? The thoughts may not seem irrational or illogical and they may not be. Some ATs make sense, but they are negative and/or not helpful to think about. If you are having difficulty identifying ATs, ask yourself the following questions:

- What doubts do I have about whether this treatment program will work for me?

- What worries do I have about the exposures?

- What doubts do I have that I will be able to make real, lasting change?

- What doubts do I have that my therapist will really be able to understand and help me? (if in therapy)

- What doubts do I still have that this therapy program could really help me? (if not in therapy)

ATs often begin with "I'm . . .," "I'm going to . . .," or "He/she will think . . .." Also look for thoughts that have a lot of emotion in them or contain emotional words (e.g., nervous, anxious, worried, hopeless) or emotionally laden labels (e.g., stupid, incompetent, idiot).

Automatic Thoughts About Starting Treatment for Social Anxiety

As I think about starting this treatment program, I am thinking about . . .

1.
2.
3.
4.
5.
6.
7.
8.

Emotions I feel as I think these thoughts *(check boxes that apply)*

☐ anxious/nervous ☐ frustrated ☐ irritated ☐ ashamed

☐ angry ☐ sad ☐ embarrassed ☐ hateful

☐ other: _____

Figure 5.2.

Over the years we have asked hundreds of people with social anxiety disorder to do this exercise about the ATs they have about treatment. There are a number of thoughts that come up repeatedly. We have listed those thoughts, along with some more rational responses to them. Again, we include the rational responses to preview what you will be learning to do for yourself starting next week.

This treatment won't work for me because my social anxiety is too severe.

What evidence, other than my own pessimism, do I have to think this is true? Do I have evidence that this treatment might possibly be helpful? This treatment has been used with many people around the world. At least some of them were probably as bad off as I am, maybe worse. Besides, if my problems are so serious, then it means I need to try even harder to make changes. I'll just do the best I can and hope it works.

I've been anxious too long. There is no way I can change.

It is true that I have had problems with social anxiety since I was a child, but does that mean I cannot change? Earlier I read that many of the people in the authors' research had social anxiety disorder most of their lives, yet most of them got better.

I won't be able to do the exposures because I'm too anxious.

I am feeling very worried about doing the exposures, but does that mean I won't be able to do them when the time comes? My therapist can help me start slowly and pick easier situations to begin with. Also, by the time the exposures start, I will have had practice with cognitive restructuring. If I work very hard on cognitive restructuring, that should help me control my anxiety.

I don't have any thoughts when I am anxious, so the cognitive restructuring won't work for me.

Again, what evidence do I have that this is the case? Although I am having difficulty figuring out what my thoughts are right now, I have not really had much chance to practice yet. The authors say that other people who could not recall their thoughts at first learned to do so later. I'll keep trying and see how it goes. If I continue to have trouble, I'll talk with my therapist about it.

It will be too hard to talk with my therapist about what I am really thinking.

It is true that I might have some thoughts that are embarrassing or seem silly. I might have thoughts that are painful to talk about. However, does this mean I can't do it? Everything I say to my therapist is private and confidential. Those thoughts that I am worried about might be the most important ones to discuss. I do not have to do it all at once, though. I can take my time.

Role playing the exposures in session sounds silly. That won't work for me.

How can I know if the role plays will work for me until I try them? Maybe I am thinking role plays are silly because I am anxious about doing them. This treatment program has helped a lot of people. There is no reason to think that I am that different from them. I'll just try and see how it goes. Besides, there are always the exposures in the homework even if the in-session exposures are not ideal for me.

I've been in therapy lots of times and nothing has ever worked for me.

Unfortunately, there are no guarantees that this treatment program will work either. However, what good do I do for myself by focusing on this point? There are a lot of scientific studies showing that it is helpful for many people. I have never done anything exactly like this in therapy. My therapist would not be recommending it if it were not appropriate for me. I know that I won't make progress on my social anxiety if I do not try it so my best option is to work hard and see how it goes.

Homework

In addition to continuing the self-monitoring of your average daily anxiety and depression, it is time to practice keeping track of the ATs you have in a situation that make you anxious during the week. Using the form entitled "Monitoring Your Automatic Thoughts"(Figure 5.3), write down a brief description of a situation you encounter that makes you anxious. A few words are sufficient. Then write down the thoughts you are having. Do not worry about spelling or grammar. Try to write down the thoughts exactly as you think them without editing to make them seem nicer or more sophisticated. If you are thinking, "I'm a damn moron!" write that down. Do not change it to "I was thinking that I was not very smart." Try to come up with at least five thoughts. Then, after you have recorded the thoughts, indicate what emotion(s) you were feeling in the situation. If the feeling you had is not listed, describe it in the space provided.

When To Do Your Homework

It is always best to fill out the form as close to the time you had the thoughts as possible. If you find yourself anxiously anticipating an event, then take a few minutes to write down your thoughts before the event even happens. You can always add some thoughts from the actual event later. Sometimes it is not reasonable to take out the paper and write down your thoughts right at the time. Try to fill out the form as soon afterwards as you can, certainly before you go to bed that night. It is especially important to record your thoughts as soon after the situation as possible if you are the sort of person who plays a situation over and over again in your mind, because doing so often changes the nature of the thoughts. We want you to capture your thoughts and feelings as they occurred to you in the situation.

Monitoring Your Automatic Thoughts

1. Situation *(Briefly describe the anxiety-provoking situation.)*

2. Automatic Thoughts *(List the thoughts you have about this situation.)*

3. Emotions you feel as you think these thoughts *(check boxes that apply)*

☐ anxious/nervous ☐ frustrated ☐ irritated ☐ ashamed

☐ angry ☐ sad ☐ embarrassed ☐ hateful

☐ other: _____

Figure 5.3.

Monitoring Your Automatic Thoughts

1. Situation (*Briefly describe the anxiety-provoking situation.*)

   Thinking about calling Amanda and asking her to go to lunch tomorrow.

2. Automatic Thoughts (*List the thoughts you have about this situation.*)

   She won't want to go with me.

   It will be awkward if she says no.

   She is probably too busy.

   I'll be even more anxious if she says yes because then I will have to go.

   I don't know what restaurant to suggest.

   I'll sound nervous.

   She will think I'm odd when my voice shakes.

3. Emotions you feel as you think these thoughts (*check boxes that apply*)

   ☑ anxious/nervous   ☑ frustrated   ☐ irritated   ☐ ashamed

   ☐ angry   ☐ sad   ☐ embarrassed   ☐ hateful

   ☐ other: _____

Figure 5.4.   **Example of a Completed Monitoring Your Automatic Thoughts**

What To Do if You Do Not Get Anxious This Week

If you do not have an anxiety-provoking situation come up this week, then take a few minutes and imagine one. You can either use something that happened in the past or something that may be coming up. Try to imagine it as vividly as possible. Then record the situation (indicating that you imagined it), your thoughts, and the accompanying emotions. See Figure 5.4 for an example of a form completed by John, who describes his automatic thoughts about calling Amanda and inviting her to lunch.

Self-Assessment

1. Actual events, rather than interpretations, are what make a person anxious. T F

2. Common emotions that occur if you feel a social situation went poorly include guilt and shame. T F

3. The thoughts you have before you enter a social situation are unlikely to influence how that situation turns out. T F

4. Simply trying to think positively will likely work to combat negative automatic thoughts. T F

5. After automatic thoughts have been identified, the next step is to question and challenge them. T F

Answers to Self-Assessment questions can be found in Appendix A.

Chapter 6

Tools to Challenge Your Automatic Thoughts

In the last chapter you learned how to identify the automatic thoughts that you have when you get anxious. Some people are very aware of their thoughts and do not have any trouble writing them down. Other people find that their ATs slip by so quickly that it takes some practice to learn to catch them. If you are having trouble identifying your ATs, do not despair! Like most things in life, it gets easier with practice.

In this chapter, we will cover the remaining steps in cognitive restructuring. These steps include analyzing the ATs for logical errors, questioning whether the ATs are really true, and developing more rational, helpful statements to make to ourselves. By the end of the chapter, you should have an entire arsenal of weapons with which to attack those anxiety-producing ATs that can ruin your life.

Defining Thinking Errors

In the last chapter we defined ATs as negative or irrational thoughts about oneself, the world, and the future. What do we mean by irrational? Irrational means that there is something about the AT that does not make any sense when you really step back and think about it, something that is illogical in some way. A number of psychologists and psychiatrists (Dr. A.T. Beck and his colleagues, Dr. Jacqueline Persons and Dr. Judith Beck, among others) have written about the types of logical errors that they have found in the thinking of their anxious and depressed clients. Over the years, we have found their ideas to be very helpful for people working to overcome social anxiety. We would like to share some of these ideas with you.

The logical errors in ATs are called Thinking Errors. We will talk about a number of different types of Thinking Errors as outlined by Dr. Judith Beck in her 1995 book *Cognitive Therapy: Basics and Beyond* (published by Guilford Press and adapted with permission of the author and publisher) and based on the work of Dr. A.T. Beck. As you read through the following sections, be sure to keep two points in mind:

1. Many ATs may contain more than one Thinking Error, depending upon which aspect of the thought you emphasize.

2. Recognizing lots of Thinking Errors in your own thoughts does not mean that your social anxiety is more severe or that you will not be able to benefit from this treatment program.

We will review each of the Thinking Errors in detail here. Figure 6.1 contains a summary of the Thinking Errors that will be a good reference for you to use as you make efforts to recognize these errors in your thinking in everyday life. Make a copy of it and keep it where you can review it frequently.

All-or-Nothing Thinking

(Also called black-and-white, polarized, or dichotomous thinking): You view a situation in only two categories instead of on a continuum.

All-or-Nothing Thinking means that something is seen as having only two distinct categories. Things are seen as black or as white, without any shades of gray. One of the categories represents goodness, success, intelligence, or attractiveness. The other category represents badness, failure, stupidity, or ugliness. Usually the good category is very small and hard to get into. The bad category, on the other hand, is large and easy to fall into. That means that if one is using All-or-Nothing Thinking to reflect on success and failure, it will be much easier to fail than succeed. There is no such thing as doing OK or partially succeeding, because everything is black and white. Let's look at some examples.

Consider the woman who had the AT: "Men will only date me if I am beautiful." In her case, "beautiful" meant looking like a movie star or a model. Thus, the category of being beautiful was very small and the opposite, "ugly" or "unattractive," included most of the women on the planet! Needless to say, this AT made her very anxious when talking with men because she always expected to be rejected at any moment. Although she was rather attractive, she did not look as though she had just stepped off the cover of a magazine.

Another example of All-or-Nothing Thinking is the businessman who became very anxious at the picnic sponsored by his wife's department at the university where she worked. His wife was a professor, and nearly everyone at the picnic had more education than he did. He had the AT "I'll say something stupid and embarrass both of us." For him, stupid things to say included everything that most people talk about all of the time—weather, sports, current events, movies, and so forth. He wanted to say only "brilliant" things, so he said nothing at all.

If an AT implies that only perfect is good enough, then it probably contains some All-or-Nothing Thinking. If you find yourself not wanting to do something because you fear you will not do it well enough, consider whether you are thinking only in terms of success or failure rather than the important gray areas of partial success or doing well but not perfectly.

Fortune Telling

You predict that something negative is going to happen in the future, as if you were gazing into a crystal ball.

There are two thinking errors that fall under the general heading of *Anticipating Negative Outcomes*. The first is Fortune Telling. Few of us believe that the fortune teller at the carnival can look into her crystal ball and accurately predict whom we will marry or how many children we will have. Yet it is very common for our clients with social anxiety to look into the future and make very confident predictions such as "I'll get anxious if I go to the party," "She won't go out with me," or "I won't have anything to say." Because they are already convinced that the situation will turn out badly, they often avoid going altogether, giving themselves "evidence" that the situation was indeed too difficult for them to handle. Even if the person does not avoid the situation, then these negative predictions can become self-fulfilling prophecies. For example, if people expect to be turned down when they ask a person out on a date, it is unlikely they will put their best foot forward when offering the invitation.

Typically when people make negative predictions about what is going to happen in a situation that makes them anxious, they have failed to consider whether there is any evidence to support their prediction. There may be good reason to believe that the situation will turn out just fine. In other cases, people believe that their negative predictions are firmly rooted in the evidence of past experience (e.g., "I always get anxious in this situation"). However, they ignore the fact that every circumstance is slightly different. Even small changes can affect what happens in a social situation. This may be especially true for you as you make progress in this program. You are becoming a different person who may act and think differently than you did in the past. Therefore, the "evidence" of past experience may no longer apply. Whenever you find yourself automatically predicting that a situation will turn out badly, beware the Fortune Telling error!

Catastrophizing

You tell yourself the *very worst* is happening or is going to happen, without considering other possibilities that may be more likely and/or less negative.

The second type of *Anticipating Negative Outcomes* is Catastrophizing, jumping to the conclusion that something is (or will turn out to be) absolutely terrible without any evidence that it is really that bad. Most often people catastrophize about the future, predicting that an upcoming event will turn out terribly, and then they act as if the prediction is true. "I'll never get a job!" is a good example of a Catastrophizing AT that our clients often report after suffering through a difficult job interview. Other examples include "I'll never find another person to love me" after a relationship ends and "I'll never get promoted" after appearing nervous with a supervisor. These Catastrophizing ATs have in common that they each suggest extremely negative consequences if things do not go well in the situation.

Sometimes Catastrophizing ATs can seem silly when said aloud. If someone gets turned down for one job, the next step is not usually to move the entire family into a cardboard box in an alley. However, these ATs can lead to very powerful feelings of anxiety, depression, and hopelessness. Sometimes our clients are so ashamed and afraid of the catastrophe they fear that they hardly admit it to themselves. We often find that the feared catastrophe comes in the form of a clear image of some awful outcome, like being home alone and lonely night after night, lying in your deathbed all alone, or seeing your children huddled in a cold alley. Once clients face these horrible images and express their fears aloud, the images almost always becomes less frightening.

Disqualifying or Discounting the Positive

You unreasonably tell yourself that your positive experiences, deeds, or qualities do not count.

This Thinking Error is one of the most common logical errors that we have seen in our work with individuals with social anxiety. As you will see in a later chapter, Disqualifying the Positive, which involves ignoring or rejecting positive experiences or events, can undermine your successes and interfere with your progress in this program. Here are some examples of Disqualifying the Positive ATs:

It went OK because she was easy to talk to.

I didn't get very anxious. I must have just been having a good day.

I don't know why I was so worried about it. It wasn't any big deal.

What do all of these thoughts have in common? An event that the person was anxious about beforehand went well, but the person refuses to take any credit for the success. Instead, "credit" goes to the other person, some vague unknown force that makes us have "good days" and "bad days," or our own stupidity for thinking something would be difficult when it was really easy all along. Disqualifying the Positive is the perfect strategy for maintaining a belief that you will not be able to handle a situation you fear—you have nothing to do with making it go well so there is no reason to be more confident next time!

Emotional Reasoning

You think something must be true because you "feel" (actually, believe) it so strongly, ignoring or discounting evidence to the contrary.

Emotions, especially feelings of anxiety, are often very strong. These feelings are truly hard to ignore. The strength of your feelings can mean that you come to believe that they represent the only reality of the situation—"I'm feeling very anxious so this conversation must be going badly." This is Emotional Reasoning. In this example, it is true that the person is feeling very anxious. However, the conversation could be going just fine. In fact, the anxiety may not be noticeable to the other person.

Another example of Emotional Reasoning is the man who felt very anxious at formal parties such as wedding receptions. He had worked all his life as a carpenter, and he felt foolish and out of place being all dressed up and having to talk with people he did not know well. His AT was "I feel so foolish, I must look really foolish." In reality, he looked quite handsome in a suit and tie, and other people were often as worried about making small talk with him as he was with them!

Labeling

You put a fixed, global label on yourself or others without considering that the evidence might more reasonably lead to a less disastrous conclusion.

The Thinking Error of Labeling involves summarizing your feelings about yourself, a situation, or another person with a negative label. Most often people with social anxiety apply negative labels to themselves, not other people. These labels cause problems because they shift your attention from something specific that you might be unhappy with (something you said or did) to a total negative judgement about your personality or character. This is the difference between saying to yourself that you made some mistakes on the project versus calling yourself an *incompetent oaf*. Not only does the label make you feel bad, it can make you feel stuck and hopeless about changing anything. Over the years our clients have come up with some colorful labels for themselves including:

foolish	incompetent	jerk
space cadet	idiot	inadequate
stupid	boring	loser
hopeless	mentally ill	loony
defective	dweeb	disgusting

As you might guess, the same people who labeled themselves with these emotionally loaded words would often be described by others who know them well as bright, competent, interesting, fun, and attractive.

When people with social anxiety apply negative labels to others, it is often because they are angry at them. In most cases, they have good reason to be angry. However, sometimes they are angry because a person has put them in a position in which they feel uncomfortable because of their anxiety. Consider the college student who described a professor as a "total jerk" and an "incompetent teacher" for insisting that the student complete a required classroom presentation. The student, who was very anxious about speaking in front of a group, felt trapped between his fear of making the presentation and his concern about failing the class. Labeling the professor was not helpful because it shifted his attention from trying to cope with his anxiety to just being angry at the professor.

Mental Filter

(Also called selective abstraction): You pay undue attention to one negative detail instead of seeing the whole picture.

The Thinking Error called Mental Filter means that you focus all of your attention on one negative detail and it colors your entire view of yourself, another person, or the situation. The negative detail can be a symptom of anxiety like a voice quaver, hand tremor, or blush. Or it can be something that happened, like spilling some food or a drink, a single argument with someone you care about, or losing your train of thought. By focusing on the negative detail, it is difficult to see the bigger picture, which is likely to contain many positive aspects as well. Mental Filter is similar to Disqualifying the Positive, in which positive experiences are discounted. In Mental Filter, positive experiences are overwhelmed by the focus on the negative detail.

As an example of Mental Filter, consider the lecturer who becomes very anxious after seeing one person yawn in an audience of 75 people. The lecturer's AT is "That person is yawning so my speech must be boring." By focusing all of the attention on the one sleepy person and filtering out the other 74, the lecturer loses the big picture. Yes, the person did yawn. Maybe she was bored by the speech—or maybe she just did not get enough sleep the night before. However, there is no reason to pay more attention to her than to the other 74 who did not yawn.

Mind Reading

You believe you know what others are thinking, failing to consider other, more likely, possibilities, and you make no effort to check it out.

Mind Reading is exactly what the name implies—you assume that someone is reacting poorly to you as if you could read his or her thoughts. Because you are sure about what the other person thinks about you, you act as if it were true without checking it out. That often keeps you from finding out that, like most people, you are not a very talented mind reader and the person was actually thinking neutral or positive thoughts about you or was thinking about something else altogether.

Consider the woman who believed that her boss thought she was incompetent because he did not recommend her for a new position that opened up in her firm. In reality her boss thought she could easily get the position, but was not aware that she wanted to be recommended. Or the man who became very anxious when he thought a sales clerk assumed he must be mentally ill because his hand shook a little as he wrote out his check. In reality, she thought he must be feeling impatient because there had been a long line at the checkout stand.

Overgeneralization

You make a sweeping negative conclusion that goes far beyond the current situation.

Overgeneralization means that a person gives too much emphasis to one event or experience, usually a negative one. This bad thing happened, so I know that is what will always happen. Overgeneralization often leads to not trying something again that did not go as well as the person would have liked last time. Overgeneralization often means not giving yourself—or someone else—a second chance. Let's look at an example.

Consider the man who was about halfway through this treatment program when his therapist suggested that it might be time to try having lunch with his co-workers. He had become very anxious in the situation before treatment and had been going to his car to eat lunch alone ever since. When asked by his therapist why he did not want to attempt this assignment, he reported the following Overgeneralization AT: "I know I won't be able to do it because I got very anxious last time I tried to eat with them." By basing his conclusion about his inability to join his co-workers for lunch on one experience, he ignored all of the skills he had learned in therapy and all of his more recent successes in other situations.

"Should" and "Must" Statements

(Also called imperatives): You have a precise, fixed idea of how you or others should behave and you overestimate how bad it is that these expectations are not met.

Should Statements are usually the easiest Thinking Errors to identify. Just look for ATs that contain the words "should," "must," "ought," or "have to." It is helpful to think of Should Statements as the rules we have about the way we need to live our lives. Having such rules is not necessarily bad. "You should not steal" is a rule that nearly everyone would agree is a good idea, not an irrational belief. The Should Statements that are Thinking Errors are rules that are extreme or perfectionistic, such as "I should always be perfect," "I should never get anxious," "I should always be in control." We have found that the Should Statements that socially anxious people use often create extremely high standards. In fact, these standards are so high that virtually no one could live up to them. Even highly paid TV anchor people on the evening news shows could not live up to the standards that some socially anxious people set for themselves, like "I should never stumble over my words" or "I should always speak clearly and fluently."

Although you will probably find that your Should Statements are directed at yourself, they can also be directed at other people. If you are feeling angry or hostile towards someone, consider whether a Should Statement is involved. Maybe you have some "rules" about how the other person should act. One of our clients was very upset with her husband and revealed the following Should Statement when discussing upcoming holiday plans: "He shouldn't ask me to spend Christmas with his family. He knows how anxious I get around them."

Maladaptive Thoughts

Consider the following thoughts:

I've never asked anyone out on a date before.

I'm feeling uncomfortable.

It's not fair that I have such severe anxiety.

Working on overcoming my anxiety is hard.

What do all of these thoughts have in common? They are not illogical. In fact, they are probably true, or they are value judgments which are neither true nor false. Since we defined ATs as "negative, illogical thoughts," these examples are not, strictly speaking, ATs. You may find that you have some thoughts like these that do not seem to fit into any of the Thinking Error categories. It turns out that a few thoughts that cause anxiety do not contain logical errors. However, if you dwell on them, they will make you feel more anxious. These thoughts also may make you perform less well in whatever you are doing. Dr. Jacqueline Persons calls these "maladaptive thoughts" rather than ATs. Fortunately, the strategies we use to challenge ATs also work for maladaptive thoughts.

A summary of the Thinking Errors appears in Figure 6.1.

Finding the Logical Errors in Your Automatic Thoughts

Before we look at the thoughts that you recorded about a time you became anxious in the past week (last week's homework assignment), let's look at Beth's thoughts as she gets ready to go for an interview for a job she really wants:

I must make a good first impression or they won't hire me.

They are going to think I don't have enough experience.

I'll never find another job as perfect as this one would be.

When she considered these ATs, Beth felt anxious and hopeless about getting the job.

List of Thinking Errors

■ **All-or-Nothing Thinking** (also called black-and-white, polarized, or dichotomous thinking): You view a situation in only two categories instead of on a continuum.

■ **Anticipating Negative Outcomes:** You expect that something negative has happened or is going to happen. Two types of thinking errors fall into this category:

   – **Fortune Telling:** You predict that something negative is going to happen in the future, as if you were gazing into a crystal ball.

   – **Catastrophizing:** You tell yourself that the very worst is happening or is going to happen, without considering other possibilities that may be more likely and/or less negative.

■ **Disqualifying or Discounting the Positive:** You unreasonably tell yourself that positive experiences, deeds, or qualities do not count.

■ **Emotional Reasoning:** You think something must be true because you "feel" (actually, believe) it so strongly, ignoring or discounting evidence to the contrary.

■ **Labeling:** You put a fixed, global label on yourself or others without considering that the evidence might more reasonably lead to a less disastrous conclusion.

■ **Mental Filter** (also called selective abstraction): You pay undue attention to one negative detail instead of seeing the whole picture.

■ **Mind Reading:** You believe you know what others are thinking, failing to consider other, more likely, possibilities, and you make no effort to check it out.

■ **Overgeneralization:** You make a sweeping negative conclusion that goes far beyond the current situation.

■ **"Should" and "Must" Statements** (also called imperatives): You have a precise, fixed idea of how you or others should behave and you overestimate how bad it is that these expectations are not met.

■ **Maladaptive Thoughts**: Problematic thoughts that do not contain logical thinking errors. These thoughts may be true. However, dwelling on them makes you feel more anxious and may interfere with your performance.

Figure 6.1.

Note. Adapted with permission from Judith S. Beck (1995), *Cognitive Therapy: Basics and Beyond*, Guilford Press, Figure 8.2, p. 119.

Look over the List of Thinking Errors and see how you would classify each thought. Remember, thoughts can fall into more than one category. For right now, do not worry about whether you think the thought is probably true. Just see which Thinking Error(s) might describe the AT.

Let's see if you found the same Thinking Errors that we found.

1. *"I must make a good first impression or they won't hire me."* This thought contains several Thinking Errors. It could fall into the Should Statement category. "I must..." is a way of battering oneself with rigid requirements or rules. There is no room for flexibility. Beth feels she has to make a good first impression or she would not get the job.

   This thought also has the flavor of All-or-Nothing Thinking in that everything depends on the first impression. Either Beth makes a good first impression and gets the job or she makes a bad first impression and does not get the job. This thought, like all ATs that fall in the All-or-Nothing category, ignores any possibilities between the two extremes. There are many first impressions that can be made besides "good" and "bad." For example, maybe Beth could make only a moderately good first impression and still get the job. Beth probably also believes that there are many ways to make a bad first impression but only one or two ways to make a good one.

   Finally, Beth is doing some Fortune Telling. She is looking into her crystal ball and seeing what is going to happen in the future. Although it probably is true that she is more likely to be offered the job if she makes a positive first impression, there is no way to predict that for sure. A lot of factors go into a hiring decision, and the first impression on an interview is only one of them.

2. *"They are going to think I don't have enough experience."* "They are going to think" or "They think" are always good clues that an AT contains the Mind Reading error. Beth has no way of knowing what the interviewers are thinking. They could have a variety of opinions about her level of experience. The interviewers could think that Beth has plenty of experience. Or they could think that she does not have very much experience but she could go through some training. If they think she only has a little experience, they might be pleased that they will not have to pay her as much at first as someone with more. In fact, the different interviewers may hold many opinions and disagree amongst themselves about her experience.

   If Beth does have quite a bit of experience for this particular job, then this AT is an example of Disqualifying the Positive. Beth could be downplaying her accomplishments rather than recognizing that her experience makes her very appropriate (or even overqualified) for the position.

   Once again, this thought contains some aspects of the Fortune Telling error in that Beth is predicting what is going to happen. You will notice that many ATs that you have in anticipation of an event that makes you anxious will contain Fortune Telling. It is easy to fall into the trap of thinking about what will happen as if it were an established fact. If the thought is making you anxious, then like Beth, you are probably predicting something bad is going to happen even though you do not actually know what will occur.

3. *"I'll never find another job as perfect as this one would be."* This is a good example of Catastrophizing and All-or-Nothing Thinking all rolled into one thought. The word "never" is often a good clue for Catastrophizing. Never having a particular opportunity again means you are anticipating the worst without considering other possible outcomes. Beth is emphasizing that this is the one possibility in a lifetime for a great job. If she misses this one, there will never be another chance. Certainly there are once-in-a-lifetime opportunities such as being an Olympic athlete, being chosen to sit on the U.S. Supreme Court, or being the first person to set foot on the surface of the moon. Most events in our lives do not offer such unique opportunities.

Finally, this AT contains some All-or-Nothing Thinking. Although this may be an excellent job for Beth, it is unlikely that every single aspect of the job would be wonderful. By describing the job as "perfect," Beth is forming an extremely positive opinion that may cause Beth problems for two reasons. First, it is unlikely to be true. In fact, until Beth has been in the job for awhile, she will not have enough information to know whether it has any negative aspects. Second, describing the job as "perfect" leads to Catastrophic thinking as discussed above in that all other jobs become "second best."

As you can see, there are often several ways to look at an automatic thought. At first it is helpful to try and find several Thinking Errors in each thought. This gives you practice in learning to think about your ATs in a more objective way. Over time most people start to learn which Thinking Errors are the most common for them. If Beth monitored and categorized her thoughts in this way over many situations, she would likely discover that certain errors appear in her thinking on a regular basis. Looking over Beth's thoughts, it appears that Fortune Telling and All-or-Nothing Thinking were the most common for this situation. Over time Beth might learn that, if she is anxious, she is likely to engage in Fortune Telling or All-or-Nothing Thinking. Then she could quickly identify the ATs that were making her anxious and challenge them using the strategies that we will cover later in this chapter. Now, let's have you practice identifying the Thinking Errors in your own thoughts.

Identifying the Thinking Errors in Your Homework ATs

Recording your ATs during an anxiety-provoking situation during the last week gave you an opportunity to practice the first skill of cognitive restructuring—identifying ATs. This assignment also gave us a list of ATs to use for practice in identifying Thinking Errors. Take out the "Monitoring Your Automatic Thoughts" form that you completed during the week for homework. Now look at the List of Thinking Errors in Figure 6.1 and see which distortions might be present in the first thought. At this point, do not worry whether you truly believe the thought is distorted or not. For the sake of the exercise, assume it contains some Thinking Error and try to identify it. If possible, see if each thought can fit in two or three categories. You might find that one category best fits the thought but practicing using several categories gives you more opportunities to view your ATs more objectively. Write the Thinking Errors in the margin next to the AT.

After you finish identifying the Thinking Errors in your own thoughts, look over your list and see if there was one that you used several times. Did one type of thinking dominate? If so, then that might be a common Thinking Error for you. As you practice monitoring and analyzing your ATs in the coming weeks, you will learn which thinking errors are most common for you.

If you found that identifying the Thinking Errors was difficult, then you might want to practice with some more thoughts before going on to the next section. You can either imagine a situation that makes you anxious and record your thoughts now or look back at some of the ATs from Chapter 4.

Challenging Your Automatic Thoughts

To this point you have learned the first two steps of cognitive restructuring:

1. Identifying your ATs and the emotions they cause

2. Examining the Thinking Errors in your ATs.

Now it is time to learn about questioning and challenging the ATs to see how realistic or helpful they are. We are going to ask you to become a rational scientist and analyze what your ATs really mean. Sometimes we will even conduct experiments to see if they are true. If you are like most of the people we have worked with, you may be surprised at what you are really thinking!

When someone is having difficulty with social anxiety, he or she may have been thinking the same automatic thoughts for a long time, maybe even most of his or her life. The thoughts may be so familiar that the person has never questioned them, never considered whether they were true or even if they made any sense. Thus, the best way to challenge ATs is to ask and answer a series of questions about the meaning of the thoughts. Note that we said "ask and answer." As you will see, answering the questions that you pose is an essential step in the process.

A number of years ago, Drs. Lawrence Sank and Carolyn Shaffer came up with a list of questions to challenge ATs that we'll call "Disputing Questions." This is a list of all-purpose questions that encourage a person to look at ATs from different perspectives. Some of the Disputing Questions are particularly appropriate for ATs with certain Thinking Errors and others work for a variety of thoughts. Over the

Disputing Questions

Use these questions to challenge your automatic thoughts. Be sure to answer each question you pose to yourself. You will find each question helpful for many different thoughts. Several examples are also presented to help you get started.

1. Do I know for certain that _____ ?

   Example: *Do I know for certain that I won't have anything to say?*

2. Am I 100% sure that _____ ?

   Example: *Am I 100% sure that my anxiety will show?*

3. What evidence do I have that _____ ?

   What evidence do I have that the opposite is true?

   Example: *What evidence do I have that they did not understand my speech?*

   What evidence do I have that they did understand my speech?

4. What is the worst that could happen? How bad is that? How can I cope with that?

5. Do I have a crystal ball?

6. Is there another explanation for _____ ?

   Example: *Is there another explanation for his refusal to have coffee with me?*

7. Does _____ have to lead to or equal _____ ?

   Example: *Does "being nervous" have to lead to or equal "looking stupid"?*

8. Is there another point of view?

9. What does _____ mean? Does _____ really mean that I am a(n) _____ ?

   Example: *What does "looking like an idiot" mean? Does the fact that I stumbled over my words really mean that I look like an idiot?*

Adapted from Lawrence I. Sank and Carolyn S. Shaffer (1984), *A Therapist's Manual for Cognitive Behavior Therapy in Groups,* Plenum Press, p. 223.

Figure 6.2.

years, we have developed a few additional Disputing Questions that our clients have found particularly helpful. A list of Sank and Shaffer's Disputing Questions with our additions appears in Figure 6.2.

Let's take a look at how the Disputing Questions can be used to challenge ATs. Assume Al has the following AT when he thinks about asking his co-worker Lois out on a date: "She won't go out with me."

Based on what we covered in the previous section, this AT is a perfect example of Fortune Telling. Even before he asks her out, Al "knows" that Lois will turn down his invitation. Using the Disputing Questions, let's see how reasonable Al's assumption might be. Al could ask himself:

> Do I know for certain that Lois won't go out with me? The answer to that question is: No, I don't know what Lois will do.

Then Al could use another Disputing Question to see how certain he is about what she will do:

> Am I 100% sure that Lois won't go out with me?

The answer is:

> I'm not 100% certain. There is probably a 50-50 chance she would go out with me. She seems very friendly and she was hinting that she did not have anything to do this weekend.

Notice that Al started out thinking that Lois would not go out with him and now he is able to say that there is a 50% chance that she would say yes. Al's change in thinking will probably lead to a change in his actions. It seems very unlikely that Al would ask Lois on a date if he believed she would refuse. However, he may ask her out now that he has reconsidered how she might respond.

These examples illustrate several important points about how to use the Disputing Questions to challenge your automatic thoughts. First, pick the Disputing Question that seems to make the most sense for the thought. If the first one does not fit, try others. Second, put the AT in the blank in the Disputing Question if there is one. You may have to change the wording of your thought so that it makes a logical question. For example, the AT "I'll make a complete fool of myself" could become "What is the worst that could happen if I made a complete fool of myself?" Third, Al had been thinking Lois would refuse to go out with him for quite a while. It would have been easy for him to get stuck on that belief and not really think through another point of view unless he put the answer to the question into words. Sometimes just writing down or saying the response to a Disputing Question aloud helps a person realize that the AT does not seem very logical or realistic.

The list of Disputing Questions in Figure 6.2 will help you get started with challenging your automatic thoughts. As you use the list, you will find that some of the questions are particularly helpful for you. You will probably also develop other Disputing Questions that are not on the list. This list is definitely not exhaustive. There are many different approaches to challenging each AT. As you gain experience with the cognitive restructuring procedures, you will develop the one that works best for you.

Now let's look more closely at the process of challenging ATs by going back to Beth and her job interview. As you will see, it is helpful to challenge a given thought with several Disputing Questions. The Disputing Questions and answers can be conceptualized as the rational coping person inside of you talking with the anxious person inside of you.

Beth's first thought about her job interview was, "I must make a good first impression or they won't hire me." We found three primary Thinking Errors in this thought: Should Statement, All-or-Nothing Thinking, and Fortune Telling. In the following dialogues, Coping Beth challenges Anxious Beth's ATs.

Anxious Beth: I must make a good first impression or they won't hire me.

Coping Beth: What evidence do you have that if you don't make a good first impression they won't hire you?

Anxious Beth: I don't have any evidence but I am more likely to get the job if I make a good first impression.

Coping Beth: Does making a less-than-good first impression mean that you won't get the job?

Anxious Beth: Probably.

Coping Beth: Are you 100% sure that making a less-than-good first impression means that you won't get the job?

Anxious Beth: No, not 100%. Sometimes you can make up for a bad first impression.

Coping Beth: So would it be fair to say to yourself that it would be better to make a good first impression but even if you don't, you could still get the job.

Anxious Beth: Yes. I have most of the qualifications and they must have a good impression of me from my resume or they would not have invited me to interview.

As you can see, Beth used three of the Disputing Questions from the list to challenge this thought. In the last "Coping Beth" statement, she turned a negative statement around to make it positive. This is a bit like the proverbial glass that is half full or half empty. Both statements may be equally true but most of us would feel better with the half-full glass. This strategy works well as a Disputing Question.

Now let's look at another one of Beth's thoughts. The three Thinking Errors we identified in this thought were Mind Reading, Disqualifying the Positive, and Fortune Telling.

Anxious Beth: They are going to think I don't have enough experience.

Coping Beth: Do you know for certain that they will think you don't have enough experience?

Anxious Beth: No, I don't know for certain. I am just worried they will think that.

Coping Beth: Let's look at your worry, then. What evidence do you have that you have enough experience?

Anxious Beth: The last two jobs I had were fairly similar to this one. The job announcement said that applicants need at least 2 years of experience. I have 3 years but the first was not full-time.

Coping Beth: So you have more than 2 years of experience and the announcement said you needed 2 years. Do you have any evidence that it is not enough?

Anxious Beth: No.

For this thought, Beth used two Disputing Questions to challenge her AT about not having enough experience. Note that "Coping Beth" again re-stated the answers to one of the questions in slightly more positive terms. "I have 3 years of experience but the first year wasn't full time" became "So you have more than 2 years of experience." Note how the first statement by Anxious Beth makes it seem that she does not have enough experience but the second statement by Coping Beth points out that she actually has more experience than required!

How do you think Beth felt before and after she applied these cognitive restructuring questions to her ATs? From her thoughts, it looks like Beth was very anxious about the interview. Think about what physical symptoms of anxiety you would have if you had those thoughts before a job interview. She probably had some butterflies in her stomach, perhaps more than a few. Do you think she felt a little less anxious after she had challenged the thoughts? It seems likely. As you read through the exchange between Anxious Beth and Coping Beth, notice that the tone of what she is saying to herself becomes more positive and optimistic. It is unlikely she would go into the interview perfectly calm. Almost everyone has some anxiety in job interviews. However, cognitive restructuring should help her feel a little calmer and make it more likely that she can think clearly and make a positive (not perfect!) first impression.

Now go back to the ATs that you examined for the exercise on Thinking Errors above. Using the worksheet "Practice Using Anxious Self/Coping Self Dialogue" (Figure 6.3), have an "anxious self/coping self" dialogue with yourself about two or three of the thoughts. Write the AT on the first line as "Anxious Self." Use one of the Disputing Questions to start to question the AT on the second line labeled "Coping Self." Then on the third line have Anxious Self answer the Disputing Question. Try to go back and forth between Anxious Self and Coping Self several times until you feel that you can see a more positive point of view or at least can see the AT from a slightly different perspective. Repeat this process with two or three ATs until you begin to feel comfortable with it. Be patient with yourself. As with any new skill, it takes time and practice to learn cognitive restructuring and it may feel awkward or even silly at first. Then we will be ready to move on to the final step in cognitive restructuring—developing a Rational Response. Keep in mind that it is very likely that your answers to the Disputing Questions may not seem right and the process may seem artificial to you. This is an indication that you are uncomfortable with these new skills. It is also an indication that you are doing the right thing, not the wrong thing!

Combating Automatic Thoughts with a Rational Response

The next step in the cognitive restructuring procedure is to develop a *Rational Response*. A Rational Response is a statement that summarizes or highlights the key points you have discovered as you worked through the Anxious Self/Coping Self dialogue. Often the Rational Response is a shorthand reminder to stay focused and think more rationally. When people are in a situation that makes them anxious, they can repeat the Rational Response to themselves as ATs arise. Let's go back to Beth's thoughts about her job interview to see what some Rational Responses might look like.

Beth's first AT that we challenged was "I must make a good first impression or they won't hire me." The Anxious Beth/Coping Beth dialogue ended with a more optimistic re-statement by Coping Beth of one of the points: "So would it be fair to say to yourself that it would be better to make a good first impression but even if you don't, you could still get the job?" This last statement is actually a Rational

Practice Using Anxious Self/Coping Self Dialogue

Anxious Self (AT):
Coping Self:
Anxious Self:
Coping Self:
Anxious Self:
Coping Self:
Anxious Self:
Coping Self:
Anxious Self:
Coping Self:
Anxious Self:
Coping Self:

Figure 6.3.

Response. However, it is quite a mouthful. For Beth to use it effectively in the job interview, it would be better if it were a little shorter. It could be shortened to "I could still get the job even if I don't make the best first impression" or even "Getting this job doesn't depend on the first impression." When Beth goes to the interview and notices herself having ATs about how good an impression she is making, she could repeat the Rational Response to herself as a reminder to think more rationally. This reminder should help her feel less anxious as she thinks more about what is going on in the interview and does less Fortune Telling and Catastrophizing about not getting the position.

To summarize, the steps in cognitive restructuring so far are:

1. Identify ATs and the emotions they cause

2. Identify Thinking Errors in the ATs

3. Use the Disputing Questions to ask and answer questions to challenge the ATs

4. Develop a Rational Response to combat the ATs when they occur.

Let's go back to Beth's final thought and see another example of using the Disputing Questions and developing a Rational Response. Beth's last thought was a common one for people with social anxiety disorder. This is an AT that comes up in many situations, from conversations to public speaking.

Anxious Beth:	I'll stumble over my words. (Fortune Telling)
Coping Beth:	Is stumbling over your words really so important or consequential?
Anxious Beth:	If I stumble over my words, I won't look competent enough for this great job that I want.
Coping Beth:	Does stumbling over your words equal being incompetent?
Anxious Beth:	If I stumble over my words a lot, I won't look very competent.
Coping Beth:	What is the likelihood that you will stumble over your words enough to look incompetent?
Anxious Beth:	It could happen. I'm sure I'll stumble over my words some, especially at the beginning of the interview. Sometimes it gets better after the first question or two, so it probably is not that likely that I will stumble over my words enough to look incompetent.

Rational Response: *Stumbling over my words a little is OK.*

This Anxious Beth/Coping Beth dialogue is a good example of how analyzing an AT reveals another AT "underneath" the first one. At first it looked like Beth was just worried about stumbling over her words. However, that was important to her because she was worried about appearing incompetent. As she thought it through more carefully with the Disputing Questions, she was able to conclude that it was unlikely she would stumble so much that she would look incompetent. That allowed Beth to develop a Rational Response that recognized that she did not have to speak perfectly to appear competent. If she notices herself stumbling in the interview, she can remind herself that "Stumbling over my words a little is OK." That reminder should help her calm down enough so that she can speak clearly.

Over the years we have found that developing a Rational Response is the most difficult part of the cognitive restructuring for many people. It seems that people have lived with their ATs so long without questioning them that it is difficult to truly take a more rational point of view. With practice, Rational Responses become easier to develop. Here are some pointers to help you get started:

1. A good Rational Response takes a positive (or at least neutral) view of the situation or symptoms. "It probably won't be a total disaster" is not a good Rational Response. "It will probably go OK" or even "It might go OK" will be more effective.

2. A good Rational Response is short. In fact, the shorter the Rational Response the easier it is to use. Sometimes it is helpful to reduce longer Rational Responses to short slogans. It is not necessary that the Rational Responses include all the details, but they should serve as a reminder for everything you thought through in the cognitive restructuring. "Nervousness ≠ rejection" is a good example of a slogan type of Rational Response.

3. You do not have to believe the Rational Responses, especially at first. In fact, it would be fairly unusual if you were able to reject your ATs so easily that the Rational Responses were totally believable right away. Cognitive restructuring is like a sculptor chipping away at a block of marble. For a while, it does not seem like much is happening, and it is hard to believe a beautiful sculpture will emerge. However, those first challenges to the ATs are essential to chip away the years of anxious thinking so that healthier, more helpful thoughts about yourself, other people, and social situations can emerge. You do not need to believe the Rational Response at first, but it is very important that you keep an open mind and be willing to consider it.

4. Rational Responses should be realistic. In other words, Rational Responses should represent rational thinking, not wishful thinking! Going back to Al who wants to ask Lois for a date, it would not be realistic for him to use a Rational Response that says "I'm sure Lois will go out with me." It is no more rational for Al to predict that Lois definitely will go out with him than to predict that she will not. A better Rational Response for Al would acknowledge that he does not know what Lois will do but that he will never know if he does not invite

her to go out. As we said in an earlier chapter, cognitive restructuring does not simply replace bad thoughts with good ones. Instead, it encourages you to think realistically about yourself, a situation, and other people.

5. If you are having trouble developing a Rational Response, try some of these that many people have found helpful. However, Rational Responses are very individualized, so just because it works for someone else does not mean it will work for you.

_____ ≠ _____ The first blank is something you are worried about such as looking nervous, being rejected, experiencing an anxiety symptom, and so forth. The second blank is an outcome you are worried about such as not getting something you want. Some examples are:

looking nervous ≠ looking foolish

being rejected ≠ being alone forever

not getting this job ≠ never getting a good job

blushing ≠ looking stupid

feeling anxious ≠ looking anxious

Sometimes it is helpful to use cognitive restructuring to figure out what the absolutely worst thing that could happen would be. That can lead to good Rational Responses. *The worst that can happen is _____ and I can live with that,* is a good Rational Response for ATs about outcomes that are unpleasant but not awful. For example, if your worst fear is that you would be rejected by someone, blush, look silly or foolish, or be temporarily humiliated, then that might be a good Rational Response for you. On the other hand, if your worst fear is something you see as more serious (such as being fired from a job, never finding a marital partner, or missing an important promotion), then it makes more sense to think about how likely such an event might be. That could lead to the Rational Response of, *The worst that can happen is _____, but that is unlikely.*

In the next chapter we will talk a lot about the last step in cognitive restructuring—setting reasonable goals for ourselves. However, attainable goals can also make good Rational Responses. Some common ones that our clients have developed over the years include:

I only have to say hello.

I only have to make it through the first couple of minutes, then I'll be OK.

I just need to get three points across.

Developing good Rational Responses takes time and practice. As you use the cognitive restructuring skills over and over, they will become routine. You might even find that you can shorten or even eliminate some of the steps. At this point, though, be sure to use all of the steps so you allow yourself to get the maximum benefit.

Homework

Between now and the next session it will be important for you to practice the cognitive restructuring skills. Look for one or two situations during the week that cause you some anxiety and work through all four steps using the worksheet in your packet entitled "Cognitive Restructuring Practice" (Figure 6.4). A completed example appears in Figure 6.5. At the top of the form is a place to describe the situation in a few words, then list your ATs. Try to list at least four or five ATs. In the column next to the ATs, identify the Thinking Errors in each one. Remember that most ATs contain more than one Thinking Error, depending upon how you think about the thought. Then pick two or three of the thoughts to challenge. Using the Disputing Questions, challenge the ATs one at a time with the Anxious Self/Coping Self dialogue. Finally, summarize the work you did with the Disputing Questions into a Rational Response. Feel free to expand the Anxious Self/Coping Self dialogue to another sheet of paper if needed.

As always, if you do not have a situation arise this week that causes anxiety, use a situation from the past or imagine something coming up in the future. Try to imagine the situation as vividly as possible so that you will be able to identify your ATs.

You should also continue the self-monitoring of your average daily anxiety and depression in the situations you are monitoring each week.

Self-Assessment

1. Paying a great deal of attention to a negative detail of a situation (versus seeing the whole picture) is an example of the Thinking Error called Mind Reading.   **T F**

2. Some kinds of thoughts, although they are not logically incorrect, can be maladaptive. They may make you feel anxious and interfere with your performance.   **T F**

3. Changing your ATs may lead to different behaviors, and therefore to different outcomes.   **T F**

4. When examining ATs and determining the appropriate Disputing Questions, it is important to actually answer these questions.   **T F**

Cognitive Restructuring Practice

1. Situation

2. Automatic Thoughts

3. Thinking Errors

Emotions *(check boxes that apply)*

- [ ] anxious/nervous
- [ ] frustrated
- [ ] irritated
- [ ] ashamed
- [ ] angry
- [ ] sad
- [ ] embarrassed
- [ ] hateful
- [ ] other: _____

4. Use Disputing Questions to Challenge ATs in Anxious Self/Coping Self Dialogue

Anxious Self (AT):
Coping Self:
Anxious Self:
Coping Self:
Anxious Self:
Coping Self:
Anxious Self:
Coping Self:
Anxious Self:

5. Rational Response(s):

Figure 6.4.

Cognitive Restructuring Practice

1. Situation

   Returning defective jacket to the store

2. Automatic Thoughts	3. Thinking Errors
The clerk will be angry.	*Mind Reading, Fortune Telling*
I'll be nervous.	*Fortune Telling*
They won't take the jacket back and I'll look stupid for having asked.	*Catastrophizing, Labeling*
It will be a big scene.	*Catastrophizing*
I should have looked the jacket over more carefully before I took it home.	*Should Statement*

Emotions *(check boxes that apply)*

☑ anxious/nervous ☐ frustrated ☐ irritated ☐ ashamed

☐ angry ☐ sad ☑ embarrassed ☐ hateful

☐ other: _____

4. Use Disputing Questions to Challenge ATs in Anxious Self/Coping Self Dialogue

Anxious Self (AT):	*The clerk will be angry.*
Coping Self:	*What evidence do you have that the clerk will get angry?*
Anxious Self:	*None I guess. I just expect the clerk will be angry because I shouldn't have to return the jacket.*
Coping Self:	*Who made the rule that you shouldn't return a defective jacket?*
Anxious Self:	*No one I guess. I just think it is "buyer beware" and I should have looked it over more carefully before I bought it.*
Coping Self:	*Do you have any evidence that you could have guessed it would be defective before you took it home?*
Anxious Self:	*No. It looked fine at the store. Then one of the seams came out the first time I wore it. I really need the jacket.*
Coping Self:	*So you did what you could but it was just defective. You need the jacket so you need to exchange it. Can you explain that to the clerk?*
Anxious Self:	*Yes. I'll just explain what happened to the clerk. It was not my fault so the clerk does not really have a reason to get angry.*

5. Rational Response(s):

   All I can do is explain to the clerk what happened and ask for an exchange.

Figure 6.5. **Completed Cognitive Restructuring Practice**

5. Disputing ATs will completely eliminate anxiety from situations   **T   F**
and you will approach all feared situations with total calm.

6. Rational Responses to ATs are short, positive, realistic statements   **T   F**
that highlight the key coping points.

7. It is critical that you believe your Rational Responses when you first   **T   F**
make them.

Answers to Self-Assessment questions can be found in Appendix A.

Chapter 7

Getting Into the Pool:
The First Exposure Session

The last two chapters have focused on developing cognitive restructuring skills. As you have seen, cognitive restructuring is a procedure that helps you examine how you are thinking and consider whether there may be a more useful way to look at a situation that makes you anxious. Cognitive restructuring, by helping to reduce the anxiety that you experience, also makes it possible for you to handle more and more difficult situations. As with any new skill, the more you practice, the better you will become at analyzing and responding to your own automatic thoughts. However, if you are still confused about the cognitive restructuring procedure, spend a little extra time practicing with your therapist.

Now it is time to begin the second component of treatment—therapeutic exposure to feared situations. This will give you a chance to start to apply the cognitive restructuring skills. Before beginning the first exposure, let's take a moment to review how exposure works and why it is such a crucial step in overcoming social anxiety.

As described in Chapter 3, therapeutic exposure means facing the situations that make you anxious. After all, the purpose of treatment is to be more comfortable with other people and so eventually you must face those fears. Remember that process will start with easier situations and work up to harder ones. You will most likely start with role plays of the situations with your therapist and gradually practice situations in your daily life. The Fear and Avoidance Hierarchy will help you and your therapist determine which situations to tackle first and which situations to save for later.

How Therapeutic Exposure is Helpful

Exposure is helpful in at least four ways.

1. **Habituation:** If you stay in a situation that makes you anxious, your anxiety will eventually level off and then decrease. This happens because your body automatically works to counteract the fear response by lowering your blood pressure and heart rate and slowing your breathing. You may not have discovered this if you have not stayed in anxiety-provoking situations long enough or if your negative thinking keeps feeding your anxiety. Also, some social situations are naturally so short that this process does not have an opportunity to occur. For example, introducing yourself to someone takes only a few moments, so it is difficult for habituation to take place. We have developed some special exposure procedures to handle those types of situations and will share these with you.

2. **Practice:** Exposure helps you overcome the behavioral component of anxiety because it gives you a chance to practice what to say and how to act in the situations that make you anxious. If someone has always avoided asking a person on a date, then practicing what to say and how to say it is essential. Even if you have been in the situation before, you might have been so anxious that you do not even remember what you said. One advantage of the role-played exposure is that the therapist can give you feedback on whether you are saying and doing things in a positive manner.

3. **Identification of ATs:** There are likely to be some very important ATs that only occur to you right in the middle of the situations that make you anxious. These ATs emerge when you are anxious and often play an important role in keeping your anxiety going. These powerful ATs have been called "hot cognitions" because they are so closely tied to your emotional experience. If you pay attention to your thoughts during exposures, you can identify the particular ATs that make your anxiety increase the most. Then, by challenging those ATs and developing Rational Responses to them, you will be well-prepared for the troublesome thoughts when they arise during the next exposure and when you face them in the real-life situation.

4. **Testing out ATs:** Another important use of exposure is to set up a situation that will allow you to test out whether or not an AT is accurate. Let's say that Alice has the AT "If there is a long silence, I won't be able to handle it" during conversations with potential dating partners. If she and her therapist want to test out that thought, she could have a conversation with her therapist in session that included a long silence in the middle. This would allow Alice to see what it felt like to sit in silence with someone for awhile. If she is like most people, she would learn two things. First, it is extremely unlikely that such a long silence would occur in an actual conversation because there is strong social pressure for each person to break the silence. In fact, Alice would probably think of several things to say. Second, although her anxiety would

initially increase, it would soon start to subside as the silence lengthened. In short, she would learn that, contrary to her AT, she can "handle" a long silence, even though it would probably be fairly uncomfortable.

As you can see, therapeutic exposure is a very powerful technique that helps with all three components of social anxiety—the physiological, the behavioral, and the cognitive. It is unlikely that one exposure to a situation will make all of your anxiety about that situation go away. It usually takes several exposures to the same situation for the anxiety to decrease dramatically. However, if you keep track of your SUDS during the exposure, you should see steady improvement as you enter a feared situation again and again. With practice, the anxiety should not rise as high and habituation should occur more quickly each time. In other words, the more times you practice, the anxiety should decrease more rapidly as you stay in the situation.

The First In-Session Exposure

In the next section we will cover all of the steps involved in completing your first exposure, including picking the situation, doing the cognitive work, setting a goal for yourself, entering the situation, and processing what you learned from the exposure. Although all of these steps might seem overwhelming and cumbersome at first, they will soon become routine.

Picking a Situation

Which situation should you use for your first exposure? There is no single answer to this question. Of all of the situations in which you experience social anxiety, it may not matter which one you attack first. However, there are some guidelines that will help make the first exposure a success. As you look at the Fear and Avoidance Hierarchy you constructed in Chapter 4 and think about possible exposure situations, look for one that meets the following guidelines:

1. *In real life (as opposed to a role play), you would get a SUDS rating of 40–50 on the 0 to 100 scale.* Remember this is *graduated* exposure—you will start with easier situations first. Save the situations with higher SUDS ratings for later. However, you do not want to start with such an easy situation that you do not benefit from the exposure, because this will not help you to get over your anxiety very quickly. If in doubt, pick a slightly easier situation for the first time.

2. *The situation should be relevant to your ultimate goals in therapy.* Many people become anxious when giving a speech. However, often that anxiety is not a problem because the person does not need to give speeches in his/her life. It does not make any difference if he or she is anxious giving speeches or not. Do not pick a situation for exposure just because it makes you anxious. Pick something that you want to change.

Usually it takes several exposures to work up to your ultimate goal, so pick an exposure that is a step along the way. For example, if Howard's ultimate treatment goal is to be more comfortable with women because he would like to get married and have a family, then one situation that makes him anxious is asking a woman to marry him. Making a proposal of marriage is not the best place to start treatment, however. For Howard, it would be better to start with casual conversations with women, then practice dating situations and expressing affection later on.

3. *The situation should be straightforward.* During the exposure you are likely to be anxious, you will be trying to use the cognitive restructuring skills, and you will be concentrating on talking and listening. All of that is complicated enough without having to confront a situation that is complex and/or difficult to stage. The first exposure should be a simple interaction or presentation that does not require extensive preparation or elaborate pretense. For example, Maria knows that she could meet some new friends if she would talk with people at her health club. Most of the women talk with one another while they are on the exercise bicycles. However, Maria usually takes a book to read because she is too nervous to participate in the conversation. As her first exposure, Maria could choose talking with someone on the adjacent exercise bicycle. However, this situation requires a role play in which both people pretend to ride a bicycle. It is difficult to make that seem realistic. In contrast, Maria could also talk with people while standing in line to use a piece of equipment. Both of these situations are equally anxiety-provoking for Maria and both would meet her goal of getting to know people. For her first exposure it would be better to stage having a conversation while waiting in line than the exercise bicycle situation.

Here are some good situations to use for the first exposure:

Conversation with a person you do not know very well who is . . .

- seated next to you on a bus, train, or plane
- standing next to you in line somewhere
- a new co-worker
- seated near you in an employee lunchroom or cafeteria

Speeches such as . . .

- telling about a recent experience or vacation as if in a casual group of people
- reading aloud from a book or magazine

If your primary concerns are about situations other than general social interaction or public speaking (such as eating or writing in front of others), then you may be able to adapt one of these suggested situations to include the specific thing you fear.

At this point, you only need a fairly general idea of the situation for the first exposure. All of the details will get filled in later. As long as you have enough information to identify the ATs, you are ready to move to the next step—cognitive restructuring to prepare yourself for the exposure.

Cognitive Restructuring

Before each exposure you will go through the steps of cognitive restructuring that were covered in the last two chapters. This cognitive preparation will allow you to begin the exposure with Rational Responses in hand for the ATs you expect to have. Cognitive preparation also makes it more likely that the exposure will be helpful in overcoming your anxiety.

Step 1. Imagine what it will be like to be in the situation you and your therapist have picked for the first exposure. It is sometimes helpful to imagine the situation as if it were on a movie screen in your head. As you "play the movie" in your imagination, pay attention to what ATs you are having. Try to write down at least four to five ATs. Think about how the ATs make you feel.

Step 2. Identify Thinking Errors in the ATs.

Step 3. Pick the one or two thoughts that seem the most troublesome or important and challenge them using the Disputing Questions. Remember to answer the question raised by each Disputing Question.

Step 4. Review the disputes and challenges to the ATs in Step 3 and summarize them into one or two Rational Responses that you will be able to use during the exposure. Write the Rational Response(s) where you will be able to read it (them) during the exposure. You are now armed and ready for success in the exposure!

Working Out the Details of the Exposure Situation

Now it is time to fill in the details of what will happen in the role-played exposure. It is not necessary to figure out exactly what each person will say as if this were a movie script. Rather, outline the *setting* in which the interaction or speech will occur (e.g., at a home or office, in a bus, around a lunch table), the *circumstances* (e.g., the person sitting next to you on a plane, the weekly staff meeting, a mid-morning coffee break) and the *roles* each person will play (e.g., a stranger, a female co-worker, your boss). The specific dialogue will simply evolve as the exposure situation proceeds. Usually for the first exposure, there are only two roles—yours (the client) and the other person's (the therapist). Later, you might include several people in the exposure situation. However, if you are completing this treatment program as part of a therapy group, you might have several people in different roles even in the first exposure.

Setting an Achievable Behavioral Goal

The fifth and last step in the cognitive restructuring before the exposure starts is to set an "achievable behavioral goal" so you will know if the exposure was a success. Everyone knows what a goal is—something you would like to accomplish. An "achievable goal" is one that you are likely to be able to meet. An achievable "behavioral" goal means that the goal is something observable and objective. In other words, the goal should be something that everyone can see and agree on whether or not you met it. The following are two lists of goals—the ones on the left are behavioral goals and the ones on the right are not.

Behavioral Goals	Non-Behavioral Goals
Say three things	Don't get anxious
Stay in the situation even if I get anxious	Feel like I did a good job
Learn two things about the other person	Make a good impression
Describe four ideas	Be helpful and friendly
Invite her to a movie	Look like I am competent
Ask him to have coffee	Make him feel comfortable
	Communicate effectively

As you can see, the behavioral goals are all based on some type of observable behavior or something that can be objectively evaluated. For example, in a presentation you may want to communicate effectively (non-behavioral goal), but it is very difficult to determine whether or not that goal is met. What one person sees as effective in a presentation, another person may see as boring or confusing. You might argue that part of communicating effectively is to get your ideas across to the audience. However, "describe four ideas" is an excellent behavioral goal because it is under your control. You can also check out whether your audience learned something about these four ideas after the presentation, but remember that your goal is to do the best job you can of describing the ideas.

Non-behavioral goals based on feelings ("feel like I did a good job" or "make him feel comfortable") are difficult to evaluate because only the person with the emotion knows exactly what it feels like. Feelings are difficult to measure objectively because other people cannot necessarily see how you feel. Also, we do not have much control over how other people feel, so setting a goal such as "make him feel comfortable" may not be achievable no matter how well you do in the exposure.

Setting the Goal of Not Being Anxious

It is often tempting to set the goal of not being anxious. Indeed, this is probably the overall goal you have for therapy—to not be anxious (or at least not very anxious) in social and/or performance situations. However, there are two problems with this goal. First, it is a big goal for a single exposure. If you have been experiencing social anxiety for even a few months, it is unlikely the problem will go away immediately. Second, as was discussed in Chapter 1, some social anxiety is a normal part of life. No matter how successful this treatment program is for you, you will probably experience anxiety from time to time. *A more appropriate long-term goal is to accomplish what you want to in situations, despite the anxiety you experience.* If you keep meeting that goal, the anxiety will take care of itself.

The Importance of Setting Goals

Why is it important to set a goal for the exposure? In our work with people with social anxiety, we have noticed that they are often their own worst critics. No matter how well someone does in an exposure, it is too easy to focus on what went wrong. This is a good example of Disqualifying the Positive. All-or-Nothing Thinking plays a role as well. Let's look at an example.

Before Andy completed an exposure of having a conversation with a new female co-worker, he was very anxious, and his ATs indicated that he was worried about even being able to say hello to her. However, after the exposure, in which he carried on a very appropriate conversation for nearly 10 minutes, he believed he had failed because he had stumbled over the punch line of a joke he was trying to tell. This is a good example of the Thinking Error of Disqualifying the Positive because Andy did not give himself credit for carrying on the conversation. He discounted his success. All-or-Nothing Thinking is evident in that stumbling at one point in the conversation equaled failure. If Andy had set an achievable behavioral goal of "saying hello and three more things" before the exposure started, he would have had good ammunition to challenge his Thinking Errors and be able to take credit for his success after the exposure was over. Reaching an achievable goal would have provided evidence to counter his tendency to Disqualify the Positive. Then the next time he faced a similar situation, he would be able to use his previous success as evidence against his ATs.

Setting an achievable behavioral goal helps you take credit for your successes after the exposure and makes preparing for future situations easier.

Completing the Exposure

During the exposure itself, you will be role playing the situation, usually with your therapist as the other person in the role play (at least for the first exposure or two). These in-session exposures are simulations, not perfect replications, of the actual situation. As discussed in Chapter 2, this has advantages and disadvantages. Role playing allows you to work on your anxiety in a relatively safe environment, without consequences if things do not go as well as you would like. On the other hand, it is sometimes difficult to pretend and you might feel silly at first. However, the exposure will be most effective if you can put yourself into the situation and try to make it as realistic as possible. If you keep telling yourself "this isn't real" or "this doesn't count," then the exposure will not be as effective in helping you to overcome your anxiety. Also try to stay "in role." This means that during the exposure you should continue with the simulation rather than interrupting to make comments or ask questions. If you focus your attention on the aspects that are realistic and act as if it were the real situation without interruption, you will be better prepared for the actual event.

If you find yourself doing something to interrupt the exposure or make it less real, then you should honestly ask yourself if this is a form of avoidance. Someone who is anxious about an exposure could avoid truly facing the fears by interrupting the exposure to ask questions or make comments. Such avoidance might include thinking, "This isn't real so it doesn't really matter how I do" or making jokes or acting silly. Doing these sorts of things to avoid fully participating in the exposure is like jumping into the pool and trying to swim but never letting go of the edge of the pool. Technically you are in the water and kicking and moving your arms. However, until you are willing to let go and fully commit yourself to moving through the water, you can never build up your skills and confidence as a swimmer. Similarly, to overcome your fear in the situations that make you anxious, you need to fully commit yourself and try to tolerate the anxiety you experience rather than sneaking away from it. As discussed above, staying with an exposure will allow the anxiety to peak and decrease through the process of habituation.

Before, during, and after the exposure your therapist will ask you to give ratings of how anxious you are feeling. These ratings will use the scale that you used when constructing your Fear and Avoidance Hierarchy. Remember this is the Subjective Units of Discomfort Scale (SUDS). The lowest rating is 0 (not at all anxious) and the highest rating is 100 (the worst social anxiety you can imagine). If you are having trouble concentrating, then your SUDS rating is at least a 50. If you are thinking that you want to get out of the situation, then your SUDS rating is at least 75. Your therapist will ask you to give a SUDS rating immediately before the exposure starts. Then, periodically, your therapist will interrupt the exposure and say "SUDS." Just quickly give a number that reflects how nervous you are feeling at that moment and get right back into the role play. At first this will be a little awkward but most people quickly adjust to it. It does not matter that you give precisely the right number. A "ballpark figure" is fine. Then as the exposure ends, the therapist will ask you for a final SUDS rating.

The SUDS ratings will be useful in several ways. First, they communicate how anxious you are feeling to your therapist as the exposure is going on. Your therapist is able to combine his or her observations of how anxious you appear and what you are saying and doing during the role play with your SUDS ratings to have a good understanding of the experience. This will help your therapist make the exposure as helpful as possible for you. Second, the SUDS ratings are useful in tracking your progress over several weeks. As you keep doing exposures, your average SUDS rating for exposures of similar difficulty should get lower.

Finally, the SUDS can be very useful in the cognitive restructuring that you will do after the exposure is over.

When your therapist asks you for SUDS ratings, he or she will also ask you to repeat your Rational Response aloud. The purpose of saying your Rational Response aloud is to encourage you to use it to combat your ATs during the exposure. It is easy to fall into the old familiar thought patterns that make you anxious without taking advantage of work you did to try and challenge those thoughts. The more you are able to use the Rational Response during the exposure, the more likely you will be to disrupt your ATs. That will make you less anxious in the long run. So remember, when you read the Rational Response, do not just say the words, but carefully consider their important implications for your life!

Do's and Don'ts of Therapeutic Exposure

As you can see, there is quite a lot going on during an exposure. Let's summarize the "Do's and Don'ts."

1. *Do* throw yourself into the role play as completely as possible.

2. *Don't* try to avoid the anxiety by interrupting the role play or making it less realistic.

3. *Do* say your Rational Response to yourself as ATs come up.

4. *Do* repeat your Rational Response aloud when you give a SUDS rating.

5. *Do* give SUDS ratings quickly without worrying about being too precise. Trying to be too precise could be a subtle way to avoid fully participating in the exposure.

6. *Do* stay in role until your therapist says it is time to stop.

7. *Don't* be discouraged if it does not goes as well as you would like. Remember it usually takes repeated exposures to fully conquer one's fears.

After the Exposure: Debriefing the Experience

The first thing to do after the exposure is to take a deep breath, relax, and congratulate yourself for having the courage to work on your fears.

There are many other helpful things to do after the exposure. We'll review some of the basic ones here.

Reviewing Your Goal

One of the first things to do after the exposure is to review your behavioral goal. We have found that it is very common for people to either totally forget what their goal was or to remember it differently than it was. That is why it is important to always write it down. Review your goal and ask yourself if you achieved it.

Be careful as you decide whether you achieved your goal. Most people with social anxiety have difficulty objectively analyzing whether they met their goal. One of the Thinking Errors, Disqualifying the Positive, may influence how you see your goal. A person might dismiss the goal as being trivial despite the fact that it was seen as quite difficult before the exposure began. Let's look at a concrete example.

Mohammed will have to deliver a speech in a few weeks at a luncheon meeting of the local Chamber of Commerce, about which he is quite anxious. For his first exposure, he and his therapist agreed that he would start to work towards this speech by just talking through the ideas he plans to present while seated. He set a behavioral goal of making two specific points about the future of business in his community. Mohammed thinks he will have more points to make during the actual speech but he and his therapist decided to set a goal of only two since this is the first time he has forced himself to think about what he will present. During the exposure, he became very anxious, with his highest SUDS rating being 95. However, despite the high anxiety, he was able to talk through several ideas, not just two. After the exposure, Mohammed told his therapist that he did not achieve his goal because he became very anxious. His therapist pointed out that "not getting anxious" was not the behavioral goal they had set. Mohammed engaged in Disqualifying the Positive because he ignored what he did well, namely making more points than he initially thought he could make. By focusing on his anxiety, he failed to give himself credit for his accomplishment. Instead of seeing the exposure as a success, it became another in a long list of perceived failures. It is important not to ignore the fact that Mohammed eventually wants to be less anxious while speaking in public. However, it is unlikely he will be able to overcome his anxiety in the long run unless he gives himself credit for what he is able to accomplish in each exposure along the way.

Reviewing ATs

Immediately after the exposure it is helpful to review the effectiveness of your cognitive restructuring efforts. This review can focus around three questions:

1. Did I have the ATs I expected to have?

2. How well did the Rational Response I had developed combat these ATs?

3. Were there ATs that I did not anticipate having?

If you had some or all of the ATs you expected to have, then the cognitive restructuring you worked on before the exposure should have helped you challenge and rebut those expected ATs. However, most people are not 100% effective at challenging these ATs the first time. For the first exposure, a realistic goal would be recognizing the thoughts as ATs (as opposed to viewing them as logical statements of fact) and attempting to use your Rational Response.

The second question is whether the Rational Response seemed to be working or whether it seemed irrelevant or "off track." Usually Rational Responses just need some fine-tuning, but sometimes a person has to start over. A Rational Response that seems fine beforehand may not seem very powerful when the person is actually in the anxiety-provoking situation.

With most exposures, you will find that there were some ATs that you did not expect to have. As you will remember, identifying these ATs that occur in the heat of the moment—the "hot cognitions" —is one of the purposes of exposure. Once they are identified, you can go through the steps of cognitive restructuring and develop a Rational Response. Then you will be prepared the next time the unexpected ATs come up.

What Did You Learn?

Usually the last thing that we say to clients as we finish debriefing an exposure is, "What can you take from this experience that you can use in the future?" As you have seen, completing an exposure is a complicated procedure with lots of different steps. As you go through the experience, you may think about yourself or the world in a new way. You may discover things about yourself that you have never considered before. You will probably experience anxiety but you may experience many other emotions such as sadness, anger, or a sense of accomplishment. You may have tried to do something—such as ask a person for a date or express your feelings—that you have never done before. Because of everything that is going on in an exposure, it is helpful to try and summarize one or two main points for yourself.

Here are some of the things our clients have said to us in response to the question, "What can you take from this experience that you can use in the future?"

If I hang in there, it gets easier.

Even though I am very anxious, I can still carry on a conversation.

Even though I am very anxious, I won't pass out.

It was harder than I thought it would be, but I still made it through.

The shaking in my hands is not as noticeable as I thought it was.

I must not look as nervous as I feel inside.

Once I get past the first couple of minutes, I can do OK.

Homework After the First In-Session Exposure

The procedures we have just described outline the procedure you and your therapist will use for role-played therapeutic exposures within your therapy sessions. Remember that the third component of treatment is homework. After you have done the first exposure in session, you and your therapist will negotiate a homework assignment for an exposure on your own. Usually this will be something that relates to the exposure you completed in the session. Because exposures in real life are often more anxiety-provoking than exposures within the session, it is a good idea to pick an assignment for your homework that is a little easier. You will also be practicing the cognitive skills during your homework. At the end of the chapter you will find more details about the homework and a worksheet to use for the cognitive restructuring.

Chuck's First Exposure: The Friday Afternoon Conversation

Now that we have talked about the various aspects of cognitive restructuring and role-playing that go into the first exposure, we will use an example to help bring these ideas to life. Chuck is a 32-year-old man who gets very nervous when he has casual conversations with other people, including people he knows fairly well. He feels much less anxious if the conversation is about something specific, such as talking with a co-worker about a project. Chuck says that he does not know how to make "small talk." One of the situations on Chuck's Fear and Avoidance Hierarchy is the Friday afternoon get-together at a local bar with people from work. Chuck would like to go regularly but has only gone twice in the last several years. Once it went well because he ended up talking with someone about work the whole time. The second time, however, everyone was talking about more personal topics, including their upcoming vacations. That time Chuck became extremely anxious and left early. Chuck and his therapist have decided to tackle this situation for his first exposure.

Chuck anticipates that he would have the following ATs during the Friday afternoon get-together:

> I don't know how to make small talk.

> I'll get very nervous.

> I won't have anything to say.

Chuck and his therapist have agreed that they should focus the cognitive restructuring on the third thought, *I won't have anything to say*. This AT makes Chuck feel anxious, and he feels he would be embarrassed if he had nothing to say. After looking at the List of Thinking Errors, Chuck recognizes that this thought might be an example of All-or-Nothing Thinking because it implies that he would have absolutely *nothing* to say. There is also some Fortune Telling in that he has predicted what will happen before even going to the bar. Chuck agrees with his therapist that he might also be discounting anything he might say as unimportant.

Using several different Disputing Questions, the therapist helped Chuck challenge this thought:

Therapist: What is the likelihood that you will have absolutely nothing to say?

Chuck: Not that likely. I'll at least say hello, and everyone usually talks about what appetizers to order. I can say something about that, but then I won't have anything else to say.

Therapist: What does everyone else usually talk about after ordering the appetizers?

Chuck: Usually just stupid stuff. That's why I don't know what to say.

Therapist: Define "stupid stuff."

Chuck: Sometimes they just joke around. Sometimes they talk about the weather. The one time I was there they talked about summer vacations. They might talk about movies they have seen.

Therapist: What evidence do you have that you cannot talk about the weather, summer vacations, or movies?

Chuck: I could probably talk about that stuff. I just don't want to sound stupid or like I don't have anything important to say.

Therapist: Does talking about the weather, summer vacations, and movies mean you sound stupid?

Chuck: Maybe.

Therapist: When your co-workers talk about the weather, summer vacations, and movies do they sound stupid?

Chuck: Not really, I guess, mostly I guess they are just relaxing and having a good time. It is good to unwind after the work week.

Therapist: So talking about the weather, summer vacations, and movies might sound stupid but it could also sound like unwinding and having a good time?

Chuck: Yes.

Chuck and his therapist go on to develop a Rational Response. Chuck wants the Rational Response to remind him that it is OK to talk about the topics he considers a little stupid because that is what everyone else does. The purpose of the Friday afternoon get-togethers is to have a good time, not to have serious conversation. To remind himself of all of that, Chuck chooses "It's OK to talk about the weather" as his Rational Response.

Chuck's therapist suggests that they set the role play up to start right after the appetizer order has been placed. That way they will not have to pretend to be ordering food and it is the more difficult part for Chuck. The therapist will play the role of one of Chuck's co-workers. They talk about how well Chuck knows this co-worker. They agree that they will not talk about work. They rearrange the furniture so it will seem like they are sitting across a table from each other. The corner of the therapist's desk serves as the table. Once the situation has been fully defined, Chuck and his therapist develop an achievable behavioral goal: Chuck will say three things that are not answers to direct questions. Chuck is worried that it would be too easy if he just had to answer questions posed by his "co-worker."

After the therapist asks for Chuck's initial SUDS rating, the role play proceeds. Chuck gives SUDS ratings and repeats his Rational Response about every minute. After about 6 minutes, the therapist ends the role play and they started to debrief the exposure. Chuck's SUDS ratings were 35 before the exposure started, and 50, 70, 70, 60, 60, 50 during the exposure. After reminding him to congratulate himself for making it through the first exposure, Chuck's therapist asks him whether he has achieved his goal. After first talking about how he felt fairly anxious during the exposure, Chuck remembers that his goal was to say three things that were not answers to direct questions. The therapist confirms Chuck's opinion that he has indeed said many more than three things and together they list about eight of them.

When Chuck and his therapist review the ATs he experienced during the exposure, Chuck reports that he had had two of the ones he anticipated having— "I don't know what to say" and "I'm getting very nervous." Chuck reports that at one point, there was a pause in the conversation and he started worrying about what to say. He then made a comment about how it was supposed to be an especially cold winter. Thus, he used his Rational Response that it was OK to talk about the weather.

Chuck also reports an unexpected AT: "My co-worker will think it's strange that I am talking so much more than I usually do." Chuck classifies this as Mind Reading because he was making assumptions about what his co-worker thought. Using the Disputing Question "Does talking more than usual necessarily mean I'm strange?" Chuck is able to arrive at a Rational Response. He decides that "Being friendlier isn't strange" would help him remember that people might be surprised if he were more talkative, but that it would probably be seen as something positive.

When Chuck's therapist asks him what he could take from this experience, he concludes that he has learned that it is OK to talk about minor, everyday things like the weather because everyone does it.

Chuck does not think he is quite ready to go to the Friday afternoon get-together immediately but he agrees to start three conversations about topics not related to work during the week. This will give him a chance to practice making small talk with co-workers. Then in a week or two, he might be ready to go to the Friday event. Chuck and his therapist discuss how it would be important for him to use the cognitive restructuring skills to help control his anxiety and make the experiences more beneficial.

Homework

After you complete the first exposure in session with your therapist it is time to try an exposure during the week on your own. This is the first step in transferring what you are learning in the therapy sessions to your real life. It is essential that you and your therapist pick an exposure situation that will be a little challenging but still be something that you are confident you can complete. Typically homework assignments relate to the in-session exposure. In the above example, Chuck picked a situation that was relevant to the role-played exposure he had completed but was not quite as difficult. This is an excellent strategy.

Right now the cognitive restructuring procedures that you do before and after the exposure probably seem very complicated. Believe it or not, they will soon become second nature to you as you get more practice with them. To help you along, we have developed a worksheet (Figure 7.1) called "Be Your Own Cognitive Coach" or "BYOCC" for short. This worksheet will take you through all of the cognitive restructuring steps before and after the exposure you do on your own. Complete the front side before the exposure, then use the back side to debrief the experience. Make copies of the BYOCC worksheet for use throughout the rest of your treatment.

The BYOCC form that Chuck completed for his homework assignment of starting conversations with three co-workers appears in Figure 7.2. As you can see, Chuck filled in a brief description of the situation he was using for homework in the top box. Then, the evening before he planned to do his homework, he sat down and considered the ATs he expected to have about the conversations and wrote them in the appropriate box. (Note that the numbers in some of the boxes coordinate with the lists of the steps for cognitive restructuring procedures that appear at various places in this manual.) In the bottom half of the AT box is a place to indicate the emotions related to these ATs. Chuck decided to focus on the AT "I don't know how to make small talk" because he had already worked on the second AT ("They will think it is strange that I'm so talkative") with his therapist. Chuck thought it was likely he would get nervous since he was doing something new so he did not challenge the third AT. You can see the Thinking Errors that Chuck identified in the box next to the ATs. There is a short list of the Thinking Errors on the BYOCC worksheet, but you will probably need to use the List of Thinking Errors (Figure 6.1) that explains them in more detail for now. Later this abbreviated list should be all you need.

After Chuck identified the Thinking Errors in the AT "I don't know how to make small talk" and the emotions he was feeling, he moved on to Step 4 in the procedure, challenging the AT using the Disputing Questions. See the questions and his answers on his BYOCC worksheet. Note that the Disputing Questions are abbreviated on the worksheet for your convenience. At first you will probably need to refer to the more extended Disputing Questions list (Figure 6.2).

Chuck's three Rational Responses appear in the box near the bottom of the page. Two are from the work he did in session with his therapist—"Being friendlier isn't strange" and "It's OK to talk about the weather." The third Rational Response he developed from the worksheet—"There isn't much small talk in short conversations." Chuck's achievable behavioral goal followed directly from the homework assignment from his therapist—"Start three conversations." He did not need to have long conversations for the assignment to be a success; he just needed to initiate them.

After he got home from work the next day, Chuck debriefed his experience with the therapeutic exposures he did for homework. Using the back of the BYOCC worksheet, he noted that he had achieved his goal of starting three conversations. He had the ATs he expected to have and felt that the Rational Responses had worked fairly well. He did not have any unexpected ATs. In the box labeled "What did you learn?" Chuck noted that people had seemed very friendly and eager to visit with him a little. This was a surprise and made him feel good about the conversations he had started.

Summary of Homework for Chapter 7

1. Continue self-monitoring as in previous weeks.

2. Complete an exposure on your own as negotiated with your therapist. Use the BYOCC worksheet (Figure 7.1) to guide the cognitive restructuring before and after the exposure.

As you go through this treatment program, you will be filling out a number of forms to help you learn about your reactions and work through the cognitive restructuring and exposures. Save all of these forms. You may find it helpful to refer back to Disputing Questions or Rational Responses that you found particularly useful. Also, in Chapters 12 and 13, you will need to review the work you have done in order to complete some of the exercises in advanced cognitive restructuring and evaluating your progress.

Be Your Own Cognitive Coach (BYOCC) Worksheet

Preparation Before the Exposure

1. Situation (Briefly describe the anxiety-provoking situation.) Date _____

2. Automatic Thoughts (ATs)
   (List the thoughts you have about this situation)

3. Thinking Errors *(See list below)*

Thinking Errors: All-or-Nothing Thinking, Overgeneralization, Mental Filter, Disqualifying the Positive, Mind Reading, Fortune Telling, Catastrophizing, Emotional Reasoning, Should Statements, Labeling, Maladaptive Thoughts

Emotions You Feel as You Think These Thoughts *(circle those that apply)*: anxious/nervous, angry, frustrated, sad, irritated, embarrassed, ashamed, hateful, other: _____

4. Challenges *(Using the Disputing Questions below, challenge the most important AT(s) you listed above. Be sure to answer the question raised by the Disputing Question.)*

Disputing Questions: Do I know for certain that _____ ? Am I 100% sure that _____ ? What evidence do I have that _____ ? What is the worst that could happen? How bad is that? Do I have a crystal ball? Is there another explanation for _____ ? Does _____ have to lead to or equal _____ ? Is there another point of view?

5. Rational Response(s) *(Summarize the challenges into a rational statement to use to combat the AT.)*

6. Achievable Behavioral Goal *(Something that is do-able and can be seen by others)*

Figure 7.1.

Debriefing After the Exposure

7. Did you achieve your goal? *(Watch out for Disqualifying the Positive!)*

8. Review the ATs you had during the exposure.

    Expected ATs *(The ATs you had that you expected to have)*

    How well did the Rational Response(s) combat these ATs? *(Revise if necessary)*

    Unexpected ATs *(Challenge and develop Rational Responses for these for next time)*

9. What did you learn? *(Summarize 1–2 main points you learned from this exposure that you can use in the future.)*

**Remember, you are
Investing Anxiety for a Calmer Future**

Figure 7.1.

Be Your Own Cognitive Coach (BYOCC) Worksheet

Preparation Before the Exposure

1. Situation (Briefly describe the anxiety-provoking situation.)   Date _____ *4/8* _____

   Start 3 conversations with co-workers

2. Automatic Thoughts (ATs)
   (List the thoughts you have about this situation)

   I don't know how to make small talk.

   They will think it is strange that I'm so talkative.

   I'll be nervous.

3. Thinking Errors *(See list below)*

   All or Nothing Thinking — either I'm perfect or incompetent at small talk with nothing in between

   Emotional Reasoning — I feel uncomfortable making small talk so I think that means I don't know how to do it.

   Thinking Errors: All-or-Nothing Thinking, Overgeneralization, Mental Filter, Disqualifying the Positive, Mind Reading, Fortune Telling, Catastrophizing, Emotional Reasoning, Should Statements, Labeling, Maladaptive Thoughts

   Emotions You Feel as You Think These Thoughts *(circle those that apply):* (anxious/nervous,) angry, frustrated, sad, (irritated,) embarrassed, ashamed, hateful, other: _____

4. Challenges *(Using the Disputing Questions below, challenge the most important AT(s) you listed above. Be sure to answer the question raised by the Disputing Question.)*

   What evidence do I have that I don't know how to make small talk? No evidence. I just feel uncomfortable.

   What evidence do I have that I know how to make small talk? I did it during the in-session exposure. There are some trivial things to talk about like the weather. These are short conversations so I shouldn't run out of things to say.

   Disputing Questions: Do I know for certain that _____ ? Am I 100% sure that _____ ? What evidence do I have that _____ ? What is the worst that could happen? How bad is that? Do I have a crystal ball? Is there another explanation for _____ ? Does _____ have to lead to or equal _____ ? Is there another point of view?

5. Rational Response(s) *(Summarize the challenges into a rational statement to use to combat the AT.)*

   Being friendlier isn't strange.
   I can always talk about the weather.
   There isn't much small talk in short conversations.

6. Achievable Behavioral Goal *(Something that is do-able and can be seen by others)*

   Just start the 3 conversations

Figure 7.2.   Completed Be Your Own Cognitive Coach (BYOCC) Worksheet

Debriefing After the Exposure

7. Did you achieve your goal? *(Watch out for Disqualifying the Positive!)*

   Yes, I started conversations with Sam, Alison, and Tim.

8. Review the ATs you had during the exposure.

   Expected ATs *(The ATs you had that you expected to have)*

   I don't know how to make small talk.

   They will think it is strange that I'm so talkative.

   I'll be nervous.

   How well did the Rational Response(s) combat these ATs? *(Revise if necessary)*

   They worked well.

   Unexpected ATs *(Challenge and develop Rational Responses for these for next time)*

   No unexpected ATs

9. What did you learn? *(Summarize 1–2 main points you learned from this exposure that you can use in the future.)*

   People seem eager to visit with me.

**Remember, you are
Investing Anxiety for a Calmer Future**

Figure 7.2. **Completed Be Your Own Cognitive Coach (BYOCC) Worksheet (continued)**

1. Habituation is the process that allows your anxiety to get more and more severe, until you must escape the situation.   **T F**

2. Exposure helps overcome social anxiety through habituation, practicing your skills in anxiety-provoking situations, helping you identify ATs, and allowing you to test ATs.   **T F**

3. Preparing for exposure by conducting cognitive restructuring makes it more likely that the exposure will help you overcome your social anxiety.   **T F**

4. Your first exposure should include enough behavioral goals that you are not likely to be able to meet them all the first time you practice the situation.   **T F**

5. The goal to not be anxious in an exposure situation is an important and appropriate goal.   **T F**

6. Interrupting an exposure, or trying to make it less real, may be a form of avoidance.   **T F**

Answers to Self-Assessment questions can be found in Appendix A.

Chapter 8

Settling Into the Journey: The Ongoing Routine of In-Session and Homework Exposures

In the last chapter we described how to do the first therapeutic exposure. Getting through the first exposure is a big step towards your ultimate goal of overcoming your social anxiety. Over the next several weeks you will use the same combination of cognitive restructuring and therapeutic exposure as you work your way up the situations listed on your Fear and Avoidance Hierarchy. This basic set of procedures is the key to conquering your fears. In this chapter we will describe how to go through a series of exposures. You will see that the emphasis will shift from exposures you do in session with your therapist to tackling real-life situations on your own.

The steps for therapeutic exposure are outlined in Figure 8.1. This one page contains the keys to the entire treatment program. You will want to refer to it often.

How To Pick Situations For Exposure

In the previous chapter, we described how to pick the situation to tackle first. Assuming that the first exposure went well, you will be ready to move on to a second situation. For some people, each exposure is a variation on a single theme. For example, all of your exposures might revolve around conversations with people. On the other hand, you might have two or three exposures on one theme (e.g., conversations with people or talking on the telephone) and then two or three exposures on another theme (e.g., speaking in front of groups or being assertive). In either case, there are a few guidelines that will help you and your therapist choose the situations for you to address and determine how you should sequence your efforts.

Tackle Easier Situations First

The Fear and Avoidance Hierarchy provides a road map for exposures. The first exposure probably involved a situation in the bottom third of the Hierarchy. Try to pick something just a bit harder each time. However, if in doubt, it is better to move too slowly than to attempt something that will create an extreme amount of anxiety. If the situation is too difficult, you might have trouble paying attention to your ATs and using your Rational Response. On the other hand, if you are only getting a little anxious in exposure situations, this is a sign that you can move on to more difficult situations more quickly. As a rule of thumb, we have found that it takes the typical client three to six exposures in the therapy session to approach the most difficult situation of a particular type.

Steps for Overcoming Social Anxiety with Exposure and Cognitive Restructuring

(Record Responses on the BYOCC Worksheet for Homework Exposures)

Before entering the exposure situation . . .

1. Pick an anxiety-provoking situation that you would like to work on.

2. As you imagine yourself in that situation, identify the ATs and emotions caused by the ATs.

3. Identify Thinking Errors in the ATs.

4. Challenge 1–2 of the ATs with Disputing Questions. Be sure to answer the questions.

5. Summarize answers to Disputing Questions into a Rational Response.

6. Think about the situation in more detail and pick an achievable behavioral goal.

Enter the exposure situation . . .

7. Complete the exposure, using the Rational Response to help control your anxiety. Stay in the situation until it reaches a natural conclusion or your anxiety decreases.

After the exposure is over . . .

8. Debrief your experience in the situation:

   ▨ Did you achieve your goal?

   ▨ Did you have the ATs you expected to have?

   ▨ How well did the Rational Response work?

   ▨ Did you have unexpected ATs? Take a moment to challenge them now (Steps 3 to 5 above).

9. Summarize what you can take from this experience that you can use in similar situations in the future.

Figure 8.1.

Each Exposure Should Build on the Last One

If you are like many individuals with social anxiety disorder, you probably have fears in several different types of situations. However, it is typically best to work on only one type of situation at a time. Consider the person who gets anxious in casual conversations, speaking in front of a group, and eating with other people. It is more helpful to work through several exposures on casual conversations before doing any exposures on speaking in front of a group or eating with other people. In this way you and your therapist can work from simpler situations to more complex ones within a single theme.

Use Exposures to Challenge ATs

Remember that one of the purposes of exposure is to set up situations in which you can test out whether or not your ATs are accurate. You and your therapist may choose a situation for exposure in which you worry that a particular negative outcome may occur and then examine whether it actually happens. Common examples of this strategy include the evaluation of what will happen in situations when there is a long silence in a conversation, an audience member asks a rude or difficult question during a speech, someone refuses an invitation for a date, or you spill food or drink at a party. By facing events like these during an exposure in the therapy session, you can practice how you would handle a particularly difficult situation before you have to face it in real life. You may also discover that ATs about catastrophic consequences turn out to be unrealistic.

How Cognitive Restructuring Changes as You Tackle Different Situations

The basic procedures for cognitive restructuring are the same throughout this workbook. However, the ATs you challenge will be somewhat different. At first your therapist will help you challenge ATs that are important but possibly somewhat superficial. By "superficial" we mean ATs that relate to the situation that makes you anxious and to your reactions and those of the other people involved. These are the types of ATs we have used in most of our examples—"I won't know what to say" or "I'll look nervous." Later you will begin to challenge what we call "core beliefs." These are ATs that relate more to your central, basic beliefs about yourself and the world. You might think of core beliefs as the engines that power your ATs in specific situations. "I'm flawed" and "I'm an impostor" are examples of core beliefs that some of our clients have discovered they have about themselves. Right now you are probably not very aware of your core beliefs. That is OK. As you continue through treatment, your therapist can help you become more aware of them. In Chapter 12, we describe some ways to discover and understand your core beliefs and then how to change the ones that cause you problems.

The Relationship Between Exposures, Cognitive Restructuring, and Homework

Each week you and your therapist will negotiate a homework assignment for an exposure that you can do on your own during the week. As we said earlier, it is very important to complete these assignments because they are the link between what happens in therapy sessions and conquering your fears in your daily life. When you do the homework, you should use the BYOCC worksheet to do the cognitive restructuring work for yourself before and after the assigned exposure. That repeated practice will assure that you have these skills firmly in place so you are prepared to handle any anxiety-provoking situations that arise after treatment is over. Remember, the goal of this treatment program is not to eliminate all social anxiety. Social anxiety is a normal part of life. Rather, the goal of treatment is to overcome the anxiety in situations that you face regularly and prepare you to cope with any anxiety that you do experience.

Over the course of the treatment sessions, your therapist will gradually help you face more and more difficult situations through the use of homework assignments. In fact, many of our clients get to the point that they no longer do in-session role-played exposures of situations first. They have made sufficient progress that they talk over the situation with the therapist, including getting the therapist's help working through the cognitive restructuring. Then, with Rational Responses in place, they tackle the situation and report back to the therapist the following week. From that point, it is usually only a short time before the client is ready to stop seeing the therapist regularly and work through the situations that arise on his or her own. You may use this client workbook as a reference guide and reminder of key points when working on your own.

Summary of the Course of the Treatment Program

As you work through the treatment program, you can summarize your progression as follows:

- From easier (less anxiety-producing) to harder (more anxiety-producing) situations

- From less complex to more complex situations

- From more superficial ATs to ATs related to your core beliefs about yourself and the world

- From working on your anxiety in session with your therapist to working on your anxiety on your own in everyday life

Frequently Asked Questions

In this chapter we tried to give you an overview of what to expect in the weeks that follow your first exposure. Now we will answer some of the most common questions that our clients have asked over the years. You should also talk about any questions or concerns you have with your therapist.

1. **Will I have to do an exposure for every single situation in which I get anxious? That will take a long time.** The answer to this question is probably not. Through a process called "generalization," what you learn in one exposure can be applied to similar situations. For example, if you are working on overcoming dating anxiety, using an exposure to practice asking out one person will probably help you be less anxious when you ask out a different person. Does that mean that exposures related to your dating anxiety will be helpful for your fear of talking with your supervisor? That varies from person to person. If you have similar ATs in both situations, then you may find that working on your dating anxiety "generalizes" so that you are less anxious talking with your supervisor. However, if you have different ATs and different fears in those two situations, then you may have to work on dating and talking with your boss separately. As you get more and more skilled at challenging your ATs and confronting situations that make you anxious, overcoming fears in new situations can be accomplished more quickly.

2. **All of these procedures are complicated. Can I leave some out? Do I have to do the cognitive restructuring?** For now we strongly recommend that you do not skip over any of the procedures. It may sometimes seem tedious to work through each step of the cognitive restructuring before the exposure then carefully debrief the experience afterwards. However, that hard work will pay off in the long run. Also remember that the procedures become easier with more practice. In fact, most of our clients find that identifying and challenging their ATs becomes "second nature" and happens almost automatically when they notice themselves becoming nervous. In fact, *anxiety should become a signal that it is time to examine your ATs*. Once you get to this point, you may find that you do not have to go through all of the steps. One client told us, "When I get nervous I know I am mind reading. I just take a moment to figure out whose mind I'm trying to read and then remind myself that I'm not 100% certain of what they are thinking." This client knew herself so well that she was able to move quickly to the Rational Response and proceed with the situation. However, that skill and self-awareness were the result of many weeks of systematic effort working through the procedures we have outlined on the BYOCC worksheet.

3. **I have been avoiding things so long, I do not have anyone to talk with for my homework. How will I be able to do the assignments?** Occasionally people have become very isolated because of their social fears. You may have come to the point that you are unemployed or work in a job with very little contact with other people. You may not participate in the

community or be a member of any organizations. You may do your grocery shopping at night so you do not have to talk with people. The first thing to do is to be honest with your therapist about your isolation from other people. Then he or she can help you think of some ways to begin to have contact with people gradually. Your therapist might have you begin greeting people whom you see only briefly, such as a shop clerk, a neighbor, the mail carrier, the receptionist in your therapist's office, and so forth. Later you can look for opportunities to get more involved with people with whom you might have common interests by attending community events or taking an adult education class.

4. **The situation that I really need to conquer only comes up once a year. How will I be able to practice that?** This is an excellent question and may present a real challenge in therapy. As you know, this treatment program relies on repeated exposures to the situations in which you experience anxiety. If those situations come up rarely, it is difficult to practice repeatedly! Infrequent but highly anxiety-provoking situations include toasts at wedding receptions, yearly business events such as the holiday party or summer picnic, or presentations at an annual meeting or conference. Usually your therapist can help you create a role play of the feared situation within the therapy session that will give you an opportunity to practice. Another solution is to try to find similar situations that you can use for exposures as homework. This might involve becoming an officer in an organization so that you have to run meetings and speak in front of the group regularly. You may be able to volunteer for work assignments or social engagements that allow you to do something similar to what you fear most.

If your social anxiety is limited to a few situations that arise very infrequently, and you have tried everything we just discussed to no avail, then you might want to talk with your therapist about whether certain types of medication could be helpful. As you will see in Dr. Liebowitz's chapter on medication at the end of this manual, there are some medications that you only have to take on the day that you need them. For some people, adding those medications to the cognitive restructuring skills you have already learned may be helpful. Then, over time, you may be able to stop using the medication as you gain more confidence.

5. **I am very busy. What if I don't have time to do the homework?** As you have discovered by now, the treatment program described in this workbook asks you to do a lot. It is much more than a weekly visit with your therapist. In fact, you will see that we will be asking you to do something every day to work on your anxiety. Completing the homework is essential to your success. If you really do not have time to do the program right now, then you should wait until you can make more time for it in your busy life. Before you decide to wait, however, ask yourself whether being "too busy" is just a sophisticated way to avoid facing your fears. Sometimes being busy allows a person to distract him- or herself from having to recognize being lonely or that life is not going the way one had hoped. An honest discussion with a therapist can

help you sort through your thoughts and feelings about taking time for this treatment program. You should also treat "I'm too busy" as an AT and work through the steps of cognitive restructuring to see if there might be some distorted thinking before making a decision to stop or delay treatment due to lack of time.

On the other hand, everyone misses a homework assignment now and then. You might become ill or have something unexpected happen. However, your progress towards a calmer, more confident self will be seriously hampered if you skip too many homework assignments. If you are having a difficult time completing the homework, then you should discuss this with your therapist. Together you should be able to develop a plan to get the homework done.

Where to Go From Here

Over the next several weeks you should work with your therapist to complete several exposures using the guidelines covered in this chapter. The next three chapters cover specific topics that may not apply to everyone. Although we encourage you to read all the chapters in case you come across a technique or Rational Response that seems particularly helpful to you, you and your therapist can decide which chapters apply the most to your individual circumstances. After you have completed at least three exposures in session and/or as homework assignments, read Chapter 12 on advanced cognitive restructuring and addressing core beliefs. Finally, as you approach the end of the program, read Chapter 13 on consolidating and maintaining your progress. This chapter will help you make the transition from working with your therapist to continuing to make progress on your social anxiety on your own.

Homework for the Rest of the Program

Weekly Exposure Homework

As we have noted several times, each week you and your therapist will negotiate a homework assignment for an exposure that you do on your own. You will use the BYOCC worksheet to guide you through this procedure. This homework is an essential part of treatment because it helps assure that the work you do in session translates into the changes you want in your daily life.

Self-Monitoring Homework

You should also continue the daily self-monitoring that you started in Chapter 4. As you track your progress each week you may notice your average daily anxiety increases in the first few weeks. This increase is most likely to happen if you have been avoiding a lot of situations that caused you anxiety. As you stop avoiding, your anxiety will naturally increase at first. However, as you gain skill with the cognitive restructuring procedures and you repeatedly enter feared situations, the anxiety will decrease. You should find yourself entering the situations you are monitoring on the homework more and more frequently. As you keep practicing, the positive benefits will be obvious on the graph summarizing the weekly ratings.

Making Overcoming Anxiety Your New Habit

Earlier we described social anxiety as something you learned, like a bad habit. The problem with the anxiety habit is that it causes so many missed opportunities and difficulties in your life. Now is the time to start creating a new habit for yourself. We would like you to get in the habit of doing some small thing *each and every day* to overcome social anxiety. For many people, these will also be the first steps in building relationships with other people. This new habit should help you make faster progress in therapy and generally enrich your life. Here's what we recommend:

Think of some small action that you will be able to do nearly every day. This action should involve making contact with another person in a way that is outside of your regular routine. Here are some examples:

1. Say "hello" and one other thing to a person you would not normally speak with.

2. Make one telephone call that you would usually put off for another day because you are anxious about the call.

3. Give someone a compliment when you normally would not say anything.

4. Speak up one extra time in a group of people or at a meeting (good for people whose fears have mostly to do with speaking in front of others).

5. Ask someone an appropriate, non-intrusive question about himself or herself that will help you get to know the person a little better.

6. Make an effort to do some small task when others may be observing, such as pour someone's coffee, put change in a vending machine, unlock a door, drive with someone in the car, write a check rather than pay cash, etc. (good for people who primarily become anxious when doing things while being observed by others).

If none of these examples seem to apply to you, work with your therapist to design something similar.

As you can see, these are very small gestures that may take only a moment. They may not even make you especially anxious. However, we have found that these types of small, daily exposures help people with social anxiety develop a new habit of reaching out to other people and make facing your fears routine. You might be pleasantly surprised at other people's responses to you.

Self-Assessment

1. When working out the order in which to conduct exposures, it is best   **T F**
   to start with the hardest one so that the rest will be easier.

2. Homework in this program is strictly optional, does not help to link   **T F**
   therapy to the real world, and is unrelated to your success with
   this program.

3. It is critical to do exposures for every single situation in which you   **T F**
   might become anxious.

4. An example of generalization is overcoming fears about talking with   **T F**
   co-workers which might lead to reduced fear in talking with other
   students with whom you are working on a group project.

5. Noticing that you are anxious in a situation signals that it is time   **T F**
   to examine your ATs.

Answers to Self-Assessment questions can be found in Appendix A.

Chapter 9

Overcoming Fears of Doing Things in Front of Others

The previous chapters covered the core parts of this treatment. Starting with this chapter, we will talk about procedures that are specific to certain types of social anxiety. This chapter will cover fears about performing various activities in front of others. These are known as the specific social phobias. Chapter 10 addresses fears about conversations and making small talk and Chapter 11 is about fears of public speaking. Read each chapter that applies to you. However, even if you do not have a particular fear, you may find helpful information in these chapters or maybe a Rational Response that seems particularly powerful for one of your own ATs.

The Original Social Phobia

Thirty-five years ago two well-known British psychiatrists, Drs. Isaac Marks and Michael Gelder, described individuals who were looking for treatment for fears about doing specific tasks in front of other people, such as signing one's name, eating, or drinking. Usually the fear was that the person's hand would shake or that he or she would spill the food or drink. These specific fears were the original "social phobias," the old name for social anxiety disorder. As we discussed in the first three chapters, social anxiety disorder is now more broadly defined to include fears of conversations, dating, public speaking, and being assertive. Fears of writing/eating/drinking in front of others are now known as the "observational fears" or "specific social phobias" to distinguish them from the more pervasive fears of interacting with other people experienced by many persons with social anxiety disorder. It is now known that worrying about being viewed negatively by others is the common thread that runs through all types of social anxiety.

The following is a list of observational fears. Some examples appear in parentheses. Make a check mark next to any that apply to you.

- ☐ fear that your hand will shake when signing your name in front of other people (writing a check, signing a credit card slip)

- ☐ fear that your hand will shake when filling out forms in front of other people (medical forms, insurance paperwork)

- ☐ fear that your hand will shake when writing on a chalkboard or easel

- ☐ fear that your hand will shake or you will spill something when eating in front of other people

- ☐ fear that you will spill or choke when drinking a beverage in front of other people

- ☐ fear that you will spill when pouring a beverage for someone

- ☐ fear that you will make errors when typing in front of someone

- ☐ fear that you will stumble or look odd when walking in front of a crowd (getting on an airplane or bus when others are seated, or walking in front of a crowded theater)

- ☐ fear that you will make errors when playing a sport (miss the ball when swinging a golf club or tennis racket, throw a wild pitch in softball)

- ☐ fear that your hand will shake or you will make an error when using any sort of tool or precision instrument in front of others (nurse giving an injection, mechanic using a wrench)

- ☐ fear that you will make mistakes while driving and this will be noticed by your passengers or other drivers

This list is not exhaustive. Almost any task in which you have to do something in a particular way or appear a particular way has the potential to become a specific social phobia.

When our clients describe their observational fears, they often describe themselves as being "self-conscious." In other words, they notice that they are paying too much attention to what they are doing. In fact, they are often paying attention to what they must look like to other people. Unfortunately, self-consciousness often produces the very outcome that they fear will happen. Let's look at an example of how this works.

Claudia is an expert typist who types well over 100 words per minute. She can type rapidly and accurately because she types whole words rather than individual letters. Instead of typing three letters—*a*, *n*, and *d*—for the word *and*, Claudia has one motion for the entire word. This motion involves the small finger on her left hand, the index finger of her right hand, and the middle finger of her left hand in rapid succession. If you ask Claudia to think about her fingertips touching each letter on the keyboard, she will probably type much more slowly and make a number of mistakes. Thus, if you ask Claudia to become self-conscious on purpose and observe her own hands as someone else would, she will lose the automatic nature of her expert typing. Somehow thinking about the process of typing interferes with actually doing it.

If you know how to touch-type, try this for yourself. Type something while saying the letters aloud and watching your fingers strike each key. You will see that becoming self-conscious makes an automatic task much more difficult. You can also try this experiment with anything at which you are so skilled that you can do it automatically (e.g., playing a musical instrument, throwing or hitting a ball, bowling). All you have to do is slow down and watch each motion as you make it.

If Claudia becomes self-conscious about her typing and she also becomes anxious about it, then typing becomes even more difficult for her. The anxiety might cause tension in the muscles in her arms, hands, and fingers, making it even more difficult for her to move her fingers smoothly and rapidly over the correct keys. Being anxious means that her thought processes are focused on ATs such as "I shouldn't make a mistake" or "I'll look incompetent." This makes it harder for her to concentrate on the typing because she is too busy thinking about the ATs.

This is the same process that occurs with observational fears. Once you become anxious about doing something such as drinking coffee in front of someone, that anxiety makes it more difficult for you to drink the coffee without shaking or spilling. Eventually you might find yourself avoiding drinking coffee altogether when other people are around.

When people who do not have observational fears hear about them for the first time, it is easy to dismiss them as trivial or unimportant. If you experience anxiety in any of these situations, however, you know that it can greatly interfere with your life. Fears about eating or drinking with others can lead to extreme social isolation. Much of the time we spend socializing with others involves meals, having coffee or tea together, or going out for a drink. Your work may involve entertaining clients at dinner or business meetings over lunch. It is very inconvenient to have to pay cash for everything because you cannot write a check or sign a credit card receipt. Imagine the hassle of having to worry about how many groceries you are buying, not because you cannot afford them, but because you only have a certain amount of cash with you. Observational fears may make urinating in a restroom when others are present very difficult or impossible. Individuals with this difficulty may restrict their intake of liquids at work or make decisions about attending events based on whether or not they will be able to avoid using a public restroom for that length of time. Many secretarial or factory jobs have occasions when someone is watching workers as part of a training program or quality control procedures. Offices or other work environments may be open so that co-workers and supervisors are constantly around, potentially observing while individuals work. In addition to the health benefits, sports and recreational activities offer many opportunities for friendships or business contacts. Many people join community softball, tennis, or bowling leagues. Others play in golf tournaments. Anxiety about performing those activities in front of others may lead to avoidance and missed opportunities. As you can see, specific social phobias can have a large impact on a person's life.

Common ATs Related to Observational Fear and How to Handle Them

Next we will look at some of the ATs that people with observational fears often report. Perhaps some of them will sound familiar to you. We will use the cognitive restructuring skills to categorize and challenge these ATs. We will suggest a situation in which each AT might occur because having a specific context makes them easier to challenge. However, you may have the same AT in a different situation. If necessary, your therapist can help you adapt our suggestions for cognitive restructuring to your particular situation. In each of our examples we list several ATs but focus only on the one that seems to occur for many people. This would not necessarily be the first AT to address during the first exposure. Your therapist will guide you in selecting which ATs to challenge at particular times as certain ATs are easier to challenge later in treatment, once you have completed some exposures.

"My Hand Will Shake"

Miguel is a businessman who travels a lot. In recent years he has become very anxious when having to sign credit card receipts because he fears his hand will shake. Because he needs to have a record of his expenses, the accounting office at his company does not want him to use cash. He is particularly anxious when other people are present, especially potential customers. The more he worries about his hand shaking, the more likely it is to shake. This fear often occurs when he has taken a customer out to lunch and must sign the credit card receipt for the bill. Let's look at Miguel's ATs in this specific situation:

My hand will shake.

The customer will see my hand shake.

The customer will think I'm incompetent and not give us any business.

He indicates that these thoughts make him feel nervous and frustrated. As he notices he is feeling frustrated, he reports one more AT—"I shouldn't have this problem." Because all of the other ATs come from "My hand will shake," let's work on that one.

Challenging Miguel's ATs

Looking at the List of Thinking Errors, we can classify this thought into several categories.

Fortune Telling: Miguel is predicting that his hand will shake at a particular upcoming lunch. That lunch has not yet happened, so he is predicting the future.

Overgeneralization: Miguel's hand has sometimes shaken in the past so he draws the sweeping conclusion that it will shake this time (and all other times as well).

Mental Filter: Miguel is focusing all of his attention on this one brief event—signing the credit slip. His concern about this event is crowding out everything else about the lunch and the rest of the meeting with the customer.

Looking at the Disputing Question list, we can see some ways to question this thought. Remember it is always important to answer the question raised by the Disputing Question.

What evidence do I have that my hand will shake? Miguel answers that on many similar occasions in the past his hand did shake. Since he is already anxious about the situation, it seems likely that his hand will shake this time. However, he has no concrete evidence his hand will shake this time because it has not happened yet!

Does my hand shaking last time have to lead to its shaking this time? Miguel answers that it seems to be a pattern that his hand shakes in this situation but it may not shake this time. Perhaps since he has been working on his anxiety he will be able to control it better.

What is the worst that could happen if my hand does shake? Miguel answers that if his hand shakes a lot, the customer would notice and think something is wrong with him. The customer might think he is on drugs. The customer might have less confidence in him and his company and take his business elsewhere. If this kept happening, Miguel could lose his job.

The worst that could happen is that Miguel could lose his job. However, this depends on the customer's seeing his hand shake and drawing a highly negative conclusion about Miguel. How likely is that? Let's use a technique called the "Pie Chart" to test out the AT that if Miguel's hand shakes, the customer will think something negative about him. Follow along on the Pie Chart in Figure 9.1 as Miguel answers each question.

How likely is it that my hand will shake at this particular lunch meeting? Miguel answers that there is a 90% chance. So there is a 10% chance that his hand will not shake. Locate the 10% slice of the pie labeled "Not Shake."

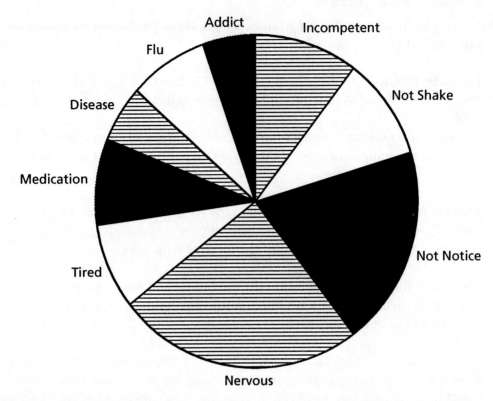

Figure 9.1. | **Pie Chart for Miguel's Automatic Thoughts About What a Customer Will Think if his Hand Shakes**

If my hand does shake, how likely is it that it will shake so much that the customer notices? The fact that the customer might not notice his hand shaking is a new idea for Miguel. As he thinks about it, however, he realizes that sometimes the tremor is so slight that it may not be visible to others. Miguel answers that there is probably a 75% chance that if his hand shakes, it will be severe enough that the customer would notice. That means there is a 25% chance that the customer would not notice. Locate the slice of the pie labeled "Not Notice" that represents this 25% chance (of the 90% chance his hand will shake).

Does my hand shaking have to lead to the customer's thinking I am incompetent? If not, what else could it mean? Miguel answers that his hand could be shaking for many reasons:

- because he is nervous
- because he is tired
- because he is taking some sort of medication
- because he is a drug addict
- because he has some sort of disease that affects the muscles in his hand

- because he has the flu

- because he is incompetent

Locate the slices of the pie that represent each of these explanations for why his hand could shake in a given situation.

As you look at the pie chart you can see that there is about a 33% chance that either his hand will not shake or the customer will not notice it. Miguel believes that either of these would be a good outcome. There is about a 30% chance that his customer would notice his hand shaking and think it was because of something that is negative but not a disaster (being tired, having the flu, having a muscular disease, or taking some sort of medication). There is a 25% chance that the customer will simply conclude that he is nervous. Miguel believes that just being thought of as nervous is not as bad as being thought of as incompetent or a drug addict. There is only a 15% chance that the customer will draw the worst conclusions. To summarize, 85% of the time, the customer will not notice or not think too negatively of him (all pie slices except "Addict" and "Incompetent"), and one out of three times (pie slices of "Not Notice" and "Not Shake"), it actually will not be a problem.

The next step in cognitive restructuring is to develop a Rational Response that summarizes what Miguel learned when he challenged his ATs. Remember, a Rational Response should be shorthand for the most important points of the cognitive restructuring that you want to remember. The Rational Response should also be short and easy to remember so that you can use it in exposures or anytime you encounter the feared situation. Miguel's fear that his hand would shake is based on his concern that the customer will draw a negative conclusion and take his business elsewhere. If Miguel lost a lot of business, he could lose his job. The following Rational Response highlights the fact that Miguel's hand might not shake, the shaking might not be noticed, and noticeable shaking will not necessarily lead to the loss of a customer.

Rational Response: *Even if my hand shakes and the customer notices it, he'll probably still do business with me.*

Notice how Miguel's definite belief that his hand would shake (that we saw in the original ATs) has now become *If my hand shakes*. The definite belief that the customer would notice his shaking hands has also become an "If"—*If. . . the customer notices.*

Achievable Behavioral Goals and the In-Session Exposure.

The next step in cognitive restructuring is to set an achievable behavioral goal. Miguel chose the goal of holding the paper out where it could easily be seen and then continuing to sign his name, even if his hand started to shake. Because signing one's name only takes a few moments, Miguel and his therapist set up the in-session exposure so that he repeatedly interrupted the conversation with the "customer" and signed fake credit card slips 30 times. Afterwards they debriefed the exposure by looking at expected and unexpected ATs. Miguel concluded that he learned that he could continue to write no matter what happened. Even if he felt anxious and his hand started to shake, he could think about his Rational Response ("Even if my hand shakes and the customer notices it, he'll probably still do business with me"). He was now ready to attempt a similar situation for homework.

Using Pie Charts to Challenge ATs

The Pie Chart helped Miguel understand that many different things could happen when he has to write in front of a customer. Some of those things are very negative, like being considered a drug addict. Although many of the possible outcomes for the situation are more neutral, he had never really considered them. Finally, the Pie Chart helped Miguel consider the possibility that his hand would not shake or that the customer would not notice a slight tremor. This cognitive restructuring will help him enter the situation with less anxiety. The Rational Response can help keep his anxiety under control while he is with the customer. If Miguel is less anxious, then it is less likely that the muscles in his hand and arm will tense up enough to cause a visible tremor.

The Pie Chart can also be used for ATs associated with many other observational fears, including fears of spilling something, choking on food or a drink, or making a mistake. In fact, you will find the Pie Chart useful any time you have ATs with Catastrophic Thinking Errors that predict something terribly bad is going to happen when, in reality, there are many possible outcomes.

"I'll Make a Mistake"

Stephanie is in nursing school, and she is approaching the point in her training where she needs to learn to draw blood. She has been told that the students will practice drawing blood from each other before trying it with actual patients. Stephanie becomes extremely nervous when she thinks about drawing blood because it is obvious whether she has done it correctly—the patient either sees the tube filling with blood or not! She has vivid images of poking someone with the needle over and over again and no blood coming out into the tube. She reacts to these images with nausea and a pounding headache. Before starting nursing school, Stephanie had spoken with the nurse at her own physician's office about her interest in nursing. When the nurse drew blood for routine testing, she commented that many people did not like to have blood drawn so she tried to get it over with as quickly as possible. The nurse then said, "You never want to make a mistake when poking a needle in someone's arm." Stephanie keeps remembering that statement when she gets anxious. Let's look at Stephanie's ATs about having to draw blood from one of her classmates:

I'll make a mistake.

I'll miss one of the steps in the procedure.

I won't be able to get any blood.

My classmates will think I'm incompetent because I can't do this.

These ATs make Stephanie feel silly and embarrassed. Since concern over making a mistake is quite common, let's look at the first AT in more detail.

Challenging Stephanie's ATs

"I'll make a mistake" can be classified into several of the Thinking Errors on the list.

All-or-Nothing Thinking: When talking with Stephanie, it becomes clear that if she does not do every step of the procedure perfectly, she would see her performance as a failure.

Fortune Telling: Stephanie is predicting that she will make a mistake. Since she has not actually tried to draw blood yet, she does not know what will happen. However, unlike most of the Fortune Telling Thinking Errors that we have discussed, this one has a greater chance of being accurate. Since she is learning a new skill, she will probably make some mistakes. However, it is important to consider whether she is likely to make a catastrophic mistake. It is more likely that she will make the mistake of missing the vein the first time than forgetting to remove the needle from the person's arm when she is done. Small mistakes that are part of the learning process are more reasonable (and more possible) than huge mistakes that are potentially dangerous to the patient.

Overgeneralization: Stephanie is making a sweeping conclusion that making a mistake will have many disastrous consequences. Not only is she worried that her classmates will think she is incompetent, but if we talked with her further, we would find out that she worries that making mistakes drawing blood means she should not be a nurse.

Now let's turn to the Disputing Questions and see if Stephanie can challenge her AT "I'll make a mistake."

Do I know for certain that I will make a mistake when I draw blood from my classmates? Stephanie answers that she cannot be 100% sure but that she will probably make a mistake because she has never done this before.

Does making a mistake when drawing blood from a classmate have such awful consequences that my entire future resides on it? Stephanie answers that if she cannot learn to draw blood she cannot be a nurse. That is probably true. However, does making a mistake in this particular instance mean that Stephanie cannot be a nurse? Probably not.

How likely is it that I will make a serious mistake drawing blood from my classmate that will get me thrown out of nursing school? Stephanie indicates that the most likely mistake would be to somehow miss the vein so that she has to try several times. She does not think this would get her thrown out of nursing school because it happens sometimes even to experienced nurses. Stephanie realizes that she would have to do something very serious to be removed from school for not drawing blood properly. It would have to be something outrageous, such as poking the needle in her classmate's eye on purpose. Not surprisingly, Stephanie thinks that such an event is extremely unlikely to occur.

Is making mistakes a normal part of learning a new skill? Stephanie answers that yes, making mistakes is a normal part of learning something new. In fact, she is able to identify several skills she has already learned in nursing school. While she made a number of mistakes at first, she was later able to perform correctly. She is able to say that that is the reason she and her fellow nursing students often practice on each other before trying the procedures on real patients. The most important thing is to learn from the mistakes and improve.

Stephanie summarizes these ideas into the following Rational Response: *Making mistakes is part of learning something new.* Notice that this Rational Response addresses the All-or-Nothing Thinking in Stephanie's AT "I'll make a mistake." It encourages her to stop thinking in terms of being perfect. Instead, the Rational Response encourages her to recognize that mistakes are a normal and expected part of learning.

Achievable Behavioral Goals and the Exposure

It would not be appropriate to have Stephanie actually draw blood during her therapy session, as this should only be done under appropriate supervision. However, she could do everything except actually sticking the needle into someone's arm. To make it more realistic, she brings all of the necessary equipment to session, although the syringe does not have a needle. She sets "Going through all of the steps in the procedure to draw blood (except the actual needle stick)" as the achievable behavioral goal. Afterwards Stephanie and her therapist debrief the exposure. Focusing on her Rational Response seemed to help control her anxiety when she had the expected AT "I'll make a mistake." When asked to summarize what she had learned from the exposure, Stephanie indicates that she knew she would be very unlikely to make a dangerous mistake and she would need to go easy on herself for making the normal mistakes that come with learning. She is now ready to use her cognitive skills to prepare for an upcoming nursing class during which the students will draw blood from each other.

General Strategies to Address Fears of Making Mistakes

In this example we worked on fears of making mistakes when learning something new. Often people with observational fears worry about making mistakes doing something that they know well. Making mistakes may be part of learning, but once you become more experienced, mistakes are less expected. Notice that we said "less expected," not "mistakes should not happen." "Mistakes should not happen" is a Should Statement that can be very destructive. If we are expert at something or it is part of our job, it is easy to have the expectation that we can do it well *every* time. However, if you think about it, that is not very realistic.

Any sports fan can tell you that even the most expert professional can make a mistake at a crucial moment. Consider the field goal kicker who misses the winning 30-yard field goal in the final seconds of a playoff game. Part of the excitement of watching sports is that the outcome is unpredictable because any player can play better or worse than usual on any given play.

In fact, it is clear that mistakes are part of the human condition. In the vast majority of situations where the consequences of a mistake are serious, there is a back-up plan if a mistake occurs. In situations where mistakes could be disastrous, such as a pilot landing a passenger jet, the pilot has the co-pilots and many safety systems that warn him or her if a mistake is being made. Manufactured products are inspected and tested to assure that a mistake has not occurred in production. These warning systems, inspections, and evaluations can be thought of as "safety nets" in case something goes wrong or someone makes a mistake.

There is no safety net for the sad ballplayer described above whose mistake cost his team the championship. That is because the consequences of this kind of mistake are not that serious. The players and the team may lose money and prestige but no one will die. Part of the challenge of sports is for players to test themselves against the opposition, recognizing that sometimes they will win but sometimes they will lose. Batting records in baseball are an excellent example of this principle. A baseball player who has a .400 batting average will certainly go to the Hall of Fame. However, a .400 average means that the player only hits the ball four out of ten times at bat. More often than not, the player makes an "out"!

If your AT is "I'll make a mistake" in a situation in which you have a lot of experience, ask yourself if there is a "safety net" if you do so. If there is, then reminding yourself of the safety net may make an excellent Rational Response. If there is not, then ask yourself how serious the consequences of making this mistake really are. Watch out for Emotional Reasoning here. The consequences may "feel" very serious. Here is an exercise that might help you put the consequences in perspective:

On the left end of the following line, identify something that could happen to you that would be unpleasant but not very serious. As an example we will fill in "stubbing my toe."

Stubbing my toe   *All of my family killed*

+——+

On the other end, fill in the absolutely worst thing that could happen to you. For most people, this is something like finding out that everyone in their family had been killed in a car accident. We filled this in on the right.

Now put a mark on the line that indicates how serious the consequences would be for the mistake you are worried about making. We'll fill it in for the football player who missed the winning field goal.

Stubbing my toe　　*Missing winning field goal*　　　　　　　　　　　　　　*All of my family killed*
+————————————+————————————————————————————+

As you can see, missing the winning field goal was far more serious than stubbing his toe, but compared to losing all of his family, it was not that serious.

Now consider where you placed the mark for the mistake that worries you. How serious is that mistake when you consider everything that is important to you? Try to develop a Rational Response that reminds you of the more realistic view of the seriousness of making a mistake. Here are some examples that our clients have used:

If _____ happens, it will be unpleasant, but I can live through it.

Even if _____ happens, I still have the most important thing in life—my family.

Exposures for Observational Fears

As we discussed in previous chapters, the exact exposures that you will complete with your therapist or as homework must be highly individualized. Everyone with social anxiety experiences the anxiety somewhat differently from situation to situation so there is no one set of exposures that should be completed by everyone. We will describe some exposures we have often used when working with individuals with observational fears. Some may apply to you, some may not. The order in which you complete the exposures will depend on what makes a situation easier or harder for you.

Some exposure situations are very brief. For example, signing your name to a credit card slip takes only a few seconds. It is best for exposures to last long enough for your anxiety to habituate (peak and start to decrease). For very short situations, this may mean setting up an artificial exposure in which you sign your name repeatedly. Your therapist can help you work this out. We offer some suggestions here on how to do exposures for these very brief feared situations for homework.

Eating in Front of Others

If you become anxious when eating with other people, start to look for situations in your life in which you could choose to dine with someone or at least in the presence of other people. Here are some examples:

▓ Dine inside the fast-food restaurant rather than using the drive-through window.

▓ Eat at a deli rather than picking up something to take home.

▓ Invite co-workers, relatives, or friends to join you for Happy Hour, lunch, dinner, or Sunday brunch either in your home or at a restaurant.

▓ Choose items to eat that you find more anxiety-provoking.

▓ Eat with chopsticks at Asian restaurants.

▓ Create extra opportunities for eating with others by bringing food to share with co-workers, family, or friends at occasions when food would be appropriate but not necessarily present.

▓ Go to restaurants when they are more or less crowded—whichever is more difficult for you.

Drinking in Front of Others

Many of the suggestions for exposures to eating in front of others also apply here. Again, look for occasions to have a beverage whenever other people are around. Although eating may not be appropriate in some circumstances (such as a formal business meeting), having a bottle of water or a cup of coffee is acceptable in most situations.

▓ Carry something to drink with you whenever possible. Take any opportunity to drink when others are present.

▓ Stop at a fast-food restaurant or coffee shop and have your drink inside rather than getting something to go.

▓ If you are a member of a church, try to take communion whenever possible.

▓ Remove the straw from a drink (or use one if that is more anxiety-provoking).

▓ Choose beverages (or types of containers) that you find more difficult to drink (or drink from) whenever possible.

▓ Invite co-workers, friends, or family to join you on occasions in which beverages will be served, such as meals, Happy Hour, etc.

▓ Take breaks at work with others and drink something.

▓ Be sure to order extra beverages when dining out, such as having a beverage and water with the dinner and coffee after dinner to provide more opportunities to practice.

Writing in Front of Others

In a society that relies more on credit and debit cards than cash, it is easy to find opportunities to sign your name in front of others. There are also many opportunities to write checks rather than pay cash. Although most people try to avoid extra paperwork, there are many opportunities to fill out forms when others are watching if you need to find them. Here are some examples of exposures to address fears of writing in front of others:

- Write a check or use a credit card rather than paying cash whenever possible.

- Do not start writing the check until it is your turn to check out at a store. Although people behind you in line may prefer that you have your check ready to go, some people do not start searching for their checkbook until they get the total from the cashier! Taking a little extra time is acceptable and can help you work on your anxiety. Be sure to fill out the complete check and all of the details in your check register in front of everyone.

- Go inside the bank rather than using the drive-through window or the automatic teller machine.

- Go to banks and stores at the busiest time.

- Volunteer to take the minutes at a meeting.

- Volunteer to write on the chalkboard or easel during a meeting or class.

- If you are making a presentation, try to write on a chalkboard or easel whenever possible.

- If there is more than one place to pay for items in a store, pay for part of your items in each place, using a check or credit card each time.

- Do your grocery shopping by purchasing a few items at several different stores, writing a check each time.

- Use a gas station where you can pay by credit card to a cashier rather than just swiping your card at the pump.

Remember that your goal is not to be an efficient shopper for now. The goal is to find as many opportunities as possible to expose yourself to the situations you fear and to practice using your Rational Responses and disputing skills as you do so.

Fears Of Making Mistakes

Sometimes people who have a specific social phobia about making mistakes find that they only become anxious in one or two particular situations. As with the nursing student described, these situations are often related to work or school. Fears of making mistakes during sports or exercise are also included here. Regardless of your primary feared situation(s), we have found that it is often helpful to put yourself in situations in which your performance will frequently fall short of perfect. Since none of us are perfect, sometimes we just need to work on making our errors a bit more public. Be sure to set your observable behavioral goal as "making a mistake and staying in the situation anyway."

- Since you are likely to make mistakes when learning something new, take on a new hobby or sport, particularly one that is taught in a class. Possibilities include instrumental or vocal music lessons, sports lessons (tennis, golf, etc.), dance classes, drawing or painting classes, arts and crafts classes, or wood-working classes.

- Take your dog to obedience classes. Even if you do everything right, your pet is likely to refuse your direction from time to time!

- Join a community sports team.

- Make harmless mistakes on purpose. Volunteer to read something aloud in a meeting and stumble over your words occasionally, pay for something with "exact change" but be over or under by a few cents, etc.

- Play games in which you are likely to make errors, such as trivia games or charades.

- If you are worried about spilling things, have a friend or family member help you by holding a glass while you pour in water. Deliberately pour in too much water so the glass overflows.

- Using water from a companion's glass in a restaurant, deliberately pour extra water into your own glass so it is difficult to drink without spilling a little. Repeatedly take a drink.

Summary

In this chapter we have discussed several common observational fears and some cognitive restructuring exercises and possible exposures to address them. Many of these will be helpful for more general fears of having conversations as well. With some creativity and the assistance of your therapist, you should be able to design exposures to address your fears, even if the particular situations arise infrequently.

Homework

We described examples of exposures that could be done both within the session and as homework assignments for exposure in your daily life. Each week you and your therapist will negotiate a homework assignment to assure that you are applying the skills you are learning. As always, be careful to use the BYOCC work-sheet to guide your homework assignment so that you work through each step of the cognitive skills.

1. As opposed to the original social phobias, social anxiety disorder   **T   F**
   now includes fears of conversations, dating, public speaking, and
   assertion, in addition to signing one's name, eating with others,
   and drinking in public.

2. Once you become anxious about performing a task, the anxiety   **T   F**
   makes the task even more difficult to complete.

3. Using a pie chart can help you see that there are many possible   **T   F**
   outcomes to a situation, including some chance that other people
   won't notice your anxiety.

4. It is reasonable to think that if you are an expert at something then   **T   F**
   you will perform perfectly every time.

5. Exposures work best if they last long enough for anxiety to get   **T   F**
   to its peak, and then they should be discontinued.

Answers to Self-Assessment questions can be found in Appendix A.

Chapter 10

Big Fears of Small Talk

I don't know what to say.

I'm not very good at making conversation.

We won't have anything to talk about.

I never have anything interesting to say.

She'll think I'm boring.

He won't be interested in what I have to say.

Do these ATs sound familiar to you? Many people who have difficulty with social anxiety worry about what to say in casual conversations. A seemingly minor encounter, such as exchanging a few words with a store clerk or neighbor, can result in anxiety for many people with social anxiety disorder. In this chapter we will explore why it is important to be able to make casual conversation. Then we will examine some of the ATs that socially anxious individuals often have in casual conversation and how to challenge those ATs.

The Big Impact of Small Talk

Most people with social anxiety tell us that they hate small talk. However, it is as necessary to life as food and water. Let's define "small talk" as the short casual conversations that people have with friends, family, acquaintances and strangers about superficial or impersonal topics. Some examples of small talk include:

- Complimenting the neighbor on the beautiful flowers on her patio when you see her out watering as you leave for work

- Asking a co-worker whether he or she did anything fun over the weekend

- Commenting to the desk clerk at the health club that the club seems fairly quiet today

- Commenting to someone while waiting for the instructor to arrive that the class is interesting but more work than you had expected it to be

- Striking up a conversation with a sales clerk by asking whether he or she has heard if the weather will be warm this weekend

As you can see from the examples, none of these conversations are about important topics. In fact, when we have clients pay attention to what people discuss when they are making small talk, clients usually are amazed at how "small" the talk is. Small talk is usually about very trivial topics. The weather is a favorite topic for casual conversations, which rarely cover major world events or great philosophical issues. By focusing on more trivial subjects or events the two people might have in common (such as, "Did you see that story in the news about that little kid getting stuck in the well?"), casual conversations provide the "grease" for people to become acquainted or just to pass the time by making contact with others. If they encounter each other frequently, then a more serious friendship or relationship might evolve. More serious or emotionally significant conversations at the right time lead to closer relationships. However, the first step in any friendship or relationship is making small talk.

Small Talk Begins Relationships

A number of years ago social psychologist Donn Byrne studied how people choose potential friends and marriage partners. He looked at a number of possible factors, including having something in common with the person and being physically attractive. Although these factors were important in picking friends and partners, another very important factor was something he called "propinquity" (pro-PIN-qui-tee), meaning "nearness" or "proximity." In Professor Byrne's research, he found that he could determine which people would become friends in a college classroom simply by assigning them to sit near each other. After a few weeks of sitting in the same nearby seats, students would become acquainted through casual conversations and, in some cases, develop friendships or dating relationships. In other studies, he found similar patterns of friendship development among neighbors. The old adage that we often marry the boy or girl next door is true, simply because they are nearby and we see them frequently.

If you have been socially anxious for a long time, you might not have any friends, or maybe only one or two people with whom you do things. You might have arranged your life so that you do not have to talk with anyone, so it may be difficult to meet new people who could become friends or dating partners. Professor Byrne's research and the work of other researchers suggests that there are two factors involved in developing friendships—you need to be around people on a regular basis and you need to start casual conversations so you can get acquainted. Before we talk about how to achieve these goals, let's discuss why it is important to have relationships with other people.

Social Support Networks

Family and friends form what is known as a "social support network." A person's social support network is the group of people that can be counted on to listen, offer advice, provide help, and do things together. Some people like to have a large network with lots of friends, family, and acquaintances, and they confide easily in one another. Other people prefer only a handful of friends and family members who are close and mutually supportive. If your social support network is too small or you do not have close relationships with the people in it, then you are likely to feel lonely and isolated. This often happens to people with social anxiety because their anxiety has interfered with their ability to make close friendships or develop romantic relationships.

An inadequate social support network can have many consequences for a person beyond feeling lonely and isolated. Many scientific studies over the last 25 years have found that social support seems to act like a buffer against the stresses in life. People with good social support networks have better physical and mental health, recover from surgery and illness faster, and may live longer than people with inadequate social support networks. Friends and family in a social support network may do things that are helpful like fixing a car or bringing chicken soup when you have the flu. Friends and family also provide emotional support by listening to your frustrations with a supervisor or reminding you that you are loved by sending a birthday card. As you can see, there are many good reasons to invest time and energy in developing a social support network that meets your needs. Now let's turn to a quick inventory of how you feel about your social support network.

Examining Your Social Support Network

Figure 10.1 is a form entitled "Your Social Support Network." Take a few moments now to answer the questions.

Count the number of different names you listed in response to the three questions. If a name appears on more than one question, count it only once. There is no "right" answer. Different people are comfortable with networks of different sizes. However, if you listed only one or two different names, your network is small. Most people would probably prefer to count on more than one or two people. On the other hand, it is hard to have close relationships with many people. If you listed 10 or more names, ask yourself how close you really are to some of the people. Consider the following questions:

1. Are you surprised about the number of people in your network? Why or why not?

2. Do you feel that your network is the right size for you? Would you like to have more people who are close to you?

Your Social Support Network

1. List the first names of everyone in whom you can confide about the things that are really important to you.

2. List the first names of everyone on whom you can count if you need help with something.

3. List the first names of everyone to whom you could turn for emotional support or advice if something bad happened to you, such as losing your job or finding out you had a serious illness.

Figure 10.1.

If you are like most people with social anxiety disorder, particularly those who get anxious in casual conversations, your social support network is probably lacking, either because there are too few people or the relationships are too superficial. It may be time to consider how to enlarge your network.

Common ATs for Casual Conversations

As we saw at the beginning of this chapter, certain ATs are commonly reported by people who have fears of casual conversations. We will look at the potential Thinking Errors in each of these thoughts and consider some ways of disputing the ATs.

"I Won't Know What to Say"

Kay is considering whether to start a conversation with her co-worker Kim. As Kay starts to get anxious anticipating the conversation, she finds herself thinking, "I won't know what to say." Next we will see how she could challenge this AT. What Thinking Errors might be in the thought, *I won't know what to say*?

Fortune Telling: Kay is making a prediction that she won't know what to say before the conversation actually happens.

Disqualifying the Positive: If Kay has things she could talk about but she has dismissed them as silly or uninteresting, then this thought would be an example of Disqualifying the Positive. She would be disqualifying what she has to say, thereby maintaining her belief that she has nothing to say in casual conversations.

Kay can use the Disputing Questions to challenge this AT. What follows is the dialogue that Kay might have with herself.

Anxious Kay:	I won't know what to say.
Coping Kay:	What evidence do you have that you won't know what to say?
Anxious: Kay:	When I think about going up to Kim and talking to her, I am unsure about what I should say.
Coping Kay:	Are you 100% certain that you do not have any ideas at all regarding what you could talk about with Kim?
Anxious Kay:	I guess I would just start with "Hello, how are you?" first.

**Coping
Kay:**   That's a good start. What else could you say after that?

**Anxious
Kay:**   I could ask her about her weekend, whether she did anything fun.

**Coping
Kay:**   Do you think she might then ask you about something, maybe what you did this weekend?

**Anxious
Kay:**   It's possible she might ask me something. If not, I could just tell her about the movie I saw on Saturday.

**Coping
Kay:**   So what is the evidence that you won't know what to say to Kim?

**Anxious
Kay:**   None. I guess there are a few things I could say.

**Coping
Kay:**   So a Rational Response to the AT "I won't know what to say" might be "I can say hello and talk about our weekends."

It is rarely the case that a person has no idea of what to say in a casual conversation. Everyone can say, "Hello, how are you?" Then it only takes one or two more topics to carry the conversation further. Doing the cognitive restructuring before starting the casual conversation will help challenge the AT "I won't know what to say." The cognitive work also has the added benefit of providing an opportunity to think of potential topics before the conversation begins. Kay now has a plan to greet Kim, ask about her weekend, and tell her about the movie she saw. This plan could easily become her achievable behavioral goal of accomplishing these three tasks. She can enter this conversation fully armed for success.

Very often ATs about not knowing what to say in casual conversations come from underlying ATs such as "I never have anything interesting to say." People with social anxiety may have difficulty finding conversation topics because they dismiss many everyday topics in their search for topics that are interesting or entertaining.

"I'm Not Very Good at Making Conversation"

Many people with social anxiety disorder believe that they do not have the skills to make conversation. When they first go to see a therapist or counselor, these individuals state that they do not know how to act or what to say in social situations. They may say that they do not know how to make small talk. In the language of psychologists, many socially anxious people believe they have poor social skills. Socially anxious people talk about their poor social skills so much that many psychologists believe them. Some of the earliest treatments for social anxiety disorder were social skills training programs. These programs included instruction and practice in what to say in different situations as well as feedback on how loud your voice is, how to make the right amount of eye contact, and so forth. These programs were fairly helpful for many people. However, in the 1980s, psychologists started to notice that many, if not most, people with social anxiety disorder did not have poor social skills. In fact, observations of individuals with social anxiety in various situations suggested that although they frequently felt anxious and uncomfortable, they actually performed just fine. Sometimes their anxiety would distract them or interfere with what they were doing but it seemed clear that most individuals with social anxiety disorder had adequate (and often excellent) social skills. Thoughts such as "I'm not very good at making conversation" were actually Thinking Errors for many people with social anxiety. Let's take a look at an example.

Alejandro is very anxious about the upcoming office Christmas Party. He dreads going every year but believes that it is important to go because the boss seems to make a mental note of who does and does not attend. Although Alejandro usually becomes very anxious talking with people, he gets along OK at work because the conversations seem to have a purpose and are generally about work-related topics. People listen to him because they are exchanging information that they both need. When anticipating the party, Alejandro imagines himself standing in a group of people totally silent. He has some ideas about what he could say but he does not know how to break in. He may laugh along with the jokes but he does not really participate in the conversation. The situation feels hopelessly awkward and Alejandro says to himself, "I'm not very good at making conversation. Other people seem to know how to take their turns and the conversation flows back and forth." Let's look at Alejandro's AT of "I'm not very good at making conversation."

First we will examine the Thinking Errors in Alejandro's AT.

Labeling: Alejandro is labeling himself "poor conversationalist" (or more honestly, perhaps, "too stupid to know how to talk to people"). He seems to see himself as fitting into a category of people that have a serious flaw—not knowing how to make conversation.

Overgeneralizing: Alejandro is using the situations in which he had trouble with conversations in the past to draw the conclusion that he will have trouble this time.

Disqualifying the Positive: Alejandro is disqualifying the conversations about work that he has every day. He seems to have the skills to carry on those conversations. Probably some of the skills are relevant to conversations at a party.

Let's look at some cognitive restructuring that Alejandro might do for himself.

Anxious
Alejandro: I'm not very good at making conversations.

Coping
Alejandro: What evidence do you have that you are not very good at making conversations?

Anxious
Alejandro: I am always miserable at these Christmas parties and usually end up standing off by myself or sticking very close to my wife all evening.

Coping
Alejandro: Is there any other reason—besides a lack of social skills—that you could feel miserable at the Christmas party?

Anxious
Alejandro: I'm embarrassed about what people will think if I am standing off by myself but my wife worries about me if I hang around her all night.

Coping
Alejandro: So it sounds like at least part of feeling miserable might be due to thoughts about what people will think if you stand by yourself. Another part might be due to thoughts about your wife's reaction if you stay with her too much.

Anxious
Alejandro: Right.

Coping
Alejandro: It sounds like your thought about your social skills is only one of the ATs that might be making you feel miserable at the party. I'm wondering if you are feeling so miserable that you do not actually attempt to talk with very many people.

Anxious
Alejandro: I usually try a few times. I start a conversation, then after a few exchanges, the person does not seem to have much to say so I excuse myself and move on, feeling like I failed.

Coping
Alejandro: Are there any other possible reasons, besides your lack of social skills, that the other person might not continue to talk?

Anxious
Alejandro: I guess some of them might be shy and not have much to say. Maybe they see someone they want to talk with. Some people try to use these parties to make points with their supervisor or the big boss by chatting with them.

Coping
Alejandro: So it sounds like some people might cut the conversation short for reasons that have nothing to do with you.

Anxious
Alejandro: Yes, I guess that is true. It takes two people to have a conversation. If they don't stick around there isn't much I can do.

Coping
Alejandro: You're right. It does take two people to have a conversation. What percentage of the conversation are you responsible for?

Anxious
Alejandro: I guess I'm only responsible for half and the other person is responsible for half.

As with many people with social anxiety, Alejandro did not have much evidence of the terrible social skills he thought he possessed. There were several reasons why he might be feeling uncomfortable at the party, including worrying about what his wife and other people thought of him. Also, he had been putting a lot of pressure on himself to carry the conversation. It is important to remember that if the other person does not want to talk, there is not much you can do about it. A good Rational Response for him might be, "I only have to do my half" or "I'm only responsible for 50% of the conversation." If he is less worried about keeping the conversation going, Alejandro should be able to be more spontaneous and better able to think of things to say.

Penny: Fear of Casual Conversations

Now that we have examined how to challenge some of the common ATs socially anxious individuals have about casual conversations, we will look at a case example that describes a series of exposures for overcoming these fears. This will allow you to see how a series of cognitive restructurings and exposures for fears of casual conversations can build on each other across treatment sessions.

Penny is 25-year-old single woman who works at a day care center. She came to treatment because she was feeling very socially isolated and had no close friends. The few friends she had from high school had all moved away or gotten married. She had not had a date in over a year. Penny stated that her primary problem was her inability to get acquainted with people. Whenever she considered starting a conversation with a stranger, she felt tongue-tied and did not know what to say. At work she was so busy with the children that she did not talk very much with the other three women who worked there. She was able to talk with the parents about the children as they came and went in the morning and evening but she kept those conversations as short as possible. Penny's goal in therapy was to become more comfortable meeting new people.

Penny participated in group therapy for social anxiety disorder. After working on cognitive skills in the first couple of sessions, it was time for Penny's first exposure. Penny and her therapist agreed that the first step in meeting new people was to make initial contact by saying "hello." They decided to do an in-session exposure in which Penny would approach each member of the group individually, offer a greeting, and say one other thing. One of Penny's ATs in anticipation of this exposure was "I'll be so nervous I won't even be able to get the words out." When she considered this thought, she felt humiliated and incompetent. With the group's help, Penny identified the Thinking Errors in this AT as two forms of Catastrophizing. Fortune Telling described her prediction, not based on evidence, that something bad will happen. She was also catastrophizing that the anxiety would be so severe that she would not be able to say even one or two sentences. Using the Disputing Question "How likely is it that I won't be able to talk at all?" Penny decided that there was no more than a 25% chance that she would not be able to talk at all. The rest of the group thought 25% was high but it seemed about right to Penny. Because a 25% chance of not being able to talk means there is a 75% chance she will be able to talk, Penny agreed to try the Rational Response "More than likely I will be able to talk." Her achievable behavioral goal was to get at least one word out to each person. With the therapist and group members standing in a circle to serve as role-play partners, Penny went around the group three times saying "Hello" or "Good Evening" and one other thing to each person, such as "How are you?" or "It's good to see you again." Her SUDS rating quickly went up to 85 as she was very anxious but slowly came down to about 60 as she completed the third time around.

Not surprisingly, Penny was able to talk with each person three times despite high anxiety, easily meeting her achievable behavioral goal. As she noticed the exercise was going OK, she felt her anxiety start to decrease. After this success, Penny agreed to approach three people she would not normally talk with during the week and say hello and one other thing. Her therapist emphasized the importance of completing the BYOCC worksheet prior to the homework so she could be fully prepared to cope with any anxiety that occurred.

Penny reported back the next session that she was able to complete her homework with the anxiety being no worse than a SUDS rating of 45 the third time. However, she did notice that it was hard to find people to talk with because she had become so isolated. At the therapist's suggestion she agreed to check into adult education classes at the community college as a way to meet new people who might have common interests. She eventually selected an 8-week photography class because she had always wanted to learn more about taking photos.

For her second in-session exposure, Penny had a brief conversation with an acquaintance. One of the other group members who became anxious when speaking in public, not in conversations, served as the role-play partner. Penny's primary AT before the exposure was "Having conversations is a normal, everyday experience. I shouldn't be anxious about it." She felt angry at herself for being anxious. The primary Thinking Error was identified as a Should Statement. After some discussion, Penny was able to ask herself whether it was really so important or consequential that she was anxious about conversations when most other people were not anxious in this situation. With the group's help, Penny concluded that everyone has their own difficulties and comparing herself to others is not very helpful. The most important thing is that she was working to overcome her fears. Thus, her Rational Response was "Everyone has their own problems, and I'm working on mine." Penny's achievable behavioral goal for the exposure was to stay in the conversation until her therapist stopped it.

Penny was very anxious at the beginning of the conversation and her SUDS rating reached 95 when she seemed to run out of things to say after the first few exchanges. However, the two soon found a topic they had in common, and the conversation proceeded fairly smoothly. Penny's SUDS rating in the final minute was 40.

After the conversation, Penny initially felt that she had failed because the conversation had not gone well at first. She said that this was when she usually found an excuse to stop talking and leave. After being reminded that her behavioral goal was simply to stay in the situation, she was able to give herself some credit for doing so. Also, she had learned that, even though they went through a few moments with nothing to say, the conversation became easier when they found a common topic. For homework, Penny agreed to try to start at least two brief conversations (three or four exchanges) with people in her photography class. She reported back the next week that these conversations had gone well and that people were friendlier than she expected them to be.

Over the next several weeks, Penny continued to practice conversations anywhere she could. She made an effort to speak more with her co-workers and the parents who came to pick up or drop off their children. She had found another single woman her age in the photography class, and they had talked several times. Something had been said about trying to go to the park together and take some photos on the weekend but it had not happened yet. When the therapist suggested that such an outing would be a logical next step, Penny indicated that it made her very nervous but she agreed to do an in-session exposure to this situation. After some discussion, Penny reported the AT, "When she gets to know me, she won't like me." After identifying this AT as Mind Reading and Catastrophizing, Penny was asked what evidence she had to support her prediction. Penny replied that she had a lot of personal problems, just like the rest of her family. She described her father as an alcoholic who had sometimes become violent when she was growing up. When asked to specify what "a lot of personal problems" meant for her, the only one Penny could list was the social anxiety disorder. The therapist and group members pointed out that this is an example of Mental Filter in which her social anxiety and father's drinking problem had colored her entire view of herself. Penny asked herself the Disputing Question, "Do my father's drinking and my social anxiety have to lead to my classmate's not liking me?" The group members were able to offer evidence that they had gotten to know her quite well and found her to be a warm, caring person. By not letting people get to know her, Penny had until now missed out on learning that other people would like her and enjoy her company. Out of this discussion, Penny developed the Rational Response, "The past is the past; I'm becoming a different person now."

Penny's goal for the role play was to share something personal about herself, because it became clear that she had been avoiding moving beyond the most superficial conversation. With one of the group members acting as the woman from the photography class, Penny revealed that she had joined the class to meet people as well as learn about photography. She had found it hard to meet people since leaving high school. Penny was less anxious during the role play than she had expected to be. Her peak SUDS rating was only 50. She agreed to try and arrange an outing with the woman from her class for the upcoming weekend.

It took a couple of weeks for Penny and her classmate to get together on the weekend but Penny reported that they both seemed to have a good time. They discovered they liked similar movies and had plans to see a new movie during the following week.

In this case, we can see that Penny's fears of casual conversations had prevented her from developing friendships and a social life. Initially her fears related to not being able to carry on casual conversations. However, it became apparent later in treatment that Penny was also fearful of more serious conversations in which she and another person would get to know one another more intimately. This fear came from longstanding beliefs about being unacceptable because of the secrecy and chaos of her alcoholic home.

This case also illustrates something that we have often found to be true when working with socially anxious people who fear casual conversations. Once people start to greet others and initiate conversations, other people usually respond positively. Those casual contacts with people eventually become an enjoyable and anticipated part of daily life. A few of the casual contacts lead to more significant friendships over time. While it is true that not all casual conversations lead to relationships, certainly all friendships and romantic relationships started with some casual conversation!

Homework

We described examples of exposures related to fears of conversations that could be done both within the session and as homework assignments for exposure in your daily life. Each week you and your therapist will negotiate a homework assignment to assure that you are applying your new skills. As always, be careful to use the BYOCC worksheet to guide your homework assignment so that you work through each step of the cognitive skills. Be sure to continue the self-monitoring to track your progress as well.

Self-Assessment

1. Small talk is irrelevant to starting new relationships.   T   F

2. Social support networks provide advice, assistance, and people   T   F
   with whom to do activities.

3. Scientific studies have shown that when individuals have good   T   F
   support networks, their health is better and they may live longer
   than those without support networks.

4. Common ATs for individuals who fear having casual conversations   T   F
   may include believing that you don't know what to say and that
   what you have to say is not interesting.

5. Being socially anxious also indicates that you have poor social skills.   T   F

Answers to Self-Assessment questions can be found in Appendix A.

Chapter 11

Public Speaking

Fear of public speaking is nearly always listed as the number-one fear experienced by the general public in national surveys in the U.S. In our own work, we have found that fear of public speaking is extremely common among individuals with social anxiety disorder. Over 90% report at least some fear about speaking in front of a group and, for most of those individuals, the fear is moderate or severe.

Not everyone who fears speaking in public seeks treatment to overcome the fear. Many find that they can easily avoid making speeches at their job or in their personal lives without great difficulty. Most socially anxious individuals come to treatment for fears about other situations such as conversations, dating, or being assertive, even though public speaking may be their most feared situation, because these other fears typically cause much more interference in their lives. Often these same individuals are able to make excellent progress on their fears of public speaking after they have addressed their most urgent concerns. However, for about one out of six people we have treated over the years, fears about speaking in front of groups is the sole reason for seeking treatment.

When someone thinks about public speaking, usually the image that comes to mind is of standing on a stage in front of hundreds of people making a formal speech. We have all seen someone do this, from the guest speaker at a graduation to the politician seeking votes. However, there are many other forms of public speaking that most people confront much more frequently. Imagine yourself in the following situations and check off the ones that would make you anxious:

☐ telling a joke to a group of people who are sitting around talking

☐ standing up in a community meeting (such as a neighborhood association or a school meeting for parents) to comment on an issue you care about

- [ ] serving as the chairperson for a committee meeting at work or a community organization

- [ ] reading scriptures or offering a prayer aloud during a religious service

- [ ] offering a eulogy at a funeral of someone you knew

- [ ] making a toast at a wedding reception or other celebration

- [ ] telling a story of an interesting experience to a group of people

- [ ] speaking up at a self-help group or twelve-step meeting

- [ ] introducing someone who is going to make a speech

- [ ] giving a report during a meeting

- [ ] teaching a class or explaining how to do something to a group of people

- [ ] making a few comments at an important occasion such as after receiving an award, at your wedding, or at a retirement party

- [ ] being called on to answer a question in a class

- [ ] making a presentation in a class

As you can see, there are many more opportunities to speak in front of a group of people than most of us might think. Many of these situations can be less anxiety-provoking than a formal public speech. These situations offer opportunities to work on speaking fears on a more gradual basis, so you do not have to work on the most difficult kind of speech first.

We will now describe two clients who sought relief from anxiety about speaking in public. In the first case, we will illustrate how you can start with easier situations and work up to harder ones. In the second, we will describe how to address public speaking fears when the anxiety occurs only in a particular situation that is infrequent but very important. For both examples, we will provide some ideas about how to tackle common ATs about public speaking.

Tom: From Computer Jock to Public Speaker

Tom was a 46-year-old man who sought treatment for fears about making presentations at work. Tom had worked in the computer department of the same large company for about 20 years, starting as a programmer who mostly worked alone or with others in small groups. Over the years he had become more involved with training new employees to use the computers, usually on a one-on-one basis. Recently, the company had converted to a new computer system, and Tom's supervisor wanted him to be in charge of training the sales staff. This would involve running training classes of 10-15 people and, occasionally, making presentations at managerial meetings on the status of the conversion. Both of these situations made Tom very anxious. He even thought about changing jobs because he feared he would not be able to carry them off. When Tom developed his Fear and Avoidance Hierarchy with his therapist, it became obvious that there were a number of situations involving speaking in front of a group that made him anxious.

Looking at Tom's Fear and Avoidance Hierarchy in Figure 11.1, you can see that speaking in front of groups in both formal settings (such as a presentation to managers) and informal settings (such as telling a humorous story at a party) produced anxiety for Tom. Using the 0-100 scales for SUDS and Avoidance, he gave lower Avoidance Ratings for teaching the class because he felt that this was something that he could not avoid—he would just have to "suffer through somehow." Tom thought that the first day of the three-day class would be the hardest because he worried about making a good impression. If the first day went well, the other two days would cause him less anxiety.

After learning the basic cognitive restructuring skills, Tom and his therapist decided to make situation 7 on his Fear and Avoidance Hierarchy—telling a humorous story at a Friday afternoon get-together with familiar co-workers—the topic of the first exposure. They planned to practice with an in-session exposure, then Tom could try the real situation for homework. When Tom's therapist asked him to imagine being out with his co-workers and telling a funny story about something that had happened to him recently, Tom reported the following ATs:

> I'll be very anxious.
>
> I'll freeze up so much that I won't be able to finish.
>
> They will see I'm nervous.

Tom felt very nervous when he considered these thoughts. The second thought caused Tom the greatest concern, so he and his therapist focused on analyzing it. Looking over the list of Thinking Errors, Tom saw that he had engaged in All-or-Nothing Thinking in that he imagined one of two extremes—either being fine or freezing up so much that he could not continue. He had not considered that he might freeze up a little bit but then be able to go on. This AT also contained aspects of Fortune Telling because he predicted ahead of time that he would freeze up and not be able to go on without considering other possible outcomes. After talking more about what Tom meant by freezing up, he and his therapist also identified Emotional Reasoning in the AT. When Tom started to feel himself getting anxious and tense, he had a sensation of being unable to move or speak. However, just because he felt that way did not mean that he actually was frozen. In fact, he sometimes had been amazed that he was able to continue despite the anxiety and tension.

Tom challenged the AT "I'll freeze up so much I won't be able to finish" using the Disputing Questions. He asked himself, "Do I know for certain that I will freeze

Fear and Avoidance Hierarchy

Subjective Units of Discomfort Scale (SUDS)

0	5	10	15	20	25	30	35	40	45	50	55	60	65	70	75	80	85	90	95	100

no anxiety, calm, relaxed   mild anxiety, alert, able to cope   moderate anxiety, some trouble concentrating   severe anxiety, thoughts of leaving   very severe anxiety, worst ever experienced

Avoidance Rating

0	5	10	15	20	25	30	35	40	45	50	55	60	65	70	75	80	85	90	95	100

never avoid   avoid once in awhile   avoid sometimes   usually avoid   always avoid

Situation	SUDS	Avoidance
#1 most difficult situation is *presentation to managers*	100	100
#2 most difficult situation is *arguing a controversial point at a community meeting—standing at my seat*	100	100
#3 most difficult situation is *first day teaching in training session for new computer system*	98	50
#4 most difficult situation is *after first day teaching in training session for new computer system*	85	20
#5 most difficult situation is *telling a humorous story at work party with group of co-workers and supervisors*	80	95
#6 most difficult situation is *making a few brief comments in a meeting with people I know—standing at my seat*	70	80
#7 most difficult situation is *telling a humorous story at Friday afternoon get-together with co-workers I know well*	60	95
#8 most difficult situation is *asking next-door neighbor to return something he has borrowed*	50	50
#9 most difficult situation is *speaking up at small departmental meetings at work*	30	25
#10 most difficult situation is *telling a funny story to several family members*	20	0

Figure 11.1.   Tom's Sample Fear and Avoidance Hierarchy

up and not be able to finish?" and "What is the likelihood that I won't be able to finish even if I do freeze up a little?" to look at whether he was overestimating the probability of his AT's coming true. After concluding that there was no more than a 20% chance that he would freeze up *and* not be able to continue, his therapist asked, "What's the worst that can happen if you do freeze up and can't continue?" Thinking about that possibility made Tom very anxious, but he was able to remember a couple of other times when he had seen people forget the punch line of a joke or lose their train of thought during a story. These situations were uncomfortable and somewhat embarrassing, but both times the person had just made a joke about getting old and everyone had laughed it off. Tom concluded that it would not be the end of the world if he did freeze up and could not finish the story.

The cognitive restructuring work resulted in the Rational Response "I'll probably be able to finish." After all, there was no more than a 20% chance he would freeze up and not be able to finish. Tom's therapist suspected that the 20% was a high estimate since it had only happened to Tom once many years ago and he had avoided telling stories in a group since then. His avoidance had deprived Tom of the opportunity to find out if he would be able to finish. Tom and his therapist established the achievable behavioral goal of "Start telling the story and stay in the situation whether you finish the story or freeze up." Tom, his therapist, and another therapist from the same office then role played sitting around talking after work on a Friday. They talked for about 10 minutes, during which Tom told a humorous story about getting stuck on his roof when the wind blew his ladder down while he was making repairs. He became quite anxious, with a peak SUDS rating of 85, but was able to finish the story despite the anxiety.

When debriefing the exposure, Tom indicated that he had felt that he was going to freeze up at one point during the story, but he had taken a deep breath and used his Rational Response "I'll probably be able to finish." That had eased his anxiety enough that he was able to continue. He had accomplished his goal of starting the story and staying in the situation whether he was able to finish the story or not. When asked what he had learned from the experience, Tom mentioned two things. First, he had noticed that starting the story was the hardest part and it became easier as he went along. Second, even if he was feeling very anxious, it was unlikely that he would not be able to continue.

For homework, the therapist and Tom agreed that he would try to tell the same story to his co-workers the next Friday after work. Tom would use the BYOCC worksheet to prepare for the exposure and set the same behavioral goal about starting the story and staying in the situation. The next week Tom reported back that he had been very anxious but was able to complete the story. Everyone had laughed, so he felt it must have gone fairly well.

Over the next few weeks, Tom and his therapist worked on several exposures related to teaching the computer training classes. Tom brought in the prepared materials and practiced different segments of the class, including introducing himself and the goals of the class the first day and answering questions. One AT kept coming up over and over: "They won't understand because I won't explain things well enough." The therapist broke the AT into two separate thoughts, "They won't understand" and "I won't explain things well enough." Let's look at how they challenged each of these ATs.

Tom and his therapist identified the Thinking Errors in the first AT "They won't understand" as Overgeneralization (one person not understanding means everyone does not understand; not understanding one part means that none of the material is understood) and Mind Reading (assuming the class did not understand even though they were not asking questions to indicate confusion). The Disputing Question that Tom found most useful for this thought was, "Could there be any other explanations for their lack of understanding?" They made a list of all of the reasons that people might not understand, *other than a poor explanation from Tom.*

Someone might not understand because he or she might . . .

- not be listening
- have their mind on something else
- not be smart enough
- not have enough background/training in computers
- not want to learn the new system
- be looking for another job so he or she does not care to learn
- not learn well with Tom's style of instruction
- need more time and hands-on instruction

After thinking about the last item in the list, Tom remembered that part of the plan was to provide individual instruction once everyone had learned the basic material. This led Tom to consider that he might be setting his standards for how much they should understand too high, because it was generally assumed that most people would need additional training before they would be able to understand the many new concepts he would be teaching them.

Once Tom had challenged the first AT, the second thought, "I won't explain things well enough" became less important. He was confident that he could use the prepared materials to give people a good introduction. Once he adjusted to a more reasonable standard of what people should know, he became more confident that he could teach to that level. Tom summarized all of this cognitive work for himself in the Rational Response "I just have to give them a general overview. Most are going to need more instruction no matter what I do."

After his in-session exposures, Tom was able to use his cognitive self-help skills to manage his anxiety in the real-life classroom. He gradually became less anxious about teaching, and *he actually began to enjoy it*. A number of people commented on how helpful the classes were to them. A couple of times his explanations became too technical, but the students asked questions indicating their confusion. This made him a little anxious, but he was able to recover and move on.

Tom's final challenge was the presentation at the managerial meeting about how the transition to the new computer system was progressing. Despite his successes, he felt very anxious every time he thought of the upcoming meeting. At the end of his therapy session one week, Tom agreed to prepare his presentation and bring it to the next session. They would then use the presentation as an in-session exposure. Tom arrived at the next session without the prepared presentation materials. He indicated that he had become anxious every time he sat down to prepare so he kept putting it off. The therapist described Tom's failure to prepare as avoidance behavior. Tom had felt anxious and, instead of using the cognitive skills to cope with his anxiety and face his fears, he had avoided the feared situation.

When Tom and his therapist examined the ATs that had led to the avoidance, his primary AT was "They'll ask a question I can't answer." When his therapist helped him explore that thought further, Tom indicated that if he were not able to answer the managers' questions, he would look incompetent. The underlying AT was "They will think I am incompetent if I can't answer their questions." This concern interfered with Tom's ability to prepare for the presentation because he could not decide what information he needed to have ready.

Tom and his therapist identified the Thinking Errors in this AT as Mind Reading (making assumptions about what the managers will think), Catastrophizing (imagining that there would be a lot of questions that he would not be able to answer), and Labeling (calling himself "incompetent" because he sometimes had doubts about whether he really knew enough to do his job). Using the Disputing Questions, Tom asked himself whether he was 100% certain the managers would ask questions he could not answer. He concluded he was not 100% certain and, in fact, no one knew his job better than he did. In response to the Disputing Question "Does not knowing the answer mean I am incompetent?" Tom was able to identify a number of things he did well on his job and noted that he had usually received good evaluations. This helped him argue against being incompetent. However, if there was something he did not know that he should have known, the best he could do was promise to find the answer as soon as possible. This led to the Rational Response, "I know my job. All I can do is promise to find out if I don't know the answer to a question."

After his cognitive restructuring work, Tom was able to prepare his presentation, using the BYOCC worksheet to cope with the anxiety he felt. He practiced the presentation in the therapy session and then did it for the managers. The achievable behavioral goal he set for the actual presentation was to just get himself there and get through it. Tom felt very anxious as he was waiting for his turn to present, but he had written the Rational Response on his notes, and it helped him stay in the room. There were a couple of questions that took him by surprise, but he felt he handled them adequately. Although Tom thought that he would always be somewhat anxious in this situation, he believed he would be able to handle it and knew it would get easier over time.

What to Take from the Case of Tom

Tom's experience overcoming his fears of public speaking is typical of many people with whom we have worked. If you have similar fears, you might have recognized one or more of his ATs.

> I'll freeze up so much I won't be able to finish.

> I won't explain things well enough so they won't understand.

> They will ask questions I can't answer.

We highlighted these ATs because they seem to come up so often for people with public speaking fears. Many people report that they worry about getting so anxious they will not be able to finish the speech. Some even describe images of themselves running out of the room because they cannot continue. One way to tackle ATs with this general theme is to look at the likelihood of such an extreme response, as we did with Tom. Almost always such extreme reactions are not that likely to occur—that is part of what makes them extreme (and thus unusual) reactions. You might find it helpful to consider all of the possible outcomes using the Pie Chart technique we described for Miguel in Chapter 9.

The purpose of public speaking is to communicate a message, and many presentations are supposed to teach new information. In these cases, individuals with public speaking fears often express ATs about not communicating clearly. Once it has been determined that the material to be presented is appropriate and well-written, then it may be helpful to think about how much people can realistically learn. We have often found that anxious presenters set very high standards about what people should learn from their presentations and then feel inadequate when that standard is not achieved. If you are able to set a more appropriate goal for what you will communicate, as Tom did, you might be surprised at your success. In-session exposures offer an excellent opportunity to ask questions of the audience to see what they learned from a presentation.

Sometimes people feel fairly confident about a speech for which they are able to prepare in advance. However, having to think on their feet in response to questions may be much more anxiety-provoking. Like Tom, this anxiety may occur in response to an underlying belief about not being as competent or smart as you might appear to be in the prepared speech. Addressing ATs about difficult questions often focuses on two points. First, consider what you know about the topic compared to what the audience knows. Second, develop a plan for what to do if you get a question you cannot answer on the spot. Depending on the situation that plan might include simply admitting you do not know and asking if the questioner or anyone else in the room has an idea, promising to get back with the answer later, or requesting that the questioner rephrase/clarify the question so you have a moment to gather your thoughts. Whatever plan you choose, it is helpful to have one in mind so you know what to do if the need arises.

Avoidance of preparing for the speech is extremely common among people with public speaking fears. In fact, when they are very anxious, people sometimes avoid preparing for so long that they have to cancel the talk at the last minute because they are not ready. It is easy to see how this can be a recipe for failure as a public speaker. If you are feeling anxious about preparing for a speech, that is a signal to get out a BYOCC worksheet and work on the thoughts that are driving your anxiety. Then you can use the Rational Response and achievable behavioral goal to help yourself prepare. If your anxiety is high, you may not be able to work on the speech for very long at a time. Instead of avoiding, however, you should work on the speech in short bursts. Set a clock for 10 or 15 minutes and allow yourself to stop and relax after the time is up. You should do your best to work for the full interval rather than quitting when your anxiety rises. That escape from anxiety will only make it worse. Remember that the reduction in anxiety from escape or avoidance only makes it more likely you will avoid or escape again next time.

LeAnn: The Overly Prepared Vice President

Tom's case represents a common type of public speaking anxiety in which the person is fearful of a range of situations related to speaking and being the center of attention. Sometimes public speaking anxiety is very focused on a particular situation, however, usually one that occurs infrequently.

LeAnn was a highly successful vice president of a medium-sized company when she came to treatment for very severe anxiety she experienced during a yearly speech at the company's annual sales meeting. At that meeting, she was expected to make a formal presentation to about 150 salespeople and managers that high-lighted some of the successes and challenges of the previous year and set goals for the upcoming year. She had made the speech in two previous years and felt more terrified as each occasion approached. LeAnn felt the fear was odd because she regularly made speeches in many other situations as part of her job and her involvement in community activities. She had overcome most of her public speaking anxiety in those situations, experiencing only a little anticipatory anxiety right before she stood up.

As LeAnn learned the basic cognitive self-help skills, her therapist helped her identify the ATs that she had about the speech. Repeatedly, LeAnn said that her worst fear was that she would look nervous. The therapist helped her explore further, revealing the following ATs:

I'll appear nervous.

I shouldn't be nervous in this situation.

It is unacceptable for a woman in my professional position to appear nervous in front of a large group of people below me in the company hierarchy.

If I get more prepared, I'll be less nervous.

When LeAnn and her therapist began to identify the Thinking Errors in the ATs, they tentatively labeled the first AT as Fortune Telling because she was predicting what would happen at this year's speech. Although there was no way to know for sure, both LeAnn and her therapist agreed that there was a realistic possibility that she might appear nervous. A couple of people had commented last year that she looked nervous and she was even more anxious about the speech this year. When they tried to explore how much nervousness would be acceptable to show, LeAnn was adamant that it was unacceptable to show any nervousness at all. This meant they would have to address the third AT that it was unacceptable for a woman in her professional position to show any nervousness in this situation.

LeAnn's therapist thought this AT contained several Thinking Errors. First and foremost, it was a Should Statement. "It is unacceptable to be nervous" is a more extreme form of "I shouldn't be nervous," the previous AT. It implies that LeAnn is violating an important rule. This AT was also an extreme form of All-or-Nothing Thinking in that there were two categories in LeAnn's mind—No Visible Anxiety (the good/acceptable category) and Any Visible Anxiety (the bad/unacceptable category).

When they began to challenge this AT with the Disputing Questions, LeAnn had difficulty accepting anything other than displaying no anxiety. She felt that showing nervousness was the worst thing that was likely to happen but that this would be terrible because she was supposed to set an example for the other employees at the meeting. Her speech was supposed to highlight their successes and inspire them to achieve even more the next year. It was also supposed to be entertaining. As the only woman vice president with a mostly male sales staff, she believed the standard for her performance was very high. Her therapist made more progress with the Disputing Question "Is this so important that your entire future rests on it?" LeAnn felt it might influence how she was perceived in the company. The nervousness could be seen as a sign of weakness. However, at worst this might influence her future professional opportunities somewhat but it would not affect the many other things that were important in her life such as her family and her health. LeAnn and her therapist concluded that they could not predict whether she would show nervousness at the upcoming speech but that it might be helpful to act as if LeAnn could not control it entirely. This led to the Rational Response, "I have to accept that I might look a little nervous but that doesn't affect any of the really important things in my life."

As LeAnn and her therapist began to set up in-session exposures to practice the speech, the last AT, "If I get more prepared, I'll be less nervous," came up. LeAnn indicated that she usually began to work on this speech weeks in advance and spent many hours editing the wording and practicing her delivery in front of the mirror. She agreed with the therapist that she prepared excessively as a strategy to help her cope with her anxiety. Unfortunately, the opposite turned out to be the case. The more she prepared, the more anxious she became. By trying to make everything perfect, she was not able to be herself in the same way she could with other speeches and presentations. Her AT was not just distorted, it was wrong! LeAnn agreed that the best exposure would be to not work on the speech too much. She and her therapist worked out a schedule that included reasonable preparation time for the speech, but they agreed that she should limit the amount of time devoted to editing and updating it. Any other time she felt like working on the speech, she agreed to work on identifying and challenging the ATs that were giving her the urge to over-prepare.

LeAnn's behavioral goal for the speech was to limit her preparation on the day of the speech to no more than 20 minutes. She also wrote an abbreviated version of the Rational Response, "The most important things are safe," at the top of each page of her speech to remind herself that showing nervousness might have some impact on her professional life but not on all of the other important things in her life. By limiting her preparation time and getting some perspective on the importance of her performance, the speech was not the overwhelmingly negative experience it had been in previous years. She did experience quite a bit of anxiety but doubted it was noticeable. She was able to congratulate herself for getting through the speech.

What to Take From the Case of LeAnn

LeAnn's situation illustrates one of the more difficult public speaking fears to treat—a situation that occurs infrequently. As you know, repeatedly facing your fears is one of the most powerful weapons in the battle against anxiety. The repeated exposure probably helped her overcome any anxiety she had in other public speaking situations. In dealing with infrequent situations, it is important to look for any aspects that can be addressed repeatedly. LeAnn's excessive over-preparation offered an opportunity to expose herself to her fear, and by making a contract with her therapist to limit her preparation time, she was able to do so. Sometimes, it may help to give the speech to a smaller audience even though this may not generate much anxiety. Another option is to practice the speech repeatedly in your imagination. This is called "imaginal exposure." Often you or your therapist can make an audiotape describing the experience of the speech that you can use for guided imagery.

For Tom, public speaking anxiety led to avoidance of preparation. For LeAnn, the opposite was true. As with most things in life, moderation is the best recommendation on the amount of preparation you should do. Look carefully to see if the preparation and planning for your public speaking is anxiety-provoking and whether you try to avoid it or repeatedly put it off. If so, then prepare more and use the cognitive self-help skills to address the anxiety. If your preparation is itself the result of an AT and is an unhelpful attempt to manage your anxiety, then limit your preparation and use the extra time to help yourself with cognitive restructuring work.

As we noted at the beginning of this chapter, public speaking makes most people nervous. It may be that, at least at first, you will have to learn to accept some level of anxiety, especially if you speak only occasionally. You may not really have enough opportunities to overcome the fear. Like LeAnn, you may find it helpful to step back and think about how important that anxiety really is in the broader scheme of your life. Many people find that as they are able to accept that they will experience some anxiety while speaking in public, it becomes less painful and less important. Those are good first steps towards having the anxiety be less of a problem.

Homework

Throughout this chapter we have mentioned various ways to practice speaking in front of a group. With Tom, we saw that one can take opportunities to speak up in informal social situations. You can also participate in community or religious organizations and take advantage of opportunities to speak there. Many people have found one organization extremely helpful both in overcoming their fears of public speaking and developing their skills as an effective speaker. This organization is Toastmasters International, a group for people interested in becoming better speakers. Most cities and towns have one or more chapters. The meetings vary widely but all offer opportunities to make speeches of many kinds and get feedback from the group. Check the telephone directory or call local colleges, universities, or the Chamber of Commerce to find a chapter in your area.

Self-Assessment

1. Although public speaking is almost always listed as the number-one fear of the general population, it is not particularly common among those with social anxiety.   **T   F**

2. One good way to dispute your ATs during public speaking is to examine possible extreme responses and evaluate their likelihood.   **T   F**

3. When an individual experiences extreme anxiety about a speaking engagement, it is common to avoid preparing for the talk.   **T   F**

4. Experiencing anxiety about an upcoming speaking engagement is a signal to avoid working on your BYOCC sheet.   **T   F**

5. When attempting exposures for situations that do not occur   **T   F**
frequently, it helps to at least look for pieces of the situation that
can be practiced repeatedly.

Answers to Self-Assessment questions can be found in Appendix A.

Chapter 12

Advanced Cognitive Restructuring: Addressing Core Beliefs

Over the last several chapters, we have focused on identifying and challenging the ATs that you experience in the situations that have typically made you anxious. We hope you now understand how changing your thoughts helps control your anxiety. You have also learned that avoidance of the situations that you fear prevents you from learning that your catastrophic thoughts do not come true. In this chapter we delve deeper into your ATs and examine some of the beliefs you have about yourself, other people, the world, and the future that underlie your ATs.

Looking for Common Themes in Your ATs

Take out the BYOCC worksheets that you have been using over the past several weeks. Also gather any other worksheets or records you have of your ATs across various situations. Do you see any patterns in your ATs? Are there any thoughts that keep coming up over and over again? Do some or all of the ATs have a common theme running through them? In the next few pages, we will discuss how to find the important themes in your thoughts and how to begin to change those that cause you difficulty. Although most people find that they need the help of their therapist to explore their core beliefs, reading this section will help you understand the process.

Experienced cognitive therapists have noticed that people who have difficulty with anxiety (and depression) usually have one or more dysfunctional core beliefs about themselves, other people, the world, or the future. Therapists often talk about finding these core beliefs by searching through the layers of ATs and emotions, similar to the process of peeling an onion. As you peel away each layer, you can see another layer below. Even though the layers underneath have always been there, you may not be able to see them until you remove the outer layers. In the same way, when you first begin to monitor your thoughts, you notice the ATs that are "on the surface." These are the ATs that come to your mind first. Usually these are more superficial and may be relatively easier to talk about with your therapist. As you have been conducting the exposures and challenging your ATs, you have probably discovered some ATs that you did not know about at first. These may feel a little more personal and may have been harder to talk about with your therapist. Maybe your therapist has had to help you think through your thoughts to peel away some of the superficial layers so you can talk about the ATs in the layers underneath. In this chapter, we will help you peel away even more layers and try to see the core of your psychological onion!

Danielle: "I should do everything perfectly"

Let's start with several examples of common core beliefs to help you understand what we are talking about. First, let's visit with Danielle. Danielle had been making excellent progress in treatment for her fears about talking with authority figures and being the center of attention. The primary situations she had been working on included conversations with her supervisor and speaking up in a group of people. Numerous ATs had been identified but two came up over and over again in various forms. These two were:

> I'll make a mistake.

> I should do a good job.

Danielle feared making various mistakes, including stumbling over her words in conversation, losing her train of thought, making an error on a work assignment, telling her supervisor the wrong information, and making some sort of social error like forgetting someone's name. Her worries about not doing a good job meant that she worked extra hard on every assignment at work, including working after hours without getting paid for it. Through the cognitive restructuring exercises, she had begun to understand that all evidence suggested that her work was very good. She also had watched other people and seen that small difficulties in conversations, such as losing one's train of thought, happened to everyone. Other people did not seem as concerned about such errors as she was. Danielle's therapist helped her peel away the layers to see the core belief underlying her primary ATs.

Therapist: When you think about making mistakes or not doing a good job, what other thoughts do you have?

Danielle: I think that a person should always try and do a good job, should try to not make mistakes. I feel awful when I make a mistake. It means I should have tried harder.

Therapist: Tell me more about feeling awful.

Danielle: I hate that feeling. When I know I have messed something up, I sometimes get a sinking feeling in my stomach. It can just be a little thing like stumbling over my words when I am talking to the group as we sit and have coffee before work. I feel even worse if it is something important. I used to be upset for days if my supervisor asked me to do something over or do it differently. I would get mad at myself because I should have done it right the first time. I still feel this way sometimes, even though I try to challenge my negative thoughts.

Therapist: So one thought you have is, "I should do things right the first time." It is important to you to do little and big things right the first time. What does it mean to do things "right?" What is "right?"

Danielle: Well, "right" is "right." It is the correct way to do it, the best way to do something.

Therapist: So doing something "right" means doing it the very best way, perfectly the first time, every time?

Danielle: I guess it does. I never thought of it that way.

Therapist: How does it feel when you think about needing to do everything perfectly the first time, every time?

Danielle: I feel overwhelmed and frustrated. I try so hard but I just cannot do it. I should be able to do better but I cannot. I guess I feel a little angry also. I feel angry that other people don't seem to care so much. One woman at work makes lots of mistakes. I end up redoing her work sometimes. But she doesn't seem to care. Even though I think my supervisor appreciates that my work is so much better than hers, she does not seem to care what he thinks. I'm not sure it's worth trying to do everything right. I feel frustrated just talking about it.

Therapist: What would happen if you did something less than perfect on purpose?

Danielle: I don't know. That would be hard. I would be very uncomfortable. It seems like it would be breaking the rules. You are supposed to try to do everything perfectly.

Therapist: So the rule is "You should do everything perfectly."

Danielle: Yes. I guess that is a Should Statement, though. That means it must be a Thinking Error. It feels like it is true. I have always believed that. "Feeling true" probably means that it's Emotional Reasoning.

Therapist: Do you remember anyone ever telling you that you needed to do things "right" or "perfectly"?

Danielle: Oh yeah. My dad used to have a saying, "If you aren't going to do it right, don't do it."

Therapist: With all due respect to your dad, do you see any of the Thinking Errors in "If you aren't going to do it right, don't do it"?

Danielle: It seems like All-or-Nothing Thinking. Either you do something perfectly, or you do not even try. There is no middle ground.

Therapist: Exactly. No wonder you sometimes feel overwhelmed and frustrated. That is a high standard to set. Can you think of some other situations in which you feel pressured to do something perfectly? Any other times you have the thought, "If I'm not going to do it right, I shouldn't do it"?

Danielle: You know I hate trying new things that I might not be good at. Remember when everyone from work was going to participate in that charity golf tournament? I was very anxious and ended up calling in sick that day. I knew that I would probably hit the ball into the water or something embarrassing. Afterwards I heard that other people who had never golfed before did just that. I was glad I did not go but I felt bad that I did not help raise money. I knew I would not be able to hit the ball very well so I didn't feel that I could go. I could not do it perfectly, so I did not even try.

Therapist: What do you think your dad meant to communicate to you when he said, "If you aren't going to do it right, don't do it"?

Danielle: I've never thought about that. I think he wanted all of his children to do well, to be successful at things. I know he believed that if you work hard, you can get the things you want in life. To some extent he was right. A lot of good things have happened to me because I work hard and do things well. I am proud of having a reputation of being a person you can count on to get the job done.

Therapist: It does sound like following your Dad's philosophy has worked well for you in many ways. However, it seems like there are ways in which it has not worked as well for you.

Danielle: Yes, I think I have taken it too far. I would like to believe that sometimes it is OK to do something "well enough" rather than "perfectly right." That would take a lot of pressure off.

Therapist: That sounds like something we can work on with exposures. We can have you try doing something "well enough" on purpose and see how it goes. I suspect you would get more comfortable with practice.

As you can see from this example, Danielle's two common ATs, "I'll make a mistake" and "I should do a good job," related to a core belief about needing to do everything perfectly. This dysfunctional core belief influenced how Danielle approached a wide range of situations. If she is able to change her dysfunctional core belief, Danielle will have more helpful thoughts as she enters situations that make her anxious. As a result, she should experience less anxiety and less pressure to perform perfectly. That will help her at work with her supervisor and in social interactions. She will also be able to try new things that she may not be able to do well at first. The therapist used several strategies to help Danielle peel away the layers of ATs and emotions to reveal her core belief. These strategies included:

1. **Asking what other thoughts came to mind as Danielle thought about the ATs.**

   One AT usually leads to others. As you start to think about your ATs and follow one to the next, you will often work towards ATs that are more important and come up in many situations.

2. **Asking Danielle to describe what certain key aspects of her ATs meant (what does "right" mean?).**

   ATs are usually so automatic that we do not stop to consider what they actually mean. By trying to define certain key words, we can begin to expand the ATs and can more easily identify the underlying assumptions we are making.

3. **Asking Danielle to focus on the emotions she experienced when she thought about her ATs.**

   Feeling upset or emotional is one of the best signs that you and your therapist are starting to identify your core belief. As you allow yourself to experience that emotion and consider what it feels like, more ATs will usually come to mind. You have probably experienced this already when completing the BYOCC worksheets. The unexpected ATs that you record on the back of the BYOCC worksheets probably come to the surface when you are anxious. Allowing yourself to experience the emotion can be difficult because none of us wants to feel sad, angry, or frightened. However, as you have learned in exposures, the fear increases at first but then decreases if you stay in the situation. Other emotions work the same way. If you let yourself feel sad or angry, the feelings will increase in intensity then decrease as you fully experience them.

4. **Asking Danielle what would happen if her ATs came true (What would happen if you did something less than perfectly?).**

   This is another way to follow the chain of ATs from one to the other. Very often we have worked so hard at keeping the ATs from coming true that we have never considered what it would mean if they did. If you find yourself working hard at avoiding something (like not being perfect, for Danielle), then there is a good chance that what you are avoiding is related to your core belief.

5. Asking Danielle to identify the source of her ATs as it seemed like they were getting close to a core belief.

Very often a core belief is something that we learned early in life about ourselves, the way the world works, what we can expect from other people, and whom and what we can trust. These things we learn function like "rules" for life that tell us what we should do and what to expect from others. In social anxiety disorder, these rules often relate to whether or not other people are trustworthy, whether one is a worthwhile person, or how we should conduct ourselves. It is important to note that you may not have any notion of the source of your core belief or that what you remember might not be accurate. That is OK. There is no reason to think that you have to understand what happened in your past that resulted in your core belief. *You can still work to change your dysfunctional belief even if you do not know where it came from.* Sometimes thinking about where a core belief came from may help you identify it more clearly but knowing the source is not essential for making changes.

Individuals with social anxiety disorder often have a core belief about the need to be perfect, as we saw with Danielle. There are some other common core beliefs that we have explored with our clients over the years. We will share how some other clients worked with their therapists to peel away the layers to address their core beliefs.

Brent: "If People Really Knew Me. . ."

Brent is a 27-year-old man with severe dating anxiety. At the beginning of treatment he had never been on a date with a woman and became quite anxious having conversations with potential dating partners. He experienced very little anxiety in other situations and ran a fairly successful lawn care business. The primary places he met women he could date were his health club and his singles bowling league. Since starting treatment he had completed several exposures in which he had conversations with women in both of those settings. These conversations seemed to go well and the next step was to ask one of the women on a date. The previous week Brent had had an extended conversation with an attractive woman at his health club. They had started to talk about movies they wanted to see and it seemed the next logical step would be to invite her to a movie. Brent was feeling extremely anxious about taking that next step despite having been very successful in previous exposures.

Brent's therapist was helping him explore the ATs that were causing his anxiety. Brent kept coming back to one AT, "She won't want to go out with me," which he identified as Fortune Telling. Using the Disputing Questions, Brent's therapist encouraged him to look for evidence to support his AT. Brent agreed that there was no evidence that she would not go out with him. In fact, he had previously predicted that women would not even want to talk with him and that had turned out not to be true. As they talked further, it became clear that Brent believed the conversations on a date would be more personal than the casual conversations he had had previously. This discussion revealed ATs such as "I'm not very good at talking about myself" and "I won't know what to say." As Brent and his therapist further discussed his concerns about not knowing what to say, Brent was able to list several things about himself that would be appropriate to discuss, including his work, his family, and where he grew up. It was not that he did not know what to say, but that he was uncomfortable talking about these personal things with someone else. Brent's therapist asked what he thought would happen if he discussed these topics with his date. With much hesitation, Brent finally admitted that he thought he really liked this woman, but he feared that if she really got to know him, she would not like him. Brent did not believe that there was something wrong with him. He just believed that he was very ordinary. As he put it, he had not been a star football player in high school, he did not make a lot of money, and he did not have a prestigious job. In short, he had never done anything interesting or spectacular. Brent feared that he was so ordinary that when anyone found that out, there would not be anything about him to like. Brent and his therapist agreed that his core belief was "If people really knew me, they wouldn't like me."

Once the core belief had been identified, Brent and his therapist treated it like any other AT. Brent agreed to try and gather evidence to see if his belief was true. He and his therapist made of list of things that his date might like about him, things that might make him special in some way. Looking at this list, Brent developed the following Rational Response: "There are some things about me that I can be proud of." He used this Rational Response to challenge his ATs and asked the woman from his health club to a movie. As with the previous conversations, the date went better than Brent expected and with each success he felt less anxious and more confident. Because he had never before taken the risk to let someone get to know him, he had never had the opportunity to find out whether people would like him or not.

Arlene: "I'm an Imposter"

Arlene was a 44-year-old married woman with two children. She was a successful attorney who sought treatment because she had recently begun to get extremely anxious when she had to meet with important clients. Sometimes in conferences that included these clients and other attorneys, she experienced panic attacks and had to step out of the room. She felt that the anxiety was beginning to interfere with her job. Over the years she had occasionally experienced social anxiety on job interviews, at work, and when meeting with her children's teachers or her husband's boss, but as she had become more and more successful at work, the anxiety had intensified. Arlene was extremely concerned about an upcoming negotiation meeting in which she would have to be very assertive on behalf of her client. When asked to imagine herself in that situation, Arlene told her therapist that she could look around the room and see everyone in their expensive suits looking very self-assured. Her AT was that she did not belong in that room with those people. Arlene identified Emotional Reasoning ("Just because I don't feel comfortable here does not mean I don't belong") and Disqualifying the Positive (discounting all of her credentials, education, and prior successes) as the Thinking Errors in that AT. With the help of her therapist, Arlene made two lists: Evidence She Should Be Participating in the Meeting and Evidence She Should NOT Be Participating in the Meeting. The first list was quite long, and the second list had nothing on it. Still Arlene seemed stuck on the AT "I shouldn't be in this meeting." Her therapist asked whether anyone else thought she should not be there. Arlene hesitated but then indicated that anyone who knew her in high school would be shocked to see her now. With her therapist's encouragement, Arlene shared that in junior high school she had been very wild, skipping school, drinking alcohol, and smoking marijuana. She became sexually active at a young age and had become pregnant. Her parents were furious when they found out, and it was agreed that she would go live with her oldest sister and her husband in a nearby town and give the baby up for adoption. Arlene recounted that during the pregnancy and long talks with her sister, she had decided that she did not like the direction her life was going. After the birth of the baby, she moved back with her parents and went to a different school. She became very serious about her schoolwork, took a part-time job, and did very little socializing. One success led to another, and she went on to law school, marriage, and children. No one, including her husband, knew about her wild background, but Arlene felt very ashamed of it. The pregnancy was never discussed in her family. Arlene lived in constant fear that someday the adopted child would turn up on her doorstep. Arlene's core belief was, "I'm an imposter. I don't deserve to be where I am in life. Someday people will find out and I'll lose everything."

Arlene and her therapist identified three primary Thinking Errors in the core belief: Mental Filter, because she allowed the mistakes of her youth to color her entire view of herself and her life; Labeling, because she called herself an "imposter" and undeserving of her family, job, and social position; and Mind Reading, because she assumed that everyone would reject her if they found out her secret. Arlene agreed to work with her therapist to test the belief "I'm an imposter." This involved several steps: 1. Acknowledging that her activities in her youth were a less important part of who she was now than everything she had done for the last 30 years. 2. Telling her husband about the previous pregnancy. 3. Talking with her parents and her sister about what had happened in the past and how she felt about it. 4. Starting to do some volunteer work with pregnant teenagers.

Arlene decided not to tell anyone at work about her past because she decided her past was private and not related to her work performance. Each of these steps was very anxiety-provoking. Arlene used the cognitive skills she had learned in treatment to help cope with the anxiety these activities caused and treated each situation like an exposure, working from the easiest to the hardest step. Facing her fears about exposing her secret helped change her thoughts about not belonging and being an imposter at work. By discussing her past with appropriate people, including her therapist, Arlene also discovered that her prediction about people's negative reactions did not come true. Rather than condemning her mistakes, people admired her strength for having gotten herself onto the right path in high school.

Discovering Your Core Beliefs

In the stories of Danielle, Brent, and Arlene, we have tried to share some of the common core beliefs that we have seen in our work with people with social anxiety disorder. These three themes are:

I have to do everything perfectly.

If people really knew me, they wouldn't like me.

I'm an imposter. There is something wrong with me/I have done something wrong.

As you examine your ATs, you may find other themes or core beliefs. You may also find that some of these themes combine. For example, people may believe they have to do everything perfectly so others do not discover they are imposters. By sharing these examples we hope to help you understand the importance of exploring your ATs in depth and being honest with yourself and your therapist about your thoughts and feelings.

Peeling Your Own Onion

In Figure 12.1 you will find a worksheet entitled "Peeling Your Onion—Discovering and Challenging Your Core Beliefs." If you have not yet started with your therapist to explore your core beliefs, this worksheet will help get you started. A sample completed worksheet for Danielle, the first client we described in this chapter, appears in Figure 12.2.

Not All Core Beliefs are Hard to Find

The case examples in this chapter offer fairly dramatic portrayals of core beliefs. If your social anxiety is less severe or you experience it in very few situations, your core beliefs may be more readily identified. To return to the metaphor of peeling the onion, your onion may not have too many layers. A few successful experiences in exposures may provide sufficient evidence to reveal and counter your core beliefs so that further exploration is unnecessary. If your anxiety and avoidance of feared situations are much improved and no longer interfere with your life, that is the best evidence that you have challenged the beliefs that are important for you.

Peeling Your Onion—Discovering and Challenging Your Core Beliefs

1. Look over all of your completed BYOCC worksheets and write down the Automatic Thoughts that seem to occur the most frequently.

2. Look over all of your completed BYOCC worksheets and write down any ATs that seem especially powerful. These could be ones that seem the most important in general or seem especially important to how you think about yourself. Also, be sure to write down any ATs that make you feel a strong emotion when you think about them.

3. Looking over what you wrote in Step 1 and Step 2, write down any themes that seem to occur in your frequent ATs and your powerful ATs.

4. Pick the one theme in Step 3 that seems the most important to how you think about yourself and your life. Write it here.

Now it is time to peel the onion and see what ATs and core beliefs might be under that theme. Each of the following boxes contains three questions. Ask yourself the question that best fits and write the answer in the box. Keep repeating this procedure until you can no longer answer the question.

5. Looking at the theme in Step 4, ask yourself one or more of the following questions. (Pick the question(s) that makes the most sense as not all questions fit for each thought.) Write down your answer to the question(s) in the box.

Why is this important?

What does it mean if this is true?

What would be bad about that?

List the emotion(s) you feel when you think about your answer

Figure 12.1.

6a. Repeat Step 5 for the answer you wrote in the previous box.

Why is this important?

What does it mean if this is true?

What would be bad about that?

List the emotion(s) you feel when you think about your answer

6b. Repeat Step 5 for the answer you wrote in the last box.

Why is this important?

What does it mean if this is true?

What would be bad about that?

List the emotion(s) you feel when you think about your answer

7. Keep peeling your onion by asking yourself the questions and considering your emotions. It should feel as if you are getting to beliefs that are more and more personal and private. If you get stuck, stop and let yourself feel the emotions and more thoughts will likely come to your mind. If you hit a dead end, go back to a previous step and work with a different answer to the question(s). Use another sheet to record your responses if necessary.

8. When you think you have arrived at the core of your onion, your core belief, write it below. Signs that this is your core belief include: (a) You feel strong emotions when you consider this belief. (b) The belief seems very personal, important, and/or true. (c) The belief feels like something that you have thought for a long time.

9. Treat your core belief like an AT and record it on one of the BYOCC worksheets. Use the Thinking Errors and Disputing Questions to challenge your core belief. Develop a Rational Response and write it here.

10. List several therapeutic exposures that would be relevant to testing out whether your core belief is accurate or helpful.

Figure 12.1.

Peeling Your Onion—Discovering and Challenging Your Core Beliefs

1. Look over all of your completed BYOCC worksheets and write down the Automatic Thoughts that seem to occur the most frequently.

   I'll make a mistake.

   I won't do a good job.

2. Look over all of your completed BYOCC worksheets and write down any ATs that seem especially powerful. These could be ones that seem the most important in general or seem especially important to how you think about yourself. Also, be sure to write down any ATs that make you feel a strong emotion when you think about them.

   I'll make a mistake.

   I messed up a project for my boss.

   I need to do a good job.

3. Looking over what you wrote in Step 1 and Step 2, write down any themes that seem to occur in your frequent ATs and your powerful ATs.

   Making mistakes, doing things right.

4. Pick the one theme in Step 3 that seems the most important to how you think about yourself and your life. Write it here.

   I am the kind of person who wants to do things right.

Now it is time to peel the onion and see what ATs and core beliefs might be under that theme. Each of the following boxes contains three questions. Ask yourself the question that best fits and write the answer in the box. Keep repeating this procedure until you can no longer answer the question.

5. Looking at the theme in Step 4, ask yourself one or more of the following questions. (Pick the question(s) that makes the most sense as not all questions fit for each thought.) Write down your answer to the question(s) in the box.

   Why is this important?

   What does it mean if this is true?

   What would be bad about that?

   It is important to do things right because that is the kind of person I want to be.

   List the emotion(s) you feel when you think about your answer

   Frustrated, guilty

Figure 12.2.   **Sample for Danielle**

6a. Repeat Step 5 for the answer you wrote in the previous box.

Why is this important?

What does it mean if this is true?

What would be bad about that?

To do things right means to do things the way they should be done. To do them perfectly.

List the emotion(s) you feel when you think about your answer

Angry, frustrated, overwhelmed

6b. Repeat Step 5 for the answer you wrote in the last box.

Why is this important?

What does it mean if this is true?

What would be bad about that?

I should do things perfectly. Dad used to say, if you aren't going to do it right, don't do it.

List the emotion(s) you feel when you think about your answer

Frustrated, guilty

7. Keep peeling your onion by asking yourself the questions and considering your emotions. It should feel as if you are getting to beliefs that are more and more personal and private. If you get stuck, stop and let yourself feel the emotions and more thoughts will likely come to your mind. If you hit a dead end, go back to a previous step and work with a different answer to the question(s). Use another sheet to record your responses if necessary.

8. When you think you have arrived at the core of your onion, your core belief, write it below. Signs that this is your core belief include: (a) You feel strong emotions when you consider this belief. (b) The belief seems very personal, important, and/or true. (c) The belief feels like something that you have thought for a long time.

I should do everything perfectly, even the first time.

9. Treat your core belief like an AT and record it on one of the BYOCC worksheets. Use the Thinking Errors and Disputing Questions to challenge your core belief. Develop a Rational Response and write it here.

Sometimes it is OK to do things "good enough."

10. List several therapeutic exposures that would be relevant to testing out whether your core belief is accurate or helpful.

Making little mistakes on purpose
Playing golf for the first time
Leaving a little bit of a mess in my living room when company is coming

Figure 12.2.　**Sample for Danielle**

This Is Not About Gaining Insight Into Your Past

Many traditional forms of psychotherapy try to uncover the causes of our problems in our past, particularly our childhood. The idea behind this approach is that if you understand the cause, the problem will go away. Scientific evidence does not suggest that this is true. Trying to understand the core beliefs that may underlie your ATs is not the same as trying to find an event that "caused" the social anxiety to develop. Also, identifying a core belief does not mean it will automatically change. As we demonstrated in the case examples, identifying the core belief means that you and your therapist know what fears you need to face through exposures. For example, Arlene's core belief involved fear of what would happen if a secret from her past became known. This led her and her therapist to set up some exposure situations in which she discussed the past with appropriate people, including her family and her therapist. By using the tools you have—the cognitive skills and therapeutic exposure—you can challenge the core dysfunctional belief. Changing that belief is one of the final steps in fully overcoming your social anxiety.

Self-Assessment

1. By continuing to examine your ATs, you may be able to get at more core beliefs.　　T　F

2. Attempting to examine other thoughts that occur along with an AT, focusing on the emotions experienced when thinking about ATs, and considering what might happen if an AT comes true are appropriate ways to attempt to get at deeper ATs, or core beliefs.　　T　F

3. It is critical to understand the past events that led to your core beliefs in order to make changes and overcome your social anxiety, because understanding the cause makes the problem go away.　　T　F

4. Common core beliefs among individuals who struggle with social anxiety often center around the belief that everything must be done perfectly and that there is something truly wrong with them.　　T　F

5. Attempting to understand the core beliefs underlying your ATs is similar to attempting to understand what events in your past led to your having social anxiety.　　T　F

Answers to Self-Assessment questions can be found in Appendix A.

Chapter 13

Getting Ready to Continue the Journey on Your Own: Consolidating Gains and Finishing Treatment

Checklist of Progress So Far

This chapter is most useful after you have spent several weeks working on managing your social anxiety in therapy. You and your therapist should review this checklist together to see how you are progressing. The chapter numbers in parentheses indicate where to go back and read more about a topic or skill.

Are you:

☐ able to identify ATs when you notice yourself becoming anxious? (Chapter 5)

☐ able to identify the Thinking Errors in your ATs? (Chapter 6)

☐ able to use Disputing Questions to challenge your ATs? (Chapter 6)

☐ able to develop Rational Responses and use them to combat anxiety in situations in which you get anxious? (Chapter 6)

☐ doing something every day to overcome your anxiety? (Chapter 8)

☐ avoiding avoidance? Looking for opportunities to enter situations that make you anxious rather than avoiding them? (Chapter 8)

☐ avoiding subtle avoidance and giving up the things that make a situation feel safer (e.g., only talking to people you already know at a party, avoiding certain conversation topics, over-preparing for speeches or meetings)? (Chapter 8)

This would also be a good time to go back and look at the situations you put on your Fear and Avoidance Hierarchy. Take out the second copy that you made in Chapter 4. This copy should not have any SUDS or Avoidance ratings on it. Without looking at your old ratings, re-rate Fear and Avoidance for each situation using the 0-100 scales we provided in Chapter 4 that are reprinted on the top of the form. After you have completed the ratings, take out your original Fear and Avoidance Hierarchy and compare the two sets of ratings. By now you should see some positive changes. Most people find that situations in the bottom half of the Fear and Avoidance Hierarchy change first. It is also common to see reductions in Avoidance Ratings before reductions in SUDS Ratings. As you have learned already, if you stop avoiding the things you fear, the fear will decrease as well.

Also review the graphs for the weekly self-monitoring averages. Although your anxiety may have gone up for awhile as you stopped avoiding situations that make you anxious, the graphs should show your anxiety decreasing as you get to week 10 or 12 on the graph.

If your new Fear and Avoidance Hierarchy ratings or the graphs of your self-monitoring show you have made progress, it is time to celebrate. If you checked off some or all of the items on the checklist above, give yourself a pat on the back for all of your hard work. As you look at your progress, you might find yourself thinking, "Yes, I've done those things, but social anxiety is still a big problem for me." That is a very destructive AT that will make you feel discouraged! Look carefully and you will see that this AT contains the Thinking Error Disqualifying the Positive. Using one of the Disputing Questions, ask yourself, "Does still having some social anxiety mean that I have not made important progress already?" Absolutely not. Just because you still have more work to do on your social anxiety does not mean that you do not get any credit for all of your hard work so far. In fact, by learning the cognitive self-help skills and how to face your fears productively, you have gained excellent tools that will help you make even more progress.

How to Continue Making Progress

Regardless of how much progress you have made in overcoming social anxiety, there are important habits you can develop to continue making progress:

1. *Avoid avoidance.*

   The sooner you stop avoiding the situations that make you anxious, the sooner you will overcome your social fears. Every time you avoid a situation that makes you anxious, you reward the anxiety and make it worse. Every time you avoid avoidance and enter a situation, even if it makes you anxious, you have an opportunity to conquer your fears. As you continue to progress, you should try to decrease your avoidance to zero.

2. *Keep using the cognitive skills.*

As you become more familiar with the treatment procedures and they become routine, it will be easy to take short-cuts or stop using the cognitive restructuring skills. As will be discussed, the cognitive skills usually become fairly automatic with practice. However, it is extremely important to work through all of the steps, preferably writing them down on the BYOCC worksheet. These skills can be very powerful aids in controlling your anxiety. Systematic efforts to identify and challenge your ATs are essential to get as much as possible from each exposure. As we saw in the last chapter, identifying the dysfunctional core beliefs that underlie the anxiety requires repeated and systematic cognitive restructuring.

3. *View an increase in anxiety as an opportunity.*

Over the years we have noticed that the individuals who make the most progress in this treatment program have a change of mindset at some point. Initially everyone tries to avoid their fears and protect themselves from embarrassment or negative evaluation. However, individuals who come to view an anxiety-provoking situation as an opportunity rather than a threat make the most rapid progress. These individuals view an increase in anxiety as a signal to charge forward into a situation rather than as a signal to stop, escape, or avoid. If you find yourself making suggestions to your therapist about how to make an exposure harder or more effective, then you have had this change in your mindset.

4. *Reward yourself for your success.*

Facing one's fears takes courage and motivation. Be sure to take every opportunity to give yourself credit for your success. Tell your therapist about each accomplishment. If you have family or friends who know you are working to overcome social anxiety, let them celebrate each success with you. Regularly take time out to think about all of the situations that are easier, all of the things you can do now that you could not do before you started treatment. Celebrate all of the ways your life has improved as you have conquered your fears.

5. *Use additional strategies to control your anxiety.*

The last chapter in this manual describes how medications can be useful for controlling anxiety. Medication is not intended to be used instead of what you have already learned but to supplement the treatment program. If you are not making as much progress as you would like, discuss with your therapist whether medication may be helpful for you.

New Situations Mean New Challenges

In our research on cognitive-behavioral treatment for social anxiety disorder, we usually have clients come back 6 to 12 months after their treatment has ended so that we can see how they are doing. Every once in awhile someone will come back for one of these follow-up appointments feeling very discouraged because of a new situation that is causing anxiety and stress. For example, one man who had never held a regular job because of his social anxiety came in after several months at a new job as a maintenance man for a large apartment complex. He had been working as part-time assistant to an experienced maintenance person who was now leaving. The owners had asked the client to take over the full-time position. This would mean more face-to-face contact with the owners and supervision of a new part-time assistant. Despite his excitement about the promotion, he was very anxious about it and felt as if all of the gains he had made in overcoming his social anxiety were lost. The therapist quickly realized that nothing could be further from the truth. This man's success in overcoming his fears had allowed him to be in situations that had never been possible before now. Because these were new situations, he was, understandably, experiencing some anxiety. The therapist helped him reframe the anxiety as a sign of his progress rather than as failure. He was then able to use everything he had learned in treatment to face these new challenges successfully.

This example illustrates how the changes in your life that result from decreases in social anxiety may mean that you are in situations with which you have had little or no experience. There may be times that it feels like your social anxiety is getting worse when it is actually improving dramatically. The good news when you stop avoiding is that you have a lot more opportunities for things that are important to you. The bad news is that these new opportunities may also be somewhat stressful. You will not have to face the anxiety of a wedding day or a relationship break-up if you have never dated. You will not have to face the anxiety of the first day on the job you always wanted if you are too anxious to go to class and finish your degree. You will not have to face the stress of losing a job if you have never had one.

As our clients have found themselves in this position, we have made two recommendations. First, go back and use the strategies that have worked so far. This is the time to pull out this manual again and refresh your memory of the cognitive self-help skills and therapeutic exposure. Second, if the anxiety seems too severe to face alone, go back and work with your therapist for a few sessions. We'll say more about returning to therapy for "booster" sessions later in this chapter.

Reactions of Family, Friends, and Other People

As people go through therapy and start to make changes in their lives, it has an impact on others around them. Family, friends, and co-workers have all become accustomed to each of us being a particular person who acts in fairly predictable ways. As you start to overcome your social anxiety, you may find that other people are unsure how to react to you. They may be so uncomfortable that in subtle ways they encourage you to go back to being anxious. For example, if one person in a marriage is overcoming social anxiety about parties, the other person may feel rejected when he or she is no longer needed to carry all of the conversation at social gatherings. Co-workers might be surprised if someone who has always been shy and withdrawn gradually starts to make conversation and join them for lunch. They may initially forget to include the person in social plans because they still think of him or her as shy and withdrawn. Friends may be uncomfortable for awhile if a person switches from always being a listener to wanting to talk and to be more assertive when they are making plans together. Not surprisingly, these reactions can be frustrating for the person who is working so hard to overcome his or her fears. There may even be subtle pressure to return to one's old socially anxious self. However, understanding these reactions can help you continue to push forward with the changes you are making. The good news is that once everyone is used to the new you, that quickly becomes the *status quo*. Then the same subtle pressure to keep the system in balance helps work to keep you more socially involved and less anxious. When everyone starts to expect you to go to parties, have conversations, make speeches, write/eat/drink in public, be assertive, or speak up in a group, then it is harder to go back to avoiding previously feared situations. This new balance will help you maintain your progress.

When to Stop Seeing Your Therapist Regularly

Most people with social anxiety disorder will find that it takes 10-20 sessions with their therapist to get the most out of this program. That assumes that you and your therapist are concentrating on the social anxiety disorder in the sessions and not spending a lot of time on other problems you may be experiencing. To the extent you spend time in treatment on depression, marital difficulties, alcohol or drug problems, work or financial difficulties, or other issues, it will take longer to work through this treatment program. If the social anxiety disorder is severe, it may take longer.

The following are signs that you may be ready to stop seeing your therapist regularly:

1. You have completed in-session exposures for the most difficult situations on your Fear and Avoidance Hierarchy and you have completed homework exposures for nearly all of the situations on your hierarchy.

2. You have met your most important treatment goal, such as going back to school, getting/changing a job, going on a few dates, or facing a specific difficult situation such as an important speech or social occasion.

3. Your social anxiety does not interfere in your day-to-day functioning in any important way. You may still have some anxiety but you feel able to handle it and rarely if ever avoid anything due to anxiety.

As we discussed in the first chapter, social anxiety is a normal part of life. There will always be some situations in which you experience anxiety. This treatment does not make you immune to anxiety! In fact, for the rest of your life you may have more trouble with social anxiety than the average person who has not had this disorder. Our research shows that people who complete this treatment successfully still experience social anxiety fairly often. However, they continue to work on their anxiety on their own and when they return 6 or 12 months after treatment to meet with their therapist, they are doing better than at the end of treatment.

Graduation Day

There are two activities that we like to complete in the last session when someone graduates from this treatment program. You might find these helpful to do with your therapist.

1. Discuss with your therapist all of the changes that you have made over the course of treatment. As with all graduation days, this is the time to celebrate your accomplishments. Using Figure 13.1, "My Accomplishments During Treatment for Social Anxiety," think about:

   ▓ the new skills you have learned

   ▓ the changes you have made in your life

   ▓ the ways in which you are more self-confident

   ▓ the things you have done that you either had never done before or had not done for a very long time

   Reviewing the changes in ratings on your Fear and Avoidance Hierarchy may help you think about some of your accomplishments as you complete this exercise.

2. Set a goal for yourself of a situation or fear you want to tackle by one month after treatment. Most people find that they "backslide" a bit the first couple of weeks after treatment is over. Without having to report back to a therapist about progress on homework, it is easy to stop pushing oneself to try new situations. Some avoidance behavior may return. By setting a goal for the first month after treatment, you will be much more able to get yourself back on track after taking the expected rest at the end of treatment. Record your goal

My Accomplishments During Treatment for Social Anxiety

1. New skills I have learned:

2. Changes I have made in my life:

3. Ways in which I am more self-confident:

4. Things I have done that I never did before or had not done for a long time:

Figure 13.1.

Goal for the First Month After Treatment Ends

By _____ (date one month after treatment ends), I want to accomplish the following:

_____

_____

_____

_____

_____

_____

_____

_____

_____

_____

_____

Figure 13.2.

on Figure 13.2, "Goal for the First Month After Treatment Ends." Be sure to make a note on your calendar to remind yourself to accomplish the goal by the one-month date.

When to Call Your Therapist for a Booster Session

As you finish regular treatment sessions, most people experience some sadness over not seeing their therapist regularly. This is normal. However, most people also are pleased to be ending therapy because it signals that they are doing better. It is also nice to end the commitment of time, money, and emotional energy. As you have discovered by now, being in therapy is hard work! On the other hand, there may come a time in the next weeks or months that you find yourself struggling with social anxiety again. As noted above, this may be because you are facing new situations that your progress in treatment has made possible. Sometimes people become more anxious again if they have something stressful happen such as personal or family crises, death of a loved one, marriage, or a new baby. Even if the event is positive, it can be stressful.

Occasionally people have a bad experience in a social or performance situation that they thought they had conquered, and their fears return temporarily. Whatever the reason, if you find your anxiety increasing or you are starting to avoid situations that make you anxious, take this manual out again and try using the cognitive self-help skills more systematically. You may want to re-read the chapter on therapeutic exposure and try to systematically put yourself in some difficult situations in order to overcome the fears again. However, if you find that this is not working, it is time to call your therapist and request a booster session. Very often one or two sessions will help get someone back on track. In fact, it is usually true that if people come back to therapy just when they are starting to have trouble, it is easier than if they wait a long time. The longer you wait, the more likely you are to get into bad habits such as avoiding anxiety-provoking situations. More booster sessions will then be required.

End of the Journey Together

The remaining chapter in this book focuses on using medication to manage anxiety. If you have not already read this chapter, you may want to do so now. However, this is the end of the standard treatment program for overcoming social anxiety. You and your therapist may be finishing your work together (or at least shifting your attention to other matters). On the other hand, this is the beginning of your journey on your own, equipped with a toolbox full of skills and increased confidence to continue to take your life in a new direction. We wish you well.

Self-Assessment

1. Once you learn how to identify your dysfunctional core beliefs, you no longer need to practice the techniques you have learned in this treatment program. **T F**

2. You may make more rapid progress if you attempt to view a situation that makes you anxious as an opportunity rather than as something to avoid. **T F**

3. Entering totally new types of situations and becoming anxious means that your social anxiety is actually getting worse. **T F**

4. People in your environment, because they are not used to your new behaviors, may be uncomfortable and may subtly encourage you to go back to your old behaviors. **T F**

5. If you have completed exposures for your most difficult situations, have met your most important treatment goals, and your social anxiety no longer interferes with your life on a daily basis, it may be time to consider stopping regular visits to your therapist. **T F**

6. "Backsliding" a bit after your treatment has ended means that the social anxiety is back and will probably get worse. **T F**

Answers to Self-Assessment questions can be found in Appendix A.

Chapter 14

Medication Treatment of Social Anxiety

By Michael R. Liebowitz, M.D.

How Medications Affect the Brain and Reduce Social Anxiety

Although we may talk about feelings coming from our heart, in reality, they come from our brains. In fact, everything we say or do starts with tiny electrical and chemical reactions in our brains. We are born with brains well-prepared for important life-sustaining functions like breathing. Other things we learn along the way cause changes in our brains that will affect what we think, feel, say, and do in the future. Thus, if we want to change how we feel or act, as in reducing anxiety and avoidance, we need to change various processes in our brain. The first 13 chapters discussed how to make these changes with cognitive-behavioral techniques. This chapter describes the medications that may also be useful for making those changes.

Several medications have been found useful in the treatment of social anxiety disorder. These medications can be grouped into broad classes based on how they work in the brain. The brain is made up of nerve cells that communicate with each other via chemical messengers called "neurotransmitters." When one nerve cell sends a message to the next cell, it releases the neurotransmitter into the tiny space between the cells (called "synapses"). The second cell accepts some of the neurotransmitter and passes the message along. The first cell soaks up any leftover neurotransmitter (this process is called "reuptake"). Medications can affect nerve cells by changing the amount of neurotransmitter that remains in the synapse or is available in the cell to be released when needed. Higher levels of a neurotransmitter in the synapse make it easier for messages to be passed from one nerve cell to another while lower levels generally makes this more difficult.

What follows are discussions of each class of medications used to treat social anxiety disorder. Figure 14.1 summarizes information about several of the useful medications, gives their trade names and generic names, starting doses, maximum doses, and the minimum time you should take each medication before you can

Representative Medications for Social Anxiety Disorder

Class	Trade Name	Generic Name	Starting Dose	Maximum Dose	Minimum Time to Test Usefulness
Selective Serotonin Reuptake Inhibitors	Paxil®	paroxetine	20mg	50mg	6–8 weeks
	Zoloft®	sertraline	50mg	200mg	8 weeks
	Luvox®	fluvoxamine	50mg	300mg	8 weeks
	Prozac®	fluoxetine	20mg	80mg	8 weeks
	Celexa®	citalopram	20mg	50mg	8 weeks
Monoamine Oxidase Inhibitors	Nardil®	phenelzine	15mg	90mg	6–8 weeks
Reversible Inhibitors of Monoamine Oxidase	Aurorix®	moclobemide	100mg	900mg	8 weeks
Beta Blockers	Inderal®	propranolol	10–20mg	40mg	**
Benzodiazepines	Klonopin®	clonazepam	0.5mg	4mg	4 weeks

**Not applicable because Inderal® is typically used on an "as needed" basis for social anxiety disorder.

Figure 14.1.

decide whether it will be helpful to you. Trade names are copyrighted brand names, and generic names are the names of the active chemicals in each medication. In this chapter, the trade names will be followed by the generic names in parentheses. More information about these medications, including potential side effects and the major difficulties with using them, are discussed in the remainder of the chapter.

Selective Serotonin Reuptake Inhibitors (SSRIs)

You have probably heard of medications like Prozac® (fluoxetine) and Paxil® (paroxetine). They have become very commonly used, with literally millions of prescriptions for these medications written each year. These drugs are from the class of medications referred to as "Selective Serotonin Reuptake Inhibitors" or "SSRIs." Serotonin is the name of one type of neurotransmitter. The SSRIs prevent the body from removing serotonin from synapses (the spaces between nerve cells) by blocking the reuptake ("soaking up") of serotonin back into the nerve cells. When you take an SSRI, serotonin remains for a longer time in the synapses in important areas of your brain, facilitating communication between your brain and nervous system.

Several good scientific studies with Paxil® (paroxetine) and a smaller number with Zoloft® (sertraline) and Luvox® (fluvoxamine) suggest these SSRIs are useful in the treatment of social anxiety disorder. Socially anxious people taking these medications become more comfortable dealing with social situations. There is less anxiety and less avoidance. Preliminary studies with Prozac® (fluoxetine) and Celexa® (citalopram), two other SSRIs, suggest that these drugs may also be helpful.

The SSRIs are usually easy and safe to take. Their side effects may be uncomfortable for some people, but they are not generally regarded as dangerous. Side effects may include weight gain, interference with sleep and sexual function, and daytime drowsiness. When you take SSRIs, it is important to monitor other medications you are taking and watch for medication interactions.

Monoamine Oxidase Inhibitors (MAOIs)

While many people have heard of the SSRIs, people are typically less familiar with the next class of drugs that we will discuss, the "monoamine oxidase inhibitors" or "MAOIs." These drugs work by inhibiting an enzyme in the body called monoamine oxidase (MAO). MAO is responsible for helping to remove excess levels of several neurotransmitters such as dopamine, norepinephrine, and serotonin. When MAO is inhibited, the removal process is blocked, and the levels of various neurotransmitters rise. Because the MAOIs cause increases in the available amounts of several neurotransmitters, they are among the most powerful medications available for social anxiety.

MAOIs have been shown in several excellent studies to be quite helpful for patients with social anxiety disorder. The best-studied MAOI is called Nardil® (phenelzine), and it has been on the market for about 30 years. Unfortunately, the MAOIs that are available in the United States, including Nardil® (phenelzine), also inhibit some of the body's protective mechanisms in the gastrointestinal system. Thus, if you take Nardil® (phenelzine) or another standard MAOI, you have to avoid a substance called *tyramine* in foods and beverages. Tyramine is an amino acid (a building block your body uses to make proteins) and tends to be found in high amounts in any kind of aged protein, especially in aged (hard) cheeses or meats that have been allowed to age. You also have to avoid too much caffeine and alcohol, as well as cold medicines, especially certain decongestants, and certain medications such as demerol, dextromethorphan, and epinephrine that are often used in local anesthetics.

You have to be very careful because if you eat foods or drink beverages that contain tyramine or take prohibited medications while you are taking an MAOI, you can have a dangerous rise in blood pressure that can even lead to a stroke.

Obviously, use of an MAOI for social anxiety should be under the supervision of a physician.

The side effects of Nardil® (phenelzine), in addition to potential high blood pressure reactions, may include weight gain, dizziness if you stand up too quickly, and interference with sleep and sexual function. These side effects can usually be managed with dosage adjustments or antidotes. However, MAOIs are not easy to handle and many psychiatrists do not like to use them. If you are considering treatment with Nardil® (phenelzine), make every effort to find a physician who has experience with both social anxiety disorder and the MAOIs. Also, you must be given a list of prohibited foods, beverages, and medicines that you should carefully review with the physician before starting the drug. The two of you should also discuss the symptoms of a high blood pressure reaction and what to do if it occurs. Some physicians will give you an antidote to deal with the high blood pressure reaction to carry around with you. Many physicians also ask their patients to carry a wallet card or wear a bracelet identifying them as someone who is taking an MAOI, in case they are involved in a car accident or other medical emergency, so that medical personnel will know that they are taking an MAOI.

The advantage of the MAOIs is that they work well, work fairly quickly, and continue to provide benefits while you take them. The disadvantage is that some people will relapse when these drugs are stopped, even if they have taken them for as long as 9 months.

Beta-adrenergic Blockers (Beta Blockers)

Some persons with social anxiety disorder experience what might be called "pure performance anxiety," characterized by difficulty in situations such as interviewing for a job, playing an instrument, giving a speech, and so forth. People with pure performance anxiety do not experience significant anxiety in other social situations. The class of medications referred to as "beta-adrenergic blockers," or "beta blockers" for short, is a mainstay for the treatment of this type of performance anxiety. These drugs block the effects of the hormone adrenaline on the body so that many of the symptoms of performance anxiety are reduced. For example, when individuals with severe performance anxiety get up to give a speech, their hearts may race, their voices quaver, their hands shake, and they may sweat. These are all symptoms of heightened arousal of the sympathetic nervous system, the part of your nervous system that prepares you for "fight-or-flight." The person becomes aware of these distracting symptoms and may worry that the audience can see his or her nervousness. These concerns may further heighten anxiety, which increases physical symptoms, which may become more and more of a distraction, setting up a vicious cycle of increasing distress and decreasing ability to proceed (as was described earlier in Chapter 2). By blocking the effects of adrenaline on the body, the beta blockers dampen the development of this vicious cycle, reducing heart rate and the intensity of other physical symptoms. So, even though you may still feel subjectively nervous, your body does not react as strongly in a nervous way.

People take beta blockers for other medical conditions, such as high blood pressure or some heart problems, one to several times every day to make sure they are "covered" around the clock. If you suffer from pure performance anxiety, however, it may be better to use these drugs on an as-needed basis, taking your medication a half-hour to an hour before a speech or other performance.

There are several types of beta blockers, and you should consult with your physician about which is best for you. However, beta blockers are not a cure-all, nor are they good for everyone with social anxiety disorder. They work best for people with pure performance fears. Although they may help you control your physical reactions, they will not help with *anticipatory anxiety*, the worry about how you are going to perform. People with severe performance anxiety often worry about a situation for weeks in advance and may lose sleep for several nights before the event. Beta blockers will not be helpful for this anxious anticipation, which will persist until you become convinced through experience or cognitive-behavioral therapy that you will be able to perform adequately.

Benzodiazepines

When people talk about taking tranquilizers, they are referring to the class of medications called "benzodiazepines." Benzodiazepines reduce anxiety by their effects on a receptor system involving a neurotransmitter called gamma amino-butyric acid ("GABA" for short). Unlike beta blockers, these medications can help with day-to-day social anxiety as well as the anxiety you may experience about a situation in which you have to perform, such as giving a speech or playing an instrument. Medications in this class include Xanax® (alprazolam), Klonopin® (clonazepam), Valium® (diazepam), and Ativan® (lorazepam). The only side effect that you need to worry about when taking benzodiazepines on an as-needed basis for performance anxiety is feeling overly sedated or drowsy.

The major downside of the benzodiazepines is the possibility that you may become addicted to them. If you take benzodiazepines on a daily basis for an extended period of time, your body becomes physically dependent on them, making it hard to stop taking them. If you do not take your medications for awhile, as might happen if you go away for a weekend and forget your pills, you will begin to experience unpleasant withdrawal symptoms, which are your body's reaction to not having the medication. Some people may even have seizures if they withdraw improperly from benzodiazepines without consulting their physician. While there has not been much research on the issue among persons with social anxiety disorder, persons with panic disorder have often had serious problems stopping their benzodiazepine medications and may experience a return of anxiety that can be quite extreme. However, if you and your physician gradually taper the dosage off over a period of weeks, withdrawal is generally tolerable. Klonopin® (clonazepam) appears to be the best of the benzodiazepines in this regard. It is easier to stop and may result in less severe withdrawal reactions than Xanax® (alprazolam), Valium® (diazepam), or Ativan® (lorazepam).

Other Medications for Social Anxiety Disorder

Other drugs such as BuSpar® (buspirone), Tofranil® (imipramine), and Selegiline (L-deprenyl) have not been very helpful in initial studies, and further study may not be warranted. A newer, safer type of MAOI, which appears to carry much less risk of high blood pressure reactions, has also recently been developed. One of these drugs is called Aurorix® (moclobemide), and it is marketed in several European countries for depression and/or social anxiety disorder. However, recent studies in the United States and Europe did not find this drug to be very useful for social anxiety disorder.

General Considerations in Undertaking Drug Therapy for Social Anxiety Disorder

All of the medications described in this chapter are prescription drugs and should be taken only if prescribed for you by your family doctor or psychiatrist. Do not borrow these drugs from someone else or use them without proper medical supervision. Do not lend your medication to another person simply because you believe they suffer the same symptoms. You should follow your physician's instructions about how to take the drug, and you should not experiment on your own with raising or lowering the dose. If a given dose is too weak or too strong, check with your physician about what you should do. Keep your physician informed about any bad reactions you experience. Your medical history and health should be checked before beginning medication treatment for social anxiety disorder, and you should be checked periodically during the treatment period. If you are taking an SSRI or MAOI, for example, blood tests should be conducted about every six months to be sure that the medication does not irritate your liver.

Another potential limitation of medication as a treatment for your social anxiety disorder is the possibility that you may need to use it indefinitely in order to maintain your gains. That is, there is not yet any strong evidence that people can use medication for a while and then stop it without the anxiety returning. However, in one of our studies, about half the patients who took Nardil® (phenelzine) for nine months and benefited from doing so were able to stop taking the medication and maintain their gains over the next 6 months.

If you have been on medication for a period of time and wish to discontinue the medication, you should gradually taper the dosage under medical supervision. Reduce your dose every several weeks by an amount agreed upon with your physician to see if there is any increase in symptoms. If there is, you might rethink whether it is the right time to get off medicine. On the other hand, if the decrease does not appear to result in any recurrence of symptoms, then it will encourage you to keep going and get off the medicine completely. Of course, the ultimate goal is to be able to live with manageable levels of anxiety, without medication if possible.

Mixing Therapy and Medication

Medicines and cognitive-behavioral therapy may work well together in several ways. Medications can make exposure to feared situations easier by reducing the severity of your anxiety symptoms. Medications may also help with changing your thinking as well. The SSRIs or MAOIs may help with any depression that you may be experiencing. Cognitive-behavioral therapy may increase the benefits that you get from your medication by pushing you to expose yourself to feared situations and see that the medication helps. Medication's greatest strength in the treatment of social anxiety disorder may be the quick reduction of anxiety, while the greatest strength of cognitive-behavioral therapy may lie in the durability of improvements and the increased self-reliance that may follow.

There are also some potential pitfalls of combining medication and cognitive-behavioral therapy for social anxiety disorder. There is some possibility that the two different kinds of treatment may work against each other in some circumstances. When you are receiving medication as well as cognitive-behavioral therapy, you may not be as willing or motivated to complete exposure exercises, possibly feeling that you do not have to work as hard because the medications will do the work for you. This assumption may undermine your progress. With cognitive-behavioral therapy, you build confidence in yourself, but over-reliance on medication may undermine this self-confidence. In addition, some medications, such as the benzodiazepines, may sedate you too much, interfering with your ability to complete exposure tasks or to benefit from them when you do. Clearly, the decision to use medications as part of the treatment for your social anxiety disorder is a very important one and should only be considered in discussion with your therapist or physician.

If you take medication while receiving cognitive-behavioral therapy, it will most often be the case that the two treatments will be administered by different people. If so, you will get the best service from both your physician and your cognitive-behavioral therapist if they work together as a team.

1. Neurotransmitters are chemical messengers in the brain that carry   **T F**
   information between brain cells.

2. Medications for social anxiety work by changing the amounts of   **T F**
   neurotransmitters.

3. Research has shown that the SSRIs may be helpful for individuals   **T F**
   with social anxiety but it is unknown what happens to your symptoms
   if you stop taking the medication.

4. If you are taking an MAOI, you must avoid certain foods.   **T F**

5. Beta blockers work to reduce adrenaline and are most useful to reduce   **T F**
   anticipatory anxiety.

6. Taking medication for social anxiety may reduce your motivation to do   **T F**
   the exposures as part of cognitive-behavioral therapy (if you are using
   both methods to help with your social anxiety).

Answers to Self-Assessment questions can be found in Appendix A.

Appendix A

Self-Assessment Answers

Chapter 1

1. **True.** Feared situations vary widely, but the most common ones are public speaking, conversations with unfamiliar people, dating, and being assertive. Also, some people are afraid of eating or drinking in front of other people, being the center of attention, talking with supervisors or other authority figures, urinating in a public bathroom, or intimate sexual situations.

2. **False.** Social anxiety is a normal part of life and most people experience it at some point during their lifetime; if it interferes with your life in important ways, treatment might be a consideration.

3. **True.** Persons with social anxiety disorder share a common fear that other people will think poorly of them—they fear negative evaluation regardless of the situations in which they are particularly afraid.

4. **True.** It is easy to continue to see the things that you would like to improve. However, it is also important to recognize the things you have accomplished; recognizing your progress will reinforce your efforts to continue to make more progress.

6. **True.** Making personal changes can be difficult; commitment and practice will help you make those changes.

Chapter 2

1. **False.** Anxiety includes behavioral, physical, and cognitive components. Avoidance is part of the behavioral component.

2. **False.** Fever is not usually associated with anxiety.

3. **True.** Approximately one in three people experience a panic attack at some point in their lifetime.

4. **True.** Anxious thoughts often involve a prediction about something bad occurring.

5. **False.** Although avoiding scary situations will make you feel immediately better because it quickly relieves your anxiety, it encourages you to continue to avoid situations in the future. However, avoidance does not reduce your social anxiety in the long run.

Chapter 3

1. **False.** Although there appears to be a genetic component to social anxiety, scientists have not isolated an associated gene.

2. **True.** There appears to be an environmental component to social anxiety and we may learn behaviors from those in our environment. Thus, if our family members behave in socially anxious ways, we may learn and imitate this behavior.

3. **True.** This is a common expectation, and in fact, people with social anxiety frequently expect that things will go poorly in the situations that make them anxious.

4. **True.** By doing exposures, you repeatedly practice feared situations and get used to the sensations you experience when you complete the whole exposure. After the exposure, you have an opportunity to examine your beliefs.

5. **False.** Cognitive restructuring does not mean that you take out the bad thoughts and replace them with good thoughts. Rather, this technique teaches you to question your beliefs, assumptions, and expectations and see if they really make sense or are helpful.

Chapter 4

1. **False.** The situations that evoke social anxiety vary a lot from person to person.

2. **True.** Understanding the larger dimensions of situations that you find anxiety-provoking will help you to determine if you might experience anxiety in new situations that have the same larger dimensions.

3. **False.** SUDS ratings are used to rate subjective distress; avoidance ratings are used to gauge avoidance.

4. **False.** Even though an avoidance rating might be low (e.g., you participate in a situation even though you would prefer not to), your anxiety might still be very high in this situation.

Chapter 5

1. **False.** It is the interpretation of an event that makes a person anxious.

2. **True.** These are typical feelings for those who struggle with social anxiety and worry about outcomes of social situations.

3. **False.** The thoughts you have about a social situation before you enter it are quite likely to influence the outcome.

4. **False.** Thoughts must be examined in more detail. In fact, simply trying to suppress negative thoughts in order to think positively may actually make the ATs worse.

5. **True.** After you identify negative thoughts, you then analyze the ATs for logical errors, challenge whether the ATs are really true, and develop more rational, helpful statements.

Chapter 6

1. **False.** Paying attention to negative details might be more representative of Mental Filter, whereas Mind Reading is believing that you know what others are thinking without considering other, more likely, possibilities.

2. **True.** Some thoughts, although they are not logically flawed, can cause anxiety if you dwell on them.

3. **True.** In the example of Al and Lois, thinking in a different way led to different actions, and therefore, possibly different outcomes.

4. **False.** It is essential to answer these questions.

5. **False.** Disputing your ATs will not remove all anxiety from situations. However, this process will help you to feel more calm and think more clearly.

6. **True.** These qualities of a Rational Response will help you make the most out of these new thoughts.

7. **False.** You do not need to believe your Rational Responses, especially at first. It takes time for healthier, more helpful thoughts about yourself, other people, and social situations to emerge.

Chapter 7

1. **False.** Habituation is the process of your body automatically working to counteract your fear response.

2. **True.** By doing exposures, you get used to the sensations you feel in those situations and you have a chance to try out your cognitive restructuring skills.

3. **True.** Cognitive preparation makes it more likely that the exposure will be helpful in overcoming your anxiety.

4. **False.** It is important to set an "achievable behavioral goal" so you will know if the exposure was a success.

5. **False.** It is most likely that you will be anxious during an exposure; trying not to be anxious is probably too big of a goal for a single exposure, and some social anxiety is a normal part of life.

6. **True.** Interrupting the exposure to ask questions or make comments may mean you are not facing your fears, which is the crux of exposure.

Chapter 8

1. **False.** It is better to start with situations that are easier, rather than very difficult.

2. **False.** Homework is an important part of this program. Completing homework makes it more likely that you will be successful in meeting your goals.

3. **False.** You do not need to do an exposure for every situation in which you get socially anxious. Your new skills are likely to eventually generalize to some new situations.

4. **True.** Generalization involves the application of what you learn in one situation to another similar but different situation.

5. **True.** Anxiety should be a signal that it is time to examine your ATs. If so, identifying and challenging your ATs will become second nature and occur almost automatically when you notice yourself becoming nervous.

Chapter 9

1. **True.** Over the past 35 years, the definition of social phobia has broadened to include all of these fears.

2. **True.** Once you become anxious about doing something, the self-consciousness makes it more difficult to complete the task.

3. **True.** Using this technique can help you to see that there are many different things that could happen during feared situations—things that you might not have considered before including neutral and positive outcomes.

4. **False.** Even experts do not perform well every time.

5. **False.** Exposures ought to continue until anxiety has peaked and then reduced some (habituation).

Chapter 10

1. **False.** Small talk is important because it is the first step in the development of any friendship or relationship.

2. **True.** A person's social support network is the group of people that can be counted on to listen, offer advice, provide help, and do things together.

3. **True.** Many scientific studies over the last 25 years have found that social support seems to act like a buffer against the stresses in life that can affect your physical and mental health.

4. **True.** These are two of the most common ATs among those who fear casual conversations.

5. **False.** Psychologists have noticed that most people with social anxiety actually perform fine in social situations.

Chapter 11

1. **False.** Public speaking is a common fear for those with and without significant social anxiety.

2. **True.** One way to tackle ATs is to look at the likelihood of the predicted outcome, which is usually an extreme one; usually, such extreme reactions are not that likely to occur.

3. **True.** Because preparing for the talk brings up this anxiety, avoidance is a common response.

4. **False.** Experiencing anxiety about an upcoming event is a distinct signal that it might be helpful to work on your ATs using the BYOCC worksheet.

5. **True.** It is important to look for any aspects of situations that can be addressed repeatedly.

Chapter 12

1. **True.** By searching through the layers of ATs and emotions, you can get at more core beliefs.

2. **True.** These are helpful strategies to get at core beliefs.

3. **False.** You may not have any notion of the source of your core beliefs nor must you understand what happened in your past that resulted in your core belief. Dysfunctional beliefs can change even if you do not know where they came from.

4. **True.** Very often individuals with social anxiety disorder have a core belief about the need to be perfect.

5. **False.** These processes are different; you do not need to understand what, if any, events in your past may be related to your social anxiety in order to understand your ATs and core beliefs.

Chapter 13

1. **False.** It is extremely important to continue to use the skills you've learned from this program. You may be able to take some shortcuts with time, but systematic efforts to identify and challenge your ATs are essential for you to continue to get as much as possible from each exposure. As we saw in the last chapter, identifying the dysfunctional core beliefs that underlie the anxiety requires repeated and systematic cognitive restructuring.

2. **True.** Every time you avoid avoidance and enter a situation that makes you anxious, you have an opportunity to conquer your fears.

3. **False.** The opposite is true. As you have been able to decrease your social anxiety, you are probably entering into situations that you would not have entered before you had these new skills. It may feel as though your social anxiety is worse because you may experience anxiety in a social situation, but things have actually improved.

4. **True.** As your behaviors change, others may be so uncomfortable that in subtle ways they encourage you to go back to being anxious.

5. **True.** As you become more skilled, you will need less support from your therapist.

6. **False.** Backsliding a little is a common experience and does not indicate a return to your former behaviors.

Chapter 14

1. **True.** The chemicals that communicate information are called neurotransmitters.

2. **True.** Medications work on nerve cells by changing the amount of neurotransmitter that is available for release, and medications for social anxiety are thought to affect this process.

3. **True.** There has not been enough research done to establish whether your treatment gains will maintain if you stop taking medication.

4. **True.** Yes, you must avoid certain foods that contain tyramine, such as hard cheeses, aged meats, and certain medications.

5. **False.** This type of medication does block adrenaline but is most effective for performance anxiety.

6. **True.** This is one of the pitfalls of combining medication and cognitive-behavioral treatments. Sometimes two different kinds of treatments may work against each other.

References

Beck, Aaron T., Rush, A. John, Shaw, Brian F., & Emery, Gary (1979). *Cognitive therapy of depression.* New York: Guilford Press.

Beck, Judith S. (1995). *Cognitive therapy: Basics and beyond.* New York: Guilford Press.

Ellis, Albert (1962). *Reason and emotion in psychotherapy.* New York: Lyle Stuart.

Marks, Isaac M. (1969). *Fears and phobias.* New York: Academic Press.

Sank, Lawrence I., & Shaffer, Carolyn S. (1984). *A therapist's manual for cognitive behavior therapy in groups.* New York: Plenum Press.

Wolpe, Joseph, & Lazarus, Arnold A. (1967). *Behavior therapy techniques: A guide to the treatment of neuroses.* Oxford: Pergamon Press.